Heinrich Heine's Contested Identities

German Life and Civilization

Vol. 26

PETER LANG
New York • Washington, D.C./Baltimore • Boston
Bern • Frankfurt am Main • Berlin • Vienna • Paris

Heinrich Heine's Contested Identities

Politics, Religion, and Nationalism in Nineteenth-Century Germany

Edited by
Jost Hermand
& Robert C. Holub

PETER LANG
New York • Washington, D.C./Baltimore • Boston
Bern • Frankfurt am Main • Berlin • Vienna • Paris

Library of Congress Cataloging-in-Publication Data

Heinrich Heine's contested identities: politics, religion, and nationalism in nineteenth-century Germany / edited by Jost Hermand and Robert C. Holub.
p. cm. — (German life and civilization; vol. 26)
Papers presented at a conference held Oct. 23–25, 1997.
Includes bibliographical references.
1. Heine, Heinrich, 1797–1856—Political and social views—Congresses.
2. Heine, Heinrich, 1797–1856—Religion—Congresses. 3. Heine, Heinrich, 1797–1856—Contemporary Germany—Congresses.
4. Germany—Politics and government—19th century—Congresses.
I. Hermand, Jost. II. Holub, Robert C. III. Series.
PT2343.P7H38 831'.7—dc21 98-25587
ISBN 0-8204-4105-8
ISSN 0899-9899

Die Deutsche Bibliothek-CIP-Einheitsaufnahme

Heinrich Heine's contested identities: politics, religion, and nationalism in nineteenth-century Germany / ed. by Jost Hermand and Robert C. Holub.
–New York; Washington, D.C./Baltimore; Boston; Bern;
Frankfurt am Main; Berlin; Vienna; Paris: Lang.
(German life and civilization; Vol. 26)
ISBN 0-8204-4105-8

The paper in this book meets the guidelines for permanence and durability of the Committee on Production Guidelines for Book Longevity of the Council of Library Resources.

Printed in the United States of America.

Contents

Preface

In 1997 Germanists from around the world celebrated the 200th anniversary of the birth of Heinrich Heine (1797-1856), the best known German author of the nineteenth century and one of the few German authors of his age to achieve worldwide recognition. To celebrate this bicentennial year, the German Department at Berkeley, in connection with the North American Heine Society, held a scholarly workshop on Heine's identities. The workshop, organized by Jost Hermand (Madison) and Robert Holub (Berkeley), who are also the editors of this volume, took place over a three-day period from October 23 to 25, 1997. This volume collects the talks that were presented at that conference in essay format.

The theme of the workshop was Heine's identity, which was formed and reformed, revised and modified, in relationship to the politics, religion, and nationalism of his era. In the context of nineteenth-century Europe Heine possessed at one point or another various identities. Indeed, one could argue that from the early 1820s until his death in 1856 Heine was in a constant struggle, both within himself and with his contemporaries to define himself. With regard to politics, Heine obviously falls somewhere on the left. But his political perspectives are never simple. Unlike many of his contemporaries, he remained on the outskirts of partisan party politics while he resided in France from 1831 until 1856, and at various points he was critical of almost every political group with which he was associated in the public mind. Known as a liberal during the 1820s in Germany, he was identified in his first decade in France with the Saint Simonists and in Germany with the Young Germans, which was a political affiliation only in the minds of the German authorities. During the 1840s he participated in various publication efforts of left Hegelians and socialists. Following the failed revolutions of 1848 he appears to resign himself to the status quo, and he expresses more ambivalence about communism, but he simultaneously insists that he remains linked to progressive forces.

Heine's religious affiliations were no less complex. Born into a Jewish family, he converted to Protestantism in 1825, although his conversion appears to be largely due to his concern for future employment in the German civil service. At the same time in his writings he deprecates Jews who converted and represents Protestantism as the latest and highest stage in a progression of Western religious thought through Judaism and Catholicism. He writes with passion in the 1830s about pantheism, but he criticizes Goethe's version of pantheism as quietistic. At various points during the 1830s and 1840s he appears to reject all religion, and his convictions come close to atheism. In his final years he proclaims himself a deist, embracing a personal God, but he also reevaluates in a positive fashion his relationship to the Judaism that he abandoned earlier.

With regard to nationality and national sentiments Heine was born in the Rhineland, and like many young people in the early part of the nineteenth century, considered himself a German first, rather than a member of a particular German state, and evidenced strong feelings for Germany throughout his life. But at various times he also exhibited an extremely strained relationship to his native land. Because of his Jewish faith, he became estranged from everything Germany in the early 1820s; in the 1830s he seems to identify more with France and French customs than with Germany; in the 1840s he attacks German nationalists, at the same time insisting that he is a true patriot; and in the 1850s he expands his purview beyond Germany and Europe, considering for the first time developments in what is now known as the third world.

The purpose of the workshop was thus to explore Heine's various identities, both the ones he himself assumed and the ones imposed upon him, in the context of the nineteenth century. The essays that resulted from that workshop indicate that we were able to arrive at a more differentiated understanding of Heine's predicaments and choices, as well as the parameters placed on him by the exigencies of the time. Most contributors chose one aspect of Heine's contested identity, and although none of the essays covers the same ground or complex of issues, there are significant overlaps. Most of the participants at one point touch upon Heine's disputed relationship to Judaism and the Jewish community, and almost every contribution contains something about Heine's relationship to the political and social issues of his time. What we have achieved with this volume therefore is not a radically new vision of Heine, but one that recognizes the ambivalences and vacillations, as well as the development and consistency, of aspects of his identity.

For the success of the workshop in October of 1997 and the production of this volume the editors owe a debt of gratitude to Matt Erlin, whose conference planning was superb, and who also assisted with the initial editing of the manuscripts. The workshop was funded primarily by the Bonwit-Heine endowment, a bequest of the late Professor Marianne Bonwit given to the University to support lectures in honor of her father Hugo Bonwit and the German poet Heinrich Heine. The Graduate Division and the German Department also assisted with monetary and logistic support. The publication of the volume has been made possible with monies from the Vilas Foundation at the University of Wisconsin-Madison.

Columbus, February 1998 RCH

Note on Bibliographical References

All references to Heine's writings are cited parenthetically in the text by volume and page number from Heinrich Heine, *Sämtliche Schriften*, ed. Klaus Briegleb, 6 volumes (Munich, 1968-1976). All correspondence is cited with volume and page number from Heinrich Heine, *Werke, Briefwechsel, Lebenszeugnisse. Säkularausgabe* (Berlin and Paris, 1970ff.) (HSA). All German from Heine's works and letters was translated into English for this volume.

Who Did Heine Think He Was?

Jeffrey L. Sammons

Contrary to my custom, I am going to begin with a sweeping, undemonstrable generalization: I think that scholars, especially scholars in the humanities, and perhaps most especially literary scholars, have great difficulty uttering the words: "I don't know."[1] One might ask why anyone should tolerate such an utterance. It is, after all, our métier to piece together some version of knowledge with sometimes the smallest clues. Furthermore, if some segments of the current theoretical discourse are to be credited, there is nothing intelligible out there anyway and we might as well just make it up. Still, one does not easily escape the sense that there are levels of security in what we talk about, for example, in our biographical grasp of people of the past. Biography and autobiography are often presented as under such disabilities in the pursuit of congruent representation as to be virtually hopeless enterprises. Even so, cases differ.

It has long been my view that Heine is a particularly difficult case, more so than is fully recognized in what has become the vast and all but unmanageable discourse that seems to know so much about him. Joseph Kruse, known as the vicar of Heine on earth, has remarked that his life is an open book,[2] and Manfred Windfuhr, whose heroic guidance of the modern critical edition has been accompanied by numerous detailed studies, has ascribed to Heine "uncommon openness."[3] Needless to say, differing from the two greatest Heine experts in the world today makes me more than a little uncomfortable; nevertheless, it seems to me that, if the book is open, the text is encrypted, and the harmonization of his private and public selves can only be achieved by replicating his self-representations, underestimating the degree of fictionalization and momentary opportunism, and repressing the underlying stresses in his personality structure. By comparison one may think in the first instance of Goethe. But he is not the clearest contrast, as he acknowledged the element of fiction in *Poetry and Truth* as a necessity for the recovery of memory and for organizing details of the past in the spirit of the present. We can see that in some places the moderating and reconciling reshapement is rather less innocent than this, for example, in the case of *The Campaign in France*. All the same, we do not think Goethe's autobiographical writings *grossly* distortive, and he is certainly ambitious for us to understand him: "it was my most earnest effort to represent and express as far as possible what was fundamentally true that, insofar as I was able to see, had prevailed over my life."[4] He does not mean to shut us out from intimate acquaintance with him, as Heine consistently does, systematically blocking and misdirecting our access to the inner sanctum of the self. A genuine contrast would be August von Platen-Hallermünde, whose diaries, despite their eventual quasi-literary shaping, record for us every nuance of life, every blunder in the management of it, every flutter of his inner disposition. On the whole, this intimacy, for all its exceptional authenticity, cannot be said to be pleasant; often the reader will share with many if not most of those who knew him the same feelings of exasperation, of a wish that he would shut up and go away.[5]

Heine does not annoy us in this way, if possibly in numerous other ways. He was well aware of the Goethean ambiguity, securing himself in the pseudo-autobiographical *Confessions* with a gesture of modest aspirations: "with the best will toward frankness no one can speak the truth about himself," only to assure us a couple of pages later: "I will always indicate my color quite exactly, so that one may know how far one may trust my judgment when I discuss people of a different color" (6/1: 447, 449-50). He does, of course, from start to finish talk about himself all the time, publicly and privately, and it is the custom of Heine scholars to reproduce and remix these utterances within a replicative discourse that remains fairly rigorously within the limits of what he would have us believe. It is extraordinary how little attention is given to such things as the details of Napoleonic governance in the Grand Duchy of Berg or political and social developments in the July Monarchy beyond Heine's own reportage. On the former point, neither Heine nor any of his commentators make anything of the circumstance that in Düsseldorf at the beginning of 1813 there was a popular uprising against Napoleon's relentless conscription of troops.[6] On the latter, commentators reproduce from book to book clichés about the July Monarchy and the dominion of finance capitalism but do not wish to account for Heine's interest in the personality of Louis-Philippe or share his at least partial awareness that François Guizot—of "enrichissez-vous" notoriety—was a significant political thinker and cosmopolitan intellectual, and Adolphe Thiers an accomplished historian of the Revolution.[7]

Heine does not begin to come even sketchily into view for us until he is around eighteen years old, and with relative clarity only around twenty-one. Of his childhood and youth we have, apart from the always uncertain anecdotal material, only his stylized accounts filtered through an imaginative matrix late in life. Some things are in all probability almost wholly fictional, such as the story of Josepha, the executioner's daughter; others rearranged in a self-allegorizing process, such as the portraits of his mother and father. The inaccessibility of the first third of his life makes psychological understanding difficult and chancy. Thus it is not surprising that psychoanalytical inquiries have come to quite various and incompatible results. If I may quote my own previous comment on this:

> Manfred Schneider's stimulating psychosocial inquiry into Heine's generation of dissidents found the problem in his relationship to his mother and the limits on her love in the interests of preparing the son for a capitalist society; Franz Futterknecht finds the mother boundlessly loving and adoring and locates the problem in disillusion with the weak father, resulting in a narcissistic, emotionally arrested self in the son; and Irene Guy, as far as I am able to follow her, applies a semiotic psychoanalysis derived from Julia Kristeva and sees the pathology emerging at the collapse of his health and the 1848 Revolution, causing him to regress into castration anxieties and fears of the "phallic" mother.[8]

Sometimes observers fall back on slogans. Wolfgang Hädecke finds the core of Heine's multiplicity of personality in a "torn consciousness,"[9] hardly a functional psychoanalytic category, and as a sociological category, in my view, like "alienation," of doubtful utility, though I shall reintroduce it later on. More recently, Ingrid Stipa has offered some stimulating suggestions, again largely derived from Kristeva, about narcissistic depression motivated by a primeval loss yet generating creativity; about the images of dismemberment and castration; and about the exotic as a realm of imagined, utopian wholeness, subject to images of disruption and discontinuity.[10] Such probes can be highly intelligent and resourceful, but it would be wise to remain constantly aware of their eminently speculative character, especially in view of the fragile state of our most ordinary biographical materials.

We do not even know with certainty what language was spoken in Heine's childhood home. I think it was German, very likely with a Judeo-German coloration, but the evidence is not unequivocal. It is remarkable, however, how often it is asserted, with greater or lesser assurance, that Heine's mother tongue was Yiddish.[11] I find no convincing evidence of this.

In the first place, it is not clear that everyone understands what would be meant by the term "Yiddish" in this case. It would not have been the now standard Yiddish based in Lithuania with its Slavicized grammar and Polish or Ukrainian vocabulary items, a descendant of the "Jew-Jargon" that martyred Heine's ears in Poland (2: 76), but Judeo-German, called, since World War II, West Yiddish, a language now regarded as extinct, which was more Hebraized in lexicon but also more of a German dialect phonetically and formally.[12] This assumption has had unfortunate consequences in claims that Heine did not have a native or natural relationship to the German language, transmitted not only in anti-Semitic screeds and their echo in Karl Kraus, but also in Adorno's dubious essay, "Heine the Wound."[13] Peter Uwe Hohendahl has usefully pointed out in this connection that at that time all poets, including the esteemed Hölderlin and Eichendorff, were initially "at home" in a regional dialect, not in the standard German that Adorno's Krausian language purism appears to presume.[14] No one, I should think, would say that a Swiss writer such as Gottfried Keller lacked an intimate relationship to the German language, even though his native Swiss is at least as distant from standard German as West Yiddish is.

For the moment I should like to attempt to achieve a little distance from Heine's relentlessly invasive pseudo-autobiographical voice, which structures so much of the modern discourse about him, and to see him somewhat more abstractly. When he first becomes visible to us, on the threshold of his young manhood, we find him progressing on two separate, not very congruent tracks. One of these is his burgeoning vocation as a poet. Heine did not decide to be a poet; he discovered within himself the inner lyric of which he was capable, without which his poetic career and œuvre would not have achieved their world-literary dimensions. It is reasonable to assume that his experience with himself generated, by the time the cycles of *Lyrical Intermezzo* and *Homecoming* were forming, a quite justifiable conviction of his superiority as a poet that was to sustain him to the end of his days. One thing that Heine thought he was, first and last, was a poet; one cannot stress this identity often enough because of the constant efforts of modern Heine studies to distract attention away from it. At the same time, this identity as poet emerges as notably other-directed. As Michael Perraudin has shown us in absorbing detail, it is oriented on and influenced by a large body of verse that occupied a large place in the cultural environment, a not insignificant part of the discourse of the bourgeois public sphere.[15] It is the verse of a late Romanticism already in process of domestication. Neither in his formative creative phase nor later in *The Romantic School* does Heine give any concentrated attention to the challengingly experimental lyric poetry of the German High Romanticism, of, say, Brentano or Novalis; of Hölderlin he seems not even to have heard. Even his Goethe canon is limited, on the whole, to Romantic love lyric and ballads, along with the inescapable "Song of Mignon" and, of special interest owing to its alternative site of exotic sensuality, the *West-eastern Divan*. One may conclude, therefore, that he was coming to think of himself not only as an artistically superior poet, but as a public poet, ambitious for prominent participation and influence in a prestigious national discourse, a high and courageous ambition, as it seems to me, perhaps requiring the narcissistic personality. It would lead too far afield to pursue here the obvious point that by identifying himself and his inner worth with poetry in this rather limited and reactive way, he worked himself into a serious dilemma concerning the durability and relevance of this already obsolescent literary mode, a dilemma that was to beset him quite soon and that he never resolved despite all the rhetoric he applied to it.

The other path is that defined by his family, toward some sort of tolerably secure situation in life. This sequence has been often described, from the successive flounderings in the realm of small business to the unloved legal studies culminating in the procurement of an academic degree that even he regarded as spurious, and it appears as one of the morality plays of the struggle of genius with philistinism. Less often noted has been the persistence with which Heine remained on this path while appearing to subvert or evade it. Indeed, what else was he to do? He cannot have conceived then of making a living by writing poetry, or writing anything. It is possible that his futile wooing of his cousin Amalie and probably also of Therese may be understood as an effort to remain bonded with the family, a reversion to an older Jewish tradition of supporting the bookish scholar with the merchant wealth of relatives. In any case, he did not abandon the path until the coincidence of his father's death with the recognition that he was not going to receive an appointment at the University of Munich and with his inability to recover his position in Cotta's publishing empire, when he was thirty-one and, as it was to turn out, his life was more than half over. If we date this path from his entry into a business school in October 1814 to his effort to obtain a municipal appointment in January 1831, he remained on it for over sixteen years.

From that perspective, his baptism in June 1825 is not mysterious, at least externally. It was motivated by the Prussian restoration of Jewish disabilities in the civil service in 1822; the closeness in time of the event to the award of the academic degree that potentially qualified him for the civil service makes this connection logical. His persistence on the path suggests a desire to please or at least to accommodate the family, especially mighty Uncle Salomon. Paradoxically, even the baptism is a sign of his desire to stay on the family path; for the family, which, as usual, primarily means Uncle Salomon, must have anticipated it as a probable prerequisite of Heine's next steps. He saw it coming more than a year and a half earlier, when he wrote to his friend Moser: "No one in my family is against it, except me," and the disgust he expresses at doing such a thing for a post "in dear Prussia!!!" is an acknowledgment of the necessity he supposed he was under, the only imaginable alternative being a private legal practice, a chancy business at that time, though he did make one desultory effort to establish himself in Hamburg.[16] The baptism was a sacrifice of personal dignity that he was soon to regret. Wilhelm Gössmann, who has written at length on Heine and religion, takes it far too lightly when he writes:

> At least one can maintain the position that with his baptism Heine did not need to undergo any inner conversion, any radical renunciation or any radical turn. It was a conscious affirmation of a secularized cultural Christianity, of a humanistic religion that had established itself literarily in European intellectual history since Lessing.[17]

The family and especially Uncle Salomon have had a rather bad press in this as in other matters, but perhaps we who are parents might have some sympathy with the family anxiety about young Heine's placement and security in a not especially hospitable society and a world that had shown itself throughout his boyhood to be extremely mutable, especially in view of all the evidence he had displayed of dreamy incompetence. Uncle Salomon was, of course, not baptized, nor is there evidence that any of his children were, except perhaps Fanny, the only one to make a non-Jewish marriage. It seems that if one could afford to remain Jewish, fine; if not, also O.K. This apparent laxity about a matter of existential significance for one who took himself as seriously as Heine must have been corrosive.

At the same time one must be struck by the quixotic way in which he appeared to meet these expectations, seeking positions for which he was no way fit and had no likelihood of obtaining, such as the Munich professorship or the post of council syndic in Hamburg. About few matters concerning him has so much nonsense been written. We have another morality play: the persecution of genius by the repressive and anti-Semitic dominant order. In fact, he was not remotely qualified for either position. The mystery about the Munich professorship is not why he did not obtain it but why the eminently conservative Bavarian minister of the interior, Eduard von Schenk, mediated it in the first place and then gave no answer of any kind. Since research has thus far discovered nothing about the disposition of the application, speculation about it is useless. The image of the savage-tempered, revolutionary-spirited Heine as corporation counsel of a city like Hamburg overstresses the imagination, not to speak of his often expressed hatred of the place. It is doubtful that he had much idea of what a council syndic was supposed to do.[18] When one contemplates these events from the perspective of his subsequent history through such things as his relations with his publisher, his resentment at the Saint-Simonian's failure to support him, the inheritance quarrel with the family, and the secret French government pension, the conclusion presents itself that he was in search of a sinecure. Thus we may postulate that he thought he was a kind of Augustan poet, in need of and deserving of a Maecenas in some form in recognition of his poetic eminence and his service to the commonweal.[19] Perhaps Heine would not have thought of himself in precisely this way, but there is a hint of it *e contrario* in his query to Horace's advice, *nonum prematur in annum*, "how one can survive nine years without eating" (2: 290).

In my observation, Heine made no systematic connection between labor and creativity on the one hand and income and material reward on the other, just as I believe he made no connection between work and wealth in the banking professions of his uncles or the Rothschilds, and the difficulty of making this disjunction functional for ease and prosperity frustrated him throughout his life. Therefore I think the frequently encountered assertion that he was the first German professional writer in the modern sense mistaken.[20] He was unable or unwilling to maintain the productivity of a professional writer, despite the recurrent urgings of his publisher. His thirty years of quarreling with and balking his publisher, potentially his most effectual ally in life, indicate an unwillingness to be professionalized. This, to be sure, provides him with another role in the modern morality play, as a resister to the commodification of literature and art. Indeed, he took this position before his literary career had actually taken shape, in his essay *On Poland*, where he complained of Germany "where the sciences are a trade and organized in guilds, and even the muse is a cow milked for a royalty until it yields pure water" (2: 88). It is difficult, or at least ambiguous, to be a professional writer while at the same time opposing the commodification of literature. Those of our time who admire Heine for this stance rarely tell us what arrangement for the economics of literature in the modern world they would prefer to the market. I think we know, however, what Heine would have preferred: an independent income, no strings attached.

Now, in sketching these abstractions, there has twice been occasion to allude to Heine's Jewishness, once in connection with the language spoken in his home, once in regard to his baptism. This topic is undergoing a very substantial change at present. In the past his Jewishness tended to be underplayed, except by Jewish commentators, who sometimes wanted to enroll him or exemplify him for some Jewish point of view or other. In the post-World-War-II period, the long and substantial history of anti-Semitic assault on him and his reputation may have motivated a recoil against foregrounding his Jewishness too explicitly. Marxists, para-Marxists, and neo-Marxists had their own reasons for relativizing Jewishness or, like Hans Mayer, absorbing it into a larger category of alienation such as the "outsider."[21] Today this reticence is undergoing a notable reversal. Not only is more and more being published about Heine's Jewishness; increasingly it is serving extensive and sometimes fundamental explanatory purposes, as the basic key to his consciousness and personality; his texts appear as codings of Jewish allusiveness and masked identity.[22] Some of this is getting to be exaggerated, and an American contemplating it may notice how exotic the commonplaces of Jewish life often remain to German observers. Solemn footnotes are supplied to explain what matzohs are and when Passover occurs, though, in regard to the latter, one would suppose anyone reasonably firm in any of the Gospels might have some notion of it, even if the German Bible insists on translating the Greek πάσχα (> Hebrew *pesach*) as "Easter." Edith Lutz, in her recent, uneven study of Heine and the Association for the Culture and Science of the Jews, charts the Passover *seder*, in order to show what fraction of it is depicted in *The Rabbi of Bacherach*, by referring extensively to a scholarly edition of the Haggadah.[23] An American wanting to examine the details of the Passover *seder* would go to a bookstore and buy a Haggadah off the shelf for a couple of dollars. An American would recognize the Yiddishisms that turn up in Heine's letters and, very occasionally, in the texts as ordinary Jewish turns of phrase, not evidence, as is sometimes argued, that he actually *spoke* Yiddish. The rising level of Judaistic scholarship in Germany is relieving this alienation somewhat, but there is still some insecurity in dealing with Jewish matters, which does not, of course, inhibit confident assertions about them.

Robert Holub, in a potentially productive effort to pick a fight with everyone, has recently asserted that the baptized author H. Heine was not a Jew and therefore not a German-Jewish writer, a classification that is "an invention of critics and literary scholars"; rather, he was a German writer of Jewish origin.[24] One may acknowledge an impropriety in regarding Jewishness as virtually a biological or existential category in permanence, a practice encountered not least among Jewish commentators, as in a Jewish attack on Heine after World War II: "You cannot choose not to be a Jew, you can only choose to be an authentic or inauthentic Jew," a formulation that runs the risk of accepting and reifying the categories of the persecutor.[25] Certainly there are writers whose Jewish or part-Jewish origin is of no detectable significance and perhaps should not be adduced at all. However, Holub would be the first to agree that Heine's case is complicated. In phases of his life he may have wished to leave Jewishness, but Jewishness would not leave him, and not only for reasons of environmental circumstances.

I have always thought that, at the outset of his career, when he first begins to come into view for us, he was not particularly exercised about his Jewishness. He did not come out of a ghetto, and if the teasing reported in his memoirs was the extent of the hostility encountered in his boyhood, it does not appear very severe or debilitating. Like other German Jews of his class and level of education, he instinctively felt himself to be under the protection, so to speak, of the brotherhood of Lessing and Mendelssohn. Jewish identity was not so much to be repudiated as simply to become less important because less defining within the universalist humanism of Enlightenment tolerance. Some combination of external and internal pressures, difficult to discriminate precisely, pushed him part way off this position: externally, the inescapable evidence that the Napoleonic advances in emancipation were to be reversed, the anti-Jewish riots of 1819, the restoration of Jewish disabilities in public service, and some unpleasant personal encounters; internally, the experiment with the Berlin Association in the early 1820s, which, as interesting and educational as it may have been, did not solve his identity problem. It is not sufficiently recognized how idiosyncratic his responses to these circumstances turned out to be. One, perhaps more a matter of psychological disposition, was a rhetoric of Jewish militance, expressed publicly in the poem "Donna Clara" or in his employment of traditional Polish Jewry with its jargon and filth as a stick with which to beat the bourgeoisified Reform Jews of Uncle Salomon's entourage (1: 156-58; 2: 76-77) and privately in "To Edom!" (1: 271) or his lament that the Jews had lost the capacity to hate (HSA 20: 72), a tone revived in his adaptation of the 137th Psalm in "Jehuda ben Halevy" (6/1: 136-37). The Jews of Heine's time were trying to make peace with their environment, not war upon it. Another is his sometimes drastic expression of repudiation of Jewishness, his denials and misdirections, transparent though they characteristically were. An example is his response, with the characteristic loss of equilibrium that beset him in the fervor of polemic, to Wolfgang Menzel's anti-Semitic innuendos directed against Young Germany: "the better educated person well knows that people who are accused of being opponents of deism cannot maintain any sympathy for the synagogue; one does not turn to the totally faded charms of the mother when the aging daughter no longer pleases" (5: 38). Another is his postulation of the horror people of the future will feel when they hear of the Eucharist:

> then perhaps one of the old men will relate that there was a time when a dead man was adored as God and celebrated with ghastly necrophagy, during which one imagined that the bread one was eating was his flesh and the wine one drank was his blood. At this tale the women's cheeks will grow pale and the wreaths visibly tremble on their beautifully tressed heads. But the men will strew new incense on the hearth-altar in order to drive away the gloomy, uncanny memories with pleasant aromas. (5: 207)

Today's anti-authoritarian readers, acknowledging no norms of decorum in public discourse, are delighted by such pugnacity without considering how eccentric and isolating it was in its own time. No one wanted to hear this, the Jews least of all.

Heine's lack of solidarity with his fellow Jews is a striking feature of his course through life in view of the high proportion of them among his acquaintances, especially in Paris.[26] He was irretrievably estranged from Orthodoxy despite his opportunistic exploitation of the Polish Jews, but also hostile to the Reform and aloof from the emancipation movement, whose paladin, Gabriel Riesser, sought to challenge him to a duel. His lack of direct and explicit interest in contemporary Jewry is marked. The main thrust of the learning of the Association, after all, was historical, and his literary response was to write a medieval Jewish novel, unlike, say, Berthold Auerbach, whose fictional biographies of Spinoza and Ephraim Kuh, despite their historical settings, more directly intersected internal Jewish concerns in the 1830s. Heine's novel, as we know, eventuated in a satire on the ghettoized Jews. Because modern commentary regularly takes his side in everything, there is a tendency to adopt his disregard for his contemporaries, to scorn them as assimilationists accommodating to the bourgeois order. This is one of the several areas where some sympathy for and understanding of someone other than Heine would not be out of place. The attitude is part of the larger context of condescension toward if not condemnation of the German Jews that has become a conspicuous feature of post-Holocaust discourse and, in the interest of justice and equity, is much in need of readjustment. Furthermore, Heine's lack of solidarity with his fellow Jews parallels his lack of solidarity with his fellow political progressives and is thus a significant feature of his personality and the management of his life.

Despite what is by now a large literature on Heine's Jewishness, there is an aspect of it that has been curiously neglected: what Philipp Veit called, in an essay published nearly a quarter of a century ago and almost totally ignored since, Heine's "Marrano Pose,"[27] that is, his strong and intensifying identification with the golden age of medieval Spanish Jewry. The Marrano pose does not mean, as it is sometimes taken to mean currently, that he was some kind of modern *converso*, nourishing a partly hidden Jewish identity in protest against the oppressive environment. Rather it is the assumption of a dignified and highly cultured Sephardic persona in contrast to the gauche philistine materialism if not outright backwardness and obscurantism associated with Ashkenazic Jewry. The Marrano pose was recognizable and quite dazzling to Emma Lazarus, who was herself of Sephardic origin on her father's side:

> We must go back to the Hebrew poets of Palestine and Spain to find a parallel in literature for the magnificent imagery and voluptuous orientalism of the "Intermezzo."... His was a seed sprung from the golden branch that flourished in Hebrew-Spain between the years 1000 and 1600.[28]

Characteristic of this pattern is a genealogy traced back to the Sephardic community of the Netherlands. Heine's former pupil from the Association recalled him as saying: "My mother ... probably descends from a noble Jewish family. The frequent expulsion of the Israelites from the European countries led my ancestors to Holland, in which land the little word *von* was changed to *van*."[29] This bit of misinformation is part of the pattern of autobiographical obfuscation characteristic of him, to which belongs the canard passed on by his acquaintances that his mother was not only of noble birth but Christian, of which Heine himself was doubtless the source.[30] Veit, to be sure, comments of those adopting this pose that "technically their aristocratic affectations were not always unfounded since they or their forebears had often been rewarded with knighthood for their public service."[31] Veit notes Heine's Sephardic personae from "Donna Clara" through *The Rabbi of Bacherach* to "Jehuda ben Halevy," but no one has built upon his initial, interpretively somewhat primitive probe. However, this is one area in which Heine did adapt a pattern of his contemporaries, a project, as Ismar Schorsch has said, of redefining the modern Jew, paradoxically, by association with a medieval "paradigm which would ground institutional rebellion in Jewish soil." "The Sephardic image," he writes, "facilitated a religious posture marked by cultural openness, philosophical thinking, and an appreciation for the aesthetic," an orientation that expressed itself in numerous ways from the Moorish style of the German-Jewish synagogue to the claimed discipleship to Spinoza. It underlay the "science of Judaism," originating in the Berlin Association and ultimately was directed against Ashkenazic culture and Polish rabbinism. Schorsch observes on this, in our time, highly volatile topic: "The course of modern Jewish scholarship cannot be understood apart from the Spanish mystique and, in fact, no other area of modern Jewish culture remained under its sway as long."[32]

This is clearly the context in which to understand the climactic amalgamation of the attributes of princely or knightly power with the balked power and martyrdom of the poet in the persona of Jehuda Halevy: "Monarch in the realm of thought, he / Is responsible to no man" (6/1: 135). A reintegration of Jewishness with poetic pride has certainly taken place in Heine's self-understanding. But at the same time it is alienated from the, in his view, uninspiring and unaesthetic life and aspirations of contemporary European Jewry into a mythified heroic age of Jewish splendor and dignity: "In the golden age of glory / Of the Arabic-Hispanic / Jewish school of poetry" (6/1: 150). When Schorsch writes that "the ultimate power and appeal of the Sephardic mystique in the age of emancipation derived from its Greek core," which enabled German Jews ambitious for cultural status "to recover a classical heritage in common with German culture,"[33] one is obliged to think of the treasure chest of ancient Persian origin, the peregrinations of which are described in an apparent digression in the third part of "Jehuda ben Halevy." Alexander made it the repository of a manuscript of Homer, but the narrator, should he acquire it and not have to pawn it, would employ it as a container for the poems of Jehuda Halevy (6/1: 145); a Jewish classic is elevated to parity with the ancient Greek avatar of German culture. It is extraordinary that Heine scholarship has not responded to Veit's initiative in this matter; even the venerable S. S. Prawer, who provides a detailed explication of the *Hebrew Melodies*, does not pursue it;[34] it is left to a Judaist like Schorsch to make the connection. Thus a study of Heine's Spanish themes several years ago waves off the Sephardic identification as ahistorical, asserting that he had no real interest in medieval Spain but employed the motifs to reflect the Jewish situation in Prussia and to oppose the German Romantic-nationalistic celebrations of Spanish triumphs over the Moors.[35] This is an example of the common practice of insisting that Heine is writing about something other than he appears to be and that is more congenial to the interests of the interpreter; in this case the observations are not wholly impertinent, but in method they deflect attention from his preoccupation with who he thought he was.

Of course, he also thought from an early date that he was an emancipator and freedom-fighter. A comprehensive reception history of Heine, which we are not likely to get soon, would show, I think, that until our own time the majority of readers world-wide did not take him altogether at his word on his heroism in the cause of freedom. Extreme examples are found in Charles Godfrey Leland's cranky and intrusive notes to his English-language edition, as when he remarks on one of Heine's claims of courage in battle—"under duress I had to take part in the pain and struggle of the times, and my participation was sincere, and I fought as well as the bravest" (3: 334):

> One would really like to know when, where, and how all this tremendous fighting, of which Heine boasts so much, ever came off, unless it is that he alludes to his ribald onslaughts on such folk as Platen, the Schlegels, Raupach, and one or two women; most of which recalls what was said of a New York journalist, that he was the bravest man who ever lived, because nobody ever beat him in

> blackguarding.[36]

There are no doubt several reasons for this resistance to his claims. One is the apparent contradiction between his highly rhetorical claims for himself and his refusal of solidarity with his liberal and radical contemporaries. Another is the centrality to his politics of sensual emancipation, which was politically, sociologically, and ideologically untimely in the middle third of the nineteenth century, as congenial as it has been to mid-twentieth-century post-adolescents. Heine constantly tried to bridge this gap with rhetorical assertiveness; thus, among many passages, the preface to the first volume of *The Salon*:

> A second, "successor generation" has seen that all my word and song blossoms forth from a great, divinely joyful springtime idea, which is, if not better, at least as respectable as that sad, moldy Ash Wednesday idea that gloomily desolated Europe of flowers and populated it with ghosts and Tartuffes. What I once rebelled against with light weapons now is the object of open, earnest warfare—I am no longer even standing in the front lines. (3: 8)

These are pipe dreams. This successor generation was imaginary in his time, if perhaps less so in our own. The modern tendency to dismiss the people of his time and elect a new one more congruent with him has been a misdirection.

But the combative revolutionary persona is a very real component of who he thought he was. It seems plausible to assume that his experience of Jewishness was a significant preparatory motive of his revolutionary spirit, even though there is no evidence for the assumption, constantly repeated by commentators, that his allegiance to Napoleon was owing to the partial and qualified emancipation of the Jews under his rule. However, Jews, experiencing at first hand the defects of the dominant order, are often found in the forefront of reform and revolution, insofar as they do not find it more convenient to be partisans of the dominant order, like Uncle Salomon or the Rothschilds. In the days of the Association and its aftermath, Heine privately foregrounded an activist allegiance to Jewish emancipation while abjuring any fidelity to Jewish religion:

> That I will be enthusiastic for the rights of the Jews and their civil equality, that I admit, and in bad times, which are inevitable, the Teutonic mob will hear my voice so that it echoes in German beer halls and palaces. But the born enemy of all positive religions will never champion the religion that first brought forth the fault-finding with human beings [*Menschenmäkeley*] that now causes us so much pain.[37]

The unusual word *Menschenmäkeley* is remembered from Lessing's *Nathan the Wise* (II, 3), actually from the prejudiced discourse of the Templar, and repeated again in the religious critique of *The City of Lucca* (2: 515). In public, however, it became his habit to divert attention from his Jewishness or even to speak of it as if it had nothing to do with him. Thus in a famous, often quoted passage in *Journey from Munich to Genoa*:

> What is this great task of our time?
> It is emancipation. Not only of the Irish, Greeks, Frankfurt Jews, West Indian blacks, and suchlike oppressed peoples, but the emancipation of the whole world, especially of Europe, which has entered its majority and now tears itself away from the iron leading strings of the privileged, the aristocracy. (2: 376)

Heine carefully encapsulates the Jews in a characteristically universalist, cosmopolitan sequence so as not to privilege their cause. Why, one might ask, particularly Frankfurt Jews? The Frankfurt Jew uppermost in Heine's mind and perhaps in the minds of many of his readers was Ludwig Börne, whose acquaintance Heine had made a year and a half before and who was certainly less in need of emancipation than the great majority of Jews. There is something mildly dismissive about the appellation and its placement, a refusal of explicit allegiance to the cause of Jewish emancipation. This strategy has met the approval of many modern observers and has been replicated by them. However, it does not appear to have been wholly settled within his inner self, as appears in his defense of Shylock in his Shakespeare book of 1838, which prefigured his readiness to respond when the Damascus pogrom of 1840 indicated that there was still something especially perilous about the Jewish condition, and thus especially demanding of attention. The most explicitly Jewish of Heine's texts, *The Rabbi of Bacherach*, is resuscitated under this provocation, and from then on, until the religious return of the last phase, there is an attempted reamalgamation of Jewish with revolutionary identity, though characteristically on explicitly subjective and isolating terms, consistently eschewing community with others.

As for the revolutionary identity itself, I think it has not been clearly seen how inevitably it was bound to come into conflict with the poetic identity. I have found this question more or less systematically obfuscated by modernist or post-modernist shadow-boxing with the autonomy of literary art or the constantly reiterated shibboleth of the "epoch of art," which I have argued both never existed and never came to an end. Rather, the problem is more elementary. The corpus of poetry upon which he modeled himself is not oppositional but affirmative, if not necessarily of the dominant order, then of its inheritor, the mass public of the folk (as distinguished from the mob). This is, indeed, the motive; Heine identified himself not with the elite, the refined, the elevated in poetry, but with the popular, as he himself aspired to be one of the folk and an acknowledged spokesman of it. But the self-representation of the folk in poetry implied conventional morality, purity of sentiment, and, in this particular context, an increasingly nationalistic spirit. Heine's radically oppositional and non-participatory stance on social, erotic, and political matters necessarily had to bifurcate from the spirit of poetry as he understood it. This bifurcation was mutual, as became evident in the clash with the practitioners of the mode into which the domesticated late Romanticism descended, designated by Heine as the Swabian School. He saw this with perfect clarity; thus his repeated repudiations of poetry and poesy as obsolete and a distraction from the imperatives of modern times. Since many of those who have worked on Heine in modern times are indifferent to or even hostile to poesy, this turn has met with approval and has been propagated as exemplary. It works for them; unfortunately, it did not work for Heine, who thought he was a poet in the most intense way, an identity essential to his self-worth.

Thus poetry continued to be the poetry he knew, late Romantic in tone, formally modeled on the folk song. His irony, his skepticism about emotion, his quotation of the inventory of motifs rescued the integrity of his poetry but alienated it from its models, which were, however, not erased or overcome, but, so to speak, sublated, still retained while repudiated. The alternative is not another kind of poetry, but noise, what Benedetto Croce called *non poesia*. Thus his difficulty in finding for himself or identifying among other poets the "new song" promised in the first caput of the *Winter's Tale* (4: 578); but thus also his constant recurrence to poetry almost to his last hour, along with a never wholly abandoned but sometimes suppressed conviction that the realm of the imagination was more habitable and humane than the realm of reality. This is his "torn consciousness," the conflict of intensely engaged but incompatible commitments in the constitution of the self. In my view, there is no dialectic, only antithesis, permanently unresolved, as appears in what has been taken to be his last poem, "I dreamed a dream upon a summer night," in which the figures of spiritualism and sensualism, of truth and beauty, erupt into an eternally cacophonous quarrel drowned out only by the hee-hawing of Balaam's ass (6/1: 349). Much of the contemporary discourse about Heine endeavors to impose resolution on him in order to make him functional for current purposes. But this is to evade or at least to metamorphize him, because it is the irresolution and the contradiction that generate the energy that keeps him memorable and fecund. Moreover, this only partially integrated self has also encouraged a separation of identities in the reception history: the preferential treatment of the poetic and lyrical Heine in the past; of the witty and ironic Heine, especially in non-German reception; of the political and revolutionary Heine in our time: for all interested persons, a Heine of one's own.

His identity—his external, visible identity, which is what I have been trying to talk about here—has the appearance of being self-created; I call it appearance because I do not believe any real self is self-created. There is always a strong motivation in him to define himself on his own terms. This has sometimes led to the view that he was uncommonly uprooted, "*quite without tradition*," as Hans Mayer insisted, "at the beginning of his career, as though he were Kaspar Hauser."[38] I think this is a categorical error. There is something Romantic about it, as though the non-contradictory integrity of the self need be organically grounded in origins; it is not without parallel to the claim that Heine had an unnatural relationship to language. He had plenty of traditions; his writings are full of them. But he chose among them and defined their relative weight and authority. The circumstance that he was the master of his external identities rather than being defined by them turned out to be a source of strength when the fortune of his life turned extremely bad in his last phase; he was able to adjust the elements of his self, his religious and philosophical postures, and his poetic practice, which became more self-sufficient, less covetous of broad public acknowledgment. The truly remarkable survival of his spirit and creativity in the "mattress-grave" may well be owing to this capacity. On the other hand, the self-created self that picks and chooses its own traditions is a self that wants no ancestors except as they are designated and configured by it, forming an ancestry that is a larger fiction; thus the insouciance about accuracy and judiciousness in his cultural-historical writings such as *On the History of Religion and Philosophy in Germany* and *The Romantic School*. There is in such a self a narcissistic tyranny over the world, past and present, which may account as much as anything for his extremely stressed relationship with that world and the people in it, and for the orbit of his life, so eccentric to that of others.

For a number of years I have believed that the project of employing Heine as medium for revolutionizing and purging German culture has accomplished about as much as it can. It was a feeling reinforced at the massive Heine congress in Düsseldorf in May 1997, where it seemed that much refinement and, sometimes, ingenuity were fueling rotation on well-worn paths and the threshing of familiar straw. The hyperbolic presence of Heine in the public domain outside the congress, not to mention the rising tide of publications in the course of this year, I find, as a foreign observer, disconcerting rather than encouraging. Perhaps by backing away from Heine somewhat, giving up requiring him to do something for us and justifying him by all and any means, applying to him some of the irony and even malice with which he appraised his world, and sorting out what we can know from what we merely suppose, we might find him richer and even more enduring.

Notes

1. Perhaps it is not so hard for poets. Nobel Prize winner Wisława Szymborska's acceptance speech was entitled "I Don't Know": *World Literature Today* 71 (1997), pp. 5-7.

2. Joseph A. Kruse, "'... alle edeln Herzen des europäischen Vaterlandes.' Heine und Europa," in *Nationale Grenzen und internationaler Austausch. Studien zum Kultur- und Wissenschaftstransfer in Europa*, ed. Lothar Jordan and Bernd Kortländer (Tübingen, 1995), p. 58.

3. Manfred Windfuhr, "Heine privat," *Rätsel Heine. Autorprofil, Werk, Wirkung* (Heidelberg, 1997), p. 51. Windfuhr's essay came to my attention after I had drafted my own. He implies that it is intended as a corrective to "an instability and indecisiveness situated in Heine's psyche that drove him to a mania for roles and personae," which he ascribes to me (p. 10, n. 3).

4. To King Ludwig I of Bavaria, January 12, 1830, *Goethes Briefe. Hamburger Ausgabe*, ed. Karl Robert Mandelkow, vol. 4 (Hamburg, 1967), p. 363.

5. As much as most people will ever want to know in Peter Bumm, *August Graf von Platen. Eine Biographie* (Paderborn, 1990).

6. See *Düsseldorf. Geschichte von den Ursprüngen bis ins 20. Jahrhundert*, vol. 2: *Von der Residenzstadt zur Beamtenstadt (1614-1900)*, ed. Hugo Weidenhaupt (Düsseldorf, 1988), pp. 331-32.

7. Jan-Christoph Hauschild and Michael Werner, *"Der Zweck des Lebens ist das Leben selbst." Heinrich Heine. Eine Biographie* (Cologne, 1997), acknowledge the question of what he did not report, but do not go into it. Ortwin Lämke, *Heines Begriff der Geschichte. Der Journalist Heinrich Heine und die Julimonarchie* (Stuttgart and Weimar, 1997), makes some progress, but for the most part the contextualization is from newspapers and contemporary discourse rather than historiography. Bodo Morawe, *Heines "Französische Zustände". Über die Fortschritte des Republikanismus und die anmarschierende Weltliteratur* (Heidelberg, 1997), draws from similar sources to mount a shrill, tendentious argument that Heine's repeated claims of monarchism were ironic and that he actually meant to agitate for a republic in France and Germany.

8. Jeffrey L. Sammons, "The Exhaustion of Current Heine Studies: Some Observations, Partly Speculative," in *The Jewish Reception of Heinrich Heine*, ed. Mark H. Gelber (Tübingen, 1992), p. 8. The sources are, respectively: Manfred Schneider, "Die Angst des Revolutionärs vor der Revolution: Zur Genese und Struktur des politischen Diskurses bei Heine," *Heine-Jahrbuch* 19 (1980), pp. 9-48; Schneider, "'... Die Liebe für schöne Frauen und Liebe für die Französische Revolution ...' Anmerkungen zum romantischen Spracherwerb und zur Ikonographie des politischen Diskurses bei Heine," in *Perspektiven psychoanalytischer Literaturkritik*, ed. Sebastian Goeppert (Freiburg im Breisgau, 1978), pp. 158-93; *Die kranke schöne Seele der Revolution: Heine, Börne, das "Junge Deutschland," Marx und Engels* (Frankfurt am Main, 1980); Franz Futterknecht, *Heinrich Heine: Ein Versuch* (Tübingen, 1985); Irene Guy, *Sexualität im Gedicht: Heinrich Heines Spätlyrik* (Bonn, 1984).

9. Wolfgang Hädecke, *Heinrich Heine: Eine Biographie* (Munich and Vienna, 1985), p. 237.

10. Ingrid Stipa, "Translating Heine's Lyrics: A Passe-partout Masquerade of the Self?" in *Poetry Poetics Translation: Festschrift in Honor of Richard Exner*, ed. Ursula Mahlendorf and Laurence Rickels (Würzburg, 1994), pp. 191-98.

11. See, for example, most recently, Helmut Koopmann, "'Nachtgedanken.' zu Heinrich Heines Gedicht 'Denk' ich an Deutschland in der Nacht,'" in Internationale Hugo-Wolf-Akademie für Gesang Dichtung Liedkunst, *Von Dichtung und Musik. "Heinrich Heine." Ein Lesebuch* (Tutzing, 1995), pp. 52-53: "We *know* that in Heine's childhood home *presumably* a kind of Yiddish was spoken" (my emphasis). Similarly, Koopmann, "Heine als Exilant in Paris," in *Romanticism and Beyond: A Festschrift for John F. Fetzer*, ed. Clifford A. Bernd, Ingeborg Henderson, and Winder McConnell (New York, etc., 1996), p. 18. There is an uninformed muddle about this in Jochanan Trilse-Finkelstein, *Gelebter Widerspruch. Heinrich Heine Biographie* (Berlin, 1997), p. 27.

12. Matthias Richter, *Die Sprache jüdischer Figuren in der deutschen Literatur (1750-1933). Studien zu Form und Funktion* (Göttingen, 1995), esp. pp. 18-35. Richter (pp. 111-12) points out that Heine's identification in *Börne* of Jewish *Mauscheln* with Frankfurt dialect (4: 24) has been shown to be inexact.

13. Theodor W. Adorno, "Die Wunde Heine," in *Noten zur Literatur I* (Frankfurt am Main, 1958), pp. 144-52.

14. Peter Uwe Hohendahl, "Language, Poetry, and Race: The Example of Heinrich Heine," in *Prismatic Thought: Theodor W. Adorno* (Lincoln, Nebraska, and London, 1995), pp. 105-17.

15. Michael Perraudin, *Heinrich Heine: Poetry in Context. A Study of* Buch der Lieder (Oxford, 1989).

16. To Moses Moser, September 27-30, 1823 (HSA 20: 113). On the semi-serious plan to open a legal practice, see to Rudolph Christiani, December 6, 1825, and to Moser, from "Damned Hamburg," December 14-19, 1825 (HSA 20: 224-26).

17. Wilhelm Gössmann, "Verschiedene Konversionen?" in *"Ich Narr des Glücks." Heinrich Heine 1797-1856. Bilder einer Ausstellung*, ed. Joseph A. Kruse et al. (Stuttgart and Weimar, 1997), p. 309. Gössmann refers for support to a passage in *Zur Geschichte der Religion und Philosophie in Deutschland* (3: 588), an example of operating with Heine's always purposively designed public utterances rather than considering as him a whole.

18. Hauschild and Werner, *"Der Zweck des Lebens ist das Leben selbst,"* p. 173: "he had no precise conception of the practical significance of a syndic's position."

19. Jan-Christoph Hochschild, "Professor Heine? Von den Lockungen einer akademischen Karriere," in *Heinrich Heine im Spannungsfeld von Literatur und Wissenschaft. Symposium anläßlich der Benennung der Universität Düsseldorf nach Heinrich Heine*, ed. Wilhelm Gössmann and Manfred Windfuhr (Hagen, 1990), pp. 41-52, sees the application for the professorship in just this light: "The model that Heine had in mind during his Munich application was the Maecenas model, the professorship that he claimed for himself an honorary professorship for which he was to be qualified by literary, not outstanding scholarly achievements" (p. 49), and points out that such a position was not without models and parallels, among them Schiller and Rückert (p. 50).

20. Hauschild and Werner, *"Der Zweck des Lebens ist das Leben selbst"*: "In reality Heine resisted the literary profession to the end, and he took this step only under the duress of external circumstances, as it became clear to him that all other possibilities were blocked... Clearly he thought, after he had met the general social and legal requirements to civic equality, that he could lie in the bed he had made for himself, as though everyone had just been waiting to indemnify him for overcoming his inner doubts and subordinating himself to the political and social constraints" (pp. 112, 114).

21. Hans Mayer, *Aussenseiter* (Frankfurt am Main, 1975), pp. 207-23, 350-66.

22. See, e. g., Jürgen Voigt, *Ritter, Harlekin und Henker. Der junge Heine als romantischer Patriot und als Jude. Ein Versuch* (Frankfurt am Main and Bern, 1982), its revision, *O Deutschland, meine ferne Liebe... Der junge Heinrich Heine zwischen Nationalromantik und Judentum* (Bonn, 1993); Klaus Briegleb, *Opfer Heine? Versuche über Schriftzüge der Revolution* (Frankfurt am Main, 1986); Walter Jens, "Heinrich Heine. Ein deutscher Jude," in *Feldzüge eines Republikaners. Ein Lesenbuch*, ed. Gerd Ueding and Peter Weit (Munich, 1988), pp. 310-18; and Trilse-Finkelstein, *Gelebter Widerspruch.*

23. Edith Lutz, *Der "Verein für Cultur und Wissenschaft der Juden" und sein Mitglied H. Heine* (Stuttgart and Weimar, 1997), pp. 240, 250.

24. Robert C. Holub, "Deutscher Dichter jüdischer Herkunft," in *"Ich Narr des Glücks,"* p. 44.

25. Martin Greenberg, "Heinrich Heine: Flight and Return. The Fallacy of Being Only a Human Being," *Commentary* 7 (Jan.-June 1949), pp. 225-31. This is contextualized in my essay, "Jewish Reception as the Last Phase of American Heine Reception," in *The Jewish Reception of Heinrich Heine*, ed. Gelber, pp. 197-214. I have come to think that Sander Gilman's various commentaries also tend in this direction.

26. See on this Michael A. Meyer, "'Der nie abzuwaschende Jude'—Heinrich Heine," in *Deutsch-jüdische Geschichte in der Neuzeit*, vol. 2, *Emanzipation und Akkulturation 1780-1871*, ed. Michael Brenner, Stefi Jersch-Wenzel, and Meyer (Munich, 1996), esp. p. 218.

27. Philipp F. Veit, "Heine: The Marrano Pose," *Monatshefte* 66 (1974), pp. 145-56.

28. Emma Lazarus, "The Poet Heine," *Century Illustrated Monthly Magazine*, 29, N.S. 7 (November 1884-April 1885), pp. 212, 215.

29. *Begegnungen mit Heine. Berichte der Zeitgenossen*, ed. Michael Werner, vol. 1 (Hamburg, 1973), pp. 67-68.

30. See Jeffrey L. Sammons, *Heinrich Heine: A Modern Biography* (Princeton, 1979), p. 17. This policy is curiously maintained by Emile Schrijver and Falk Wiesemann, eds., *Die von Geldern Haggadah und Heinrich Heines "Der Rabbi von Bacherach"* (Vienna and Munich, 1997), which replaces the locative "van Geldern" with an implied aristocratic "von Geldern" throughout, even altering it from sources.

31. Veit, "Heine: The Marrano Pose," p. 146.

32. Ismar Schorsch, "The Myth of Sephardic Supremacy," in *From Text to Context: The Turn to History in Modern Judaism* (Hanover and London, 1994), pp. 71, 79, 81-82. The distinction was socially visible and clearly articulated in nineteenth-century France: Michel Espagne, *Les Juifs allemands de Paris à l'époque de Heine. La Translation ashkénaze* (Paris, 1996), esp. "La rève sépharde des ashkénazes," pp. 220-25. In time, Jewish race theorists attempted, by measurement of skulls, to support the racial superiority of Sephardim over Ashkenazim: Bernd Rother, "Rassenwahn und Rassenstolz. Sephardische Reaktionen auf die Judenverfolgung," *Menora: Jahrbuch für deutsch-jüdische Geschichte* (1997), p. 203.

33. Schorsch, "The Myth of Sephardic Supremacy," p. 87.

34. S. S. Prawer, *Heine's Jewish Comedy: A Study of his Portraits of Jews and Judaism* (Oxford, 1983), pp. 552-603. Prawer lists Veit's essay in his bibliography, but, as far as I can see, nowhere employs it.

35. Karlheinz Fingerhut, "Spanische Spiegel. Heinrich Heines Verwendung spanischer Geschichte und Literatur zur Selbstreflexion des Juden und des Dichters," *Heine-Jahrbuch* 31 (1992), pp. 106-36, esp. pp. 113-14, 128. As is customary in German studies of such matters, there is no mention of Veit's essay. The same is true of Gerhart Hoffmeister, "Granada und

Jerusalem oder 'Poesie-Orient' versus Real-Orient: Referenzbeziehungen zwischen Heine, Arnim und Byron," in *Heinrich Heine und die Romantik. Heinrich Heine and Romanticism*, ed. Markus Winkler (Tübingen, 1997), pp. 159-72, which shows in observant detail "how the two places, Jerusalem and Granada, converge in motif" (p. 160) while merely brushing by the assumed Sephardic identity (p. 171).

36. *The Works of Heinrich Heine*, translated from the German by Charles Godfrey Leland (Hans Breitmann), vol. 4 (London and New York, 1892-1906), p. 245. Of Heine's often quoted designation of himself as "a good soldier in mankind's war of liberation," (2: 382), Leland remarks that Heine, "though he assures us that he was a brave [sic] soldier in the cause of freedom, would have been rather too nervous, or weepy and fainty, for a turn under fire" (vol. 7, p. 282).

37. To Moses Moser, August 2, 1823, *HSA* 20, p. 107.

38. Hans Mayer, "Die Ausnahme Heinrich Heine," in *Von Lessing bis Thomas Mann. Wandlungen der bürgerlichen Literatur in Deutschland* (Pfullingen, 1959), pp. 275-76, several times republished.

History versus Memory: Heinrich Heine and the Jewish Past[1]

Christhard Hoffmann

I

The emergence of the modern Jewish conception of history was closely tied to the process of emancipation and social integration of the Jews in Europe. For premodern Jewry the collective past was made present not as historiography—that is, through the narrative representation of a continuous historical trajectory—but through a sacralized culture of memory.[2] For medieval Jews, "history" was first and foremost a religiously understood story of the origins of the Jewish people, authoritatively narrated in the Bible, and regularly recalled through ritual and recitation. The past had no value in and of itself in this conception. Only through the meaning accorded it by religious categories could the past be meaningfully structured and serve as a means for the production of (religious) knowledge. The meaning of history, which might remain dark and hidden in the events of the present, was easily recognized in the historical representations of the Bible, as for example, in the accounts of the exodus from Egypt or of the wandering through the desert. The clearly ordered phases of Jewish history as set out in the canonical texts could be considered a valid historical paradigm for all time; they constituted the key to the meaning to be accorded every historical happening.[3] This valorization and making absolute of the canonically prescribed "model history," which only intensified after the destruction of the second temple and the onset of rabbinic Judaism,[4] led to a typological or archetypal notion of history: for those who had internalized the paradigmatic structure of biblical history, the further course of history appeared only as a repetition of typical constellations and foundational situations. Every actual oppressor of the Jewish people was thus seen as Pharaoh or Haman revisited; Diaspora was read as a return of the Babylonian exile; suffering was God's penalty for sins committed against Him.[5] On this view, history contains nothing essentially new prior to the transition to the messianic age. A closer engagement with history was worthless and represented, as Maimonides remarked, a "waste of time."[6] Only the study and interpretation of the biblical history of salvation promised true knowledge. The valorization of biblical history led in this manner to a largely static, "timeless" conception of history and a corresponding neglect of historiography.

Pre-modern Jewish historical consciousness was thus constituted by an anamnestic making-present of the biblical history of origins and a personal identification with it. Standing since Abraham and Moses in an uninterrupted continuum of tradition, this consciousness was central to Jewish self-understanding. The imperative "Zakhor - Remember" was understood as a religious command.[7] The religious obligation becomes especially clear at the Passover Seder, "that quintessential exercise in Jewish group memory."[8] The course of the festival seeks to effect a full identification with the ancestors who left Egypt: one eats only unleavened bread (mazzot), because the forefathers in Egypt fled in great haste; one eats bitter herbs (maror), because the Egyptians embittered their lives through slave labor; finally, the history of the Exodus is related as an answer to the question posed by the youngest child, why this night differs from all others. In an act of personal identification ("when *I* left Egypt"), the planes of present and past blend. Characteristic of this attitude is the saying of Rabbi Gamliel, who demanded: "In each and every generation let each person regard himself as though *he* had emerged from Egypt."[9]

Through its internalization and actualization in the form of ritual reconstruction, the story of Exodus became a "foundational story" of the Jewish people, a "myth," if one understands the term with Jan Assmann, as a "story with which one gains orientation with respect to one's self and the world", as a "truth of a higher order, a truth not merely accepted as truth, but one which actively posits normative claims and exerts formative powers."[10] Memory was sacralized and ritualized in Judaism through the transformation of festivals honoring nature into religious festivals, which referred to specific events of Jewish history. In this way, the collective identity of Jews was rendered independent from state or religious institutions (the monarchy, or the temple), and independent of territory. A "spiritual 'Israel'" emerged, "which might be found anywhere a group came together in order to revive the memory of the holy texts through their study."[11] The Jews had with the Torah—so Heine—a "portable Fatherland," (6/I: 483) which enabled the preservation of their religious-national identity in the Diaspora even without state cohesion. The survival of the Jewish people since antiquity may well be attributable to the development of this specific culture of memory.

The heightened import—in comparison with other cultures—of religious collective memory for the formation and preservation of traditional Jewish identity favored a concomitant neglect of "history." The impulse to record current historical experiences showed itself—if at all—in a form that could be integrated into the ritual and liturgy of the religious culture of memory, for example, in the prayers for repentance (selichot), in memorial books, or in the establishment of certain holidays like a "second Purim," enacted in memory of the Jews' salvation from persecution.[12] The present was experienced, understood, and captured through the pre-determined patterns of perception, interpretation, and representation of tradition; continuity with origins was thus preserved.

I have purposefully entered in somewhat detailed fashion into the specific tradition of Jewish religious collective memory, because only against this background do the changes wrought by modernity become recognizable—and the specific relation of Heinrich Heine to the Jewish past along with them. This static, premodern conception of history changed with the dissolution of the traditional Jewish group structure and the advent of acculturation at the end of the eighteenth and beginning of the nineteenth centuries. The relation of Jews—or at least of a leading class of intellectuals—to their own tradition was transformed under the influence of the rise of historicism to the position of leading cultural power: in the emerging Science of Judaism this relation was worked through and historicized along the lines of source-criticism, while its normative claim was relativized. At the same time, conceptions of time and history became more dynamic: past, present and future were experienced and interpreted as constituent parts of a comprehensive process of development.[13] The task of the newly emerging historiography was to represent the past in such a way that the unity of history, its "meaning," would become clear, thereby enabling meaningful action in the present.[14] Modern Jewish historiography, which expanded and with time replaced the traditional forms of Jewish collective memory, thus served as a medium for the self-definition and self-assertion of Jews in the age of acculturation. "History"—at least for those German Jews who wished in some form to retain their Judaism—became an important medium for the erection and preservation of a Jewish identity in the modern, secular world; it became, to use the formulation of Yerushalmi, "the faith of fallen Jews."[15]

This process of transformation of the Jewish conception of history—from a premodern, religiously-stamped collective memory to a modern, meaning-bestowing, and in so far as it worked through sources in a critical manner, scientific historiography—ran its course in no way so straight a manner as my preceding argument may suggest. Rather, this process was marked by specific problems that arose from the peculiarities and long tradition of Christian monopolization of Jewish history. I will name only three of the most important conceptual and interpretive problems with which the emerging Jewish historiography was confronted in the first half of the nineteenth century: (1) What is the subject of Jewish history? Wherein lies its unifying principle? This question posed itself with particular force, for there was no territorial, religious-institutional or linguistic continuity in the Jewish diaspora. (2) What is the relation between Jewish and more general history, between the history of a self-contained community and the history of its relations with the outside world, between autonomy and heteronomy? Or from another perspective: in what does the contribution of the Jews to the history of humanity, to a universal history, consist? This question derived its urgency from the fact that Jewry was deprived of any cultural importance following the rise of Christianity—both in the Christian notion of history and in its derivative product, the secular, idealistic philosophy of history in Germany.[16] Its present and future were seen correspondingly as "unreasonable" and essentially unjustified. This philosophical undermining of Jewish existence in modernity understandably represented a special challenge for Jewish historians. (3) How could the long phases of persecution and suffering be interpreted as "meaningful" in a secular context? Or, in the words of the time: Does a slave even have a history?[17] These basic questions of Jewish historical discourse were first systematically discussed among the members of the "Association for the Culture and Science of Jews (Culturverein)," founded in Berlin in November of 1819. Turning now to the discourse of history within the Culturverein, we come one decisive step closer to the actual theme of my essay—Heinrich Heine's representation of Jewish history.

II

In the literature on the Culturverein it is rightly emphasized that its members were bound more by similar questions and perceptions of problems than by unified suggestions for solutions or a common ideology.[18] This is certainly true with regard to their conception of history. It would therefore be inaccurate to speak, as sometimes happens, of "the" conception of history of the Culturverein. Common to the Jewish intellectuals who found themselves together in the Culturverein, and whose efforts towards acculturation were threatened by the renewed outbreak of anti-Semitism in the period of the Restoration, was basically the attempt to find a new answer to the dilemma of emancipation, to achieve, as Ismar Schorsch has put it, "the pursuit of individual integration without the loss of a distinct collective identity."[19] They sought, in contrast to the generation of Moses Mendelssohn in the era of Enlightenment, a Jewish self-definition no longer confined to the realm of philosophy, but, in tune with the new leading values of the nineteenth century, in the realms of "history" and "science" (Wissenschaft).[20] Crucial to this was the effort to lead Jewry out of its spiritual isolation and to bring it through "science" to the fore of modern development.[21] The key figure in this undertaking was Leopold Zunz, who already in 1818 in his programmatic work "On Rabbinic Literature" (*Etwas über die rabbinische Literatur*)[22] had applied to the future Jewish science the new approach and method of classical philology, learned first hand from the teachings of his mentors Friedrich August Wolf and August Boekh at the Berlin University.[23] For Zunz philology became the foundational science: just as classical philology worked through classical texts according to modern philological-critical methods, so should Hebrew literature be approached in the science of Judaism. The difference between holy and profane texts was dissolved; the entire tradition was grasped as a secular, national literature. In a manner similar to Boekh, who had shaken and overcome the classicist approach to antiquity through his studies of Attic finances and his postulate of a comprehensive exploration of Greek life, his student Zunz wished to expand and replace the exclusively religious interpretation of Hebrew tradition with a comprehensive, secular approach. In this way, the unknown contribution of Jewry to the culture of humanity—from statecraft and philosophy to mathematics, geography, astronomy, the study of nature and medicine, to music and poetry—would become clear, and Jewry would be liberated from its isolation from world literature. Zunz's approach, derived from the practice of classical philology, implied not only a relativization of tradition, but also the notion that the vital development of Hebrew literature had come to an end, and that for precisely this reason it had become amenable to scientific investigation.[24] Zunz's philological orientation essentially reduced Jewish history to a history of literature and culture, and to a history of Jewish contributions to the world. His approach was determined by the leading ideas of historicism and, one could almost say, by an antiquarian spirit. There may have been a pluralistic juxtaposition of different manifestations of Jewish spirit, but no unified "development," let alone a teleological concept of progress. Zunz's ideal of scientific distance and objectivity set narrow limits for an appropriation of his historical writing for the interpretative needs of the present. This was, however, completely different for those members of the Culturverein whose historiography was stamped by Hegelian philosophy— scholars like Eduard Gans, Moses Moser, or Immanuel Wolf. For them, the need to provide a speculative interpretation of Jewish existence in modernity outweighed the need for historical-philological grunt-work. Hegel's concept of history was famously based upon the premise, "that also in the course of world history things take place in accordance with reason."[25] For Hegel, the task of the philosophy of history is to apprehend the self-unfolding of spirit in history and thus to work out the "necessity" of history. This knowledge alone makes possible meaningful action in the present. The Jewish intellectuals influenced by Hegel were confronted with a special problem: how could the Jewish past be understood in the context of a universal history conceived as unity and progress. For Hegel himself, Judaism possessed a certain universal-historical meaning, but only as a precursor to Christianity; Jewry no longer retained significance after the establishment of Christianity, let alone in the present. The Jews of the present appeared to him as a people that had outlived its historical epoch.[26] The Hegelians of the Culturverein sought to overcome this verdict precisely with the concepts and patterns of thought of Hegelian philosophy. Eduard Gans justified the thousand-year-old separation of Jewish history from world history, a state of affairs deemed all the more wanting given the physical proximity of Jewish and Christian communities, by pointing to the incomplete development of a European society that excluded Jews. He saw it as the task of the Jews of the present, no longer to isolate themselves from the totality of European life, but rather to reintegrate themselves into the course of world history. The sense that Jewish ideas had become through Christianity a part of the European whole would facilitate this process of reintegration. Gans imagined the return of the Jews to the course of history as a "rising-up" into history and not a "dissolution," but on this point he remained conceptually vague: "Rising up [into history] is not dissolution. Only that form of independence that disrupts and reflects only upon itself shall be annihilated, not that which is subordinated to the whole; that which serves totality shall not need to lose that which is substantial to it."[27] And further: "Therefore neither can the Jews perish nor can Judaism dissolve; but in the great movement of the whole it shall seem to have perished and yet live on as the current lives on in the ocean."[28]

The attempt of Gans and others to bind Jewish history to a universal history conceived along Hegelian lines led inevitably to an abstract determination of Judaism as an idea. Wolf defined this idea, which he found expressed in the tetragrammaton, as "the vital unity of all being in eternity"[29]; later scholars, influenced by the Jewish reform movement, saw the essence of Jewry in a specific ethical monotheism and derived the existential justification of the Jews in history and in the present from their task as protectors and guardians of this religious idea.[30] Jewish history was understood here exclusively as the history of Judaism, and not as the history of Jews. The external history of Jews was seen as the mere hull or shell of the kernel of actual Jewish essence. This was to become a basic concept in the emerging Jewish historiography in the first half of the nineteenth century.[31] Zunz believed that a nation divided performs no deeds; its suffering might bring forth chroniclers and poets, but no historiographers. No "history," understood as a meaningful development between past, present and future, might be recognized in the external events of Jewish pasts.[32] A slave, so Zunz and others argued, has no history. Jewish history was at hand in its actual sense, that is, in the realm of spirit, only in the history of literature and religion. To be sure, Isaac Markus Jost had written between 1820 and 1829 a nine-volume "History of the Israelites from the Time of the Maccabees through our Days." This consisted, however, of countless stories lacking any inner relation or connection. His work provided in many respects the best confirmation of the generally accepted thesis that a Jewish history could only be written meaningfully as a history of Judaism, either as a history of religion or as a history of ideas.

Set against this general intellectual background Heinrich Heine's specific approach to the Jewish past becomes readily recognizable.[33] Heine, who joined the Culturverein in August of 1822, developed his own approach to Jewish history in part as an adoption of ideas represented in the Verein, and in part in sharp opposition to them. Like the others, he sought in the realm of history an answer to the problem of Jewish identity in German society of the Restoration period, a problem only sharpened by processes of integration and exclusion. In particular, he turned his attention to the history of Jewish suffering in the Christian Middle Ages, a theme wholly ignored by others in the Verein despite Moser's programmatic demand of 1819 that the Verein should work on the history of the Jewish nation "in the sorrowful times of its dispersal."[34] Heine's reconstruction and representation of the Jewish past thus achieved its personal profile in clear opposition to the idealistic tendencies of the Hegelians in the Culturverein. In letters to Moser, he clearly expressed his anger at Gans attempt to reduce Jewish historical life to abstract ideas: "For God's sake.

say not once more that I am merely an idea! I get terrifically angry about that. For all I care, you can all become ideas, just leave me undisturbed (*ungeschoren*)" (HSA 20: 97). Already in an earlier letter to Wohlwill, he had sharply criticized the religious attempts at reform that sought to make Judaism timely through accommodation to Protestant models: "A few corn-cutters [*Hühneraugenoperateurs*] (Friedlander & Co) have sought to heal with bloodletting the fatal boils and skin-ulcers that afflict the body of Jewry, and on account of their clumsiness and crazy bandages of reason Israel must bleed. ... We no longer have the strength to wear a beard, to fast, to hate, and out of hate to tolerate; that is the motive of our reformation" (HSA 20: 71-72). Heine's polemic against the idealization of Jewish historical consciousness and against the "modernization" of Jewish religion was not based on traditional belief in the law. More clearly than others he saw the loss of substance, of the emotional capacity for community and the strength to live, that went hand in hand with the "rationalization" of Judaism. This knowledge determined his representation and valuation of the Jewish past.[35] Heine wrote—so I will argue in detail—no "history" in the modern sense of the term. He performed neither Zunz's brand of source-criticism nor did he attempt, like Gans, to find the meaning of Jewish history in teleological-philosophical speculations. By contrast, he sought to give literary shape to the multiplicity, the vitality and contradictoriness of Jewish life in the past, and in such a way that they became immediately comprehensible to the readers of his time. This form of historical narration had structurally more in common with traditional Jewish group memory than with the emerging historiography. Whereas those who construed the past as a reasonably ordered series of events, as meaningful development, precisely as "history" (in its modern sense), and who correspondingly chose or left out facts that would corroborate or invalidate their presumptions, the form of Jewish group memory, structured as it was by memorial days and archetypal situations (like "bondage," "liberation," or "Exile"), permitted the expression of immediate and in part completely contradictory experiences. If the conception of history of a Gans, obsessed as it was with idealization, reduced the complexity of the Jewish past to an idea, then Heine emphasized precisely (and in clear opposition) the concreteness of Jewish life. The Jews of the past in his portrayals are no "bloodless" vessels of an abstract idea, but men of flesh and blood.

III

Heine's approach to the Jewish past was that of the poet, not that of the historian. He expressed the opposition in the following manner:

> [A people] demands its history from the hand of the poet rather than that of the historian. It does not ask for faithful reporting of naked facts; what it wants is to see these dissolved again into the original poetry from which they sprang. The poets know this, and they secretly take a malicious pleasure in remodeling, in whatever ways they see fit, what the people's memory has preserved; as a means, perhaps, of pouring scorn on historians proud of their dryness and on state-archivists as desiccated and dull as the parchment of their documents. (2: 330)

Heine was convinced that Walter Scott's novels had reproduced English history in a manner more faithful to its spirit than did Hume's historical writing. Scott's novels (so Heine argued in a selection from *The North Sea III*) evinced a specifically modern pain over the loss of traditional identity:

> [Scott's] subject is not simply an elegy over the gradual undermining of Scottish nationality and independence by foreign rule and foreign manners and modes of thought. It is rather a tragic wail over the loss of national peculiarities that are swallowed up by the general advance of modern culture; a wail that finds an echo in the heart of every nation, for national instinct has deeper roots than is commonly believed. Try the effect of disinterring the old images, and you will see in a single night the old love spring up and blossom again. This is no figure of speech, but a simple fact. (2: 236)

In a manner similar to Scott, Heine strove to render vital the "spirit of Jewish history" by reproducing the "original poetry" of the Jews, by exhuming their "old images," and through direct reference to Jewish collective memory. The most important document of this effort is the Rabbi of Bacherach, Heine's fragmentary novel in which he depicts Jewish life in the Germany of the late Middle Ages.[36] Heine's attempt at the literary reconstruction and resuscitation of traditional Jewish collective memory is clearly recognizable above all in the first chapter, in which he depicts the Passover feast and the sudden flight of Rabbi Abraham and his wife Sara from the threat of a pogrom instigated by rumors of ritual-murder. In the experiential world of the protagonists, biblical paradigm and contemporary event, private and collective memory mix together in an organic whole. It is this consciousness of the simultaneous sublation of and imbeddedness in a thousand-year old historical continuum that constitutes the "poetry" of Jewish memory. For Abraham and Sara, biblical history is no abstract past, but is intimately linked with their own, personal lives. Like their biblical counterparts, they have remained childless, but nevertheless nurture the hope that the promises of progeny extended to the biblical Sara will be extended to them as well. Just as the biblical Rachel and Jacob had to wait seven years for one another, so, too, did the beautiful Sara have to hold out seven years for the return of her fiancé, Abraham, from his studies in Spain. Just as the children of Israel left Egypt by night in flight, so, too, did Abraham and Sara flee from Bacherach, when they discovered that they were about to become the victims of an accusation of ritual murder. In the ensuing flight over the Rhein, the story of the exodus from Egypt—precisely the story recalled on the eve of the Seder—merges in Sara's fearful dreams with the exeriences of the present:

> The Rhine seemed to murmur the melodies of the *Agade*, and from its waters the pictures, large as life and in strange exaggerated guise, came forth one by one. ... King Pharaoh swimming in the Red Sea, holding his zigzagged gold crown tight in his teeth, frogs with men's faces swimming behind him, and the waves foaming and roaring, while a dark giant-hand rises threatening from the deep. (1: 473)[37]

And as the Passover Haggada ends with the salvation of the Jews and the messianic hope for redemption, so, too, does the vision of the holy city Jerusalem finally drive away Sara's nightmares. In this dream-image, biblical elements merge with personal and private memories as well:

> Then all at once the oppressive gloom and darkness passed away, the sombre curtain was torn from heaven, and there appeared, far above, the holy city Jerusalem, with its towers and gates; the Temple gleamed in golden

> splendour, and in its fore-court Sara saw her father in his yellow Sabbath dressing-gown, smiling as if well pleased. All her friends and relations looked out from the round windows of the Temple, merrily greeting her; in the Holy of Holies knelt pious David, in his purple mantle and golden crown; sweetly rang his song and the tone from his harp, and smiling happily Beautiful Sara fell asleep. (1: 474)

Heine's poetic reconstruction of premodern Jewish collective memory does not aspire to the historicist ideal of scientific exactitude, though Heine had, in preparation for the Rabbi, engaged in an intensive course of reading in historical literature.[38] His almost ethnographic image of the customs normative to the Jewish past is written out of the modern consciousness of loss and of the disappearance of the traditional Jewish life-world. The Jewish world of the Middle Ages is not represented—in consonance with the historicist ideal—as an epoch "for itself" in its otherness and foreignness; rather, it is perceived through the gate of his own memories of childhood and of contemporary experiences of alienation, and is imagined as his own past. In this respect, the familiarity of religious ritual on the one hand, and the "Judenschmerz"—that is, the experience of Jewish oppression and suffering in Christian surroundings—on the other, serve as emotional bridges between past and present. It is therefore no coincidence that Heine places at the center of the first chapter precisely the Passover feast—"that quintessential exercise in Jewish group memory" (to cite Yerushalmi once again). The detailed depiction of the Seder evening serves not only technical and compositional requirements (as occasion for the accusation of ritual murder and for the demonstration of the parallels between remembered and lived experiences of Exodus), but forges as well a link between narrated time and the time of the author, between the medieval world and the personal, mnemonic world of the nineteenth-century reader. Thus, Heine explicitly has the narrator emphasize that Jews throughout the world "even now" celebrate this festival "to perpetuate the memory of their liberation from Egyptian bondage," (1: 464) and that even those Jews who have deserted the faith of their fathers remain enchanted with its magic. The use of the present tense helps to express the timelessness and universal validity of this effect:

> *Mournfully* merry, seriously playful, and mysteriously secret is the character of this nocturnal festival, and the usual traditional singing intonation with which the *Agade* is read by the father, and now and then re-echoed in chorus by the hearers, at one time thrills the inmost soul as with a shudder, anon calms it as if it were a mother's lullaby, and anon startles it so suddenly into waking that even those Jews who have long fallen away from the faith of their fathers and run after gentile joys and honours, are moved to their very hearts when by chance the old well-known tones of the Passover songs ring in their ears. (1: 465)

Heine made present the Seder evening from the perspective of a child engaged in the act of remembering. The feast's content lay not in religious or theological theorems, but in the colorful images of the Passover Haggada, suspended in memory and often only half-understood. They show

> how Abraham smashes with a hammer the stone idols of his father, how the angels come to him, how Moses slays the Mitzri, how Pharaoh sits in state on his throne, how the frogs give him no peace even at table, how he—thank God!—is drowned, how the children of Israel go cautiously though the Red Sea; how they stand open-mouthed, with their sheep, cows and oxen, before Mount Sinai, how pious King David plays the harp; and finally, how Jerusalem, with the towers and battlements of its temple, shines in the splendor of the sun. (1: 466-67)

Heine's attempt to open up the Jewish past for the readers of his time through the medium of memory did not aspire to a return or reproduction of religious tradition. This was evident in the fact that Heine not only included details of Jewish festivals and rituals, but also the mnemonic stuff of the non-Jewish, German milieu. It is not only the Jewish religion, but the intimate landscape of the Rhineland, with its fables and legends, that lent Sara a sense of hope and security in her time of flight. Again the universal validity and timelessness of this effect is indicated through the use of the present tense, which thus produces a link to the present.

> For in truth old, kind-hearted Father Rhine cannot bear that his children shall weep, so, calming their crying, he rocks them on his trusty arm, and tells them his most beautiful stories, and promises them his most golden treasures, perhaps even the ancient long-sunk Nibelungen hoard. Little by little the tears of Beautiful Sara ceased to flow; her worst sorrow seemed to be washed away by the eddying, whispering waves, the night lost its sinister horror, while her native hills bade her the tenderest farewell. (1: 471)

That the Rhineland Jews of the fifteenth century knew the Nibelungen tale and other local stories (like the one of the Kedrich) is, from an historical perspective, more than improbable. Heine thus employed a literary trick—the aunt from Lorch told these old stories to the young Sara against the will of her father—in order to make the story halfway plausible. Historical precision was not his concern. Decisive instead was the high value which the landscape of the Rheinland, its fables and legends, had for him personally. He projected onto the period of the late Middle Ages the nineteenth-century romanticism of the Rhineland so central to his own memories of childhood.[39] The Passover festival and a Rhine landscape steeped in legend are the conduits of memory—marked by the switch to the present tense—which link present and past, personal experience with collective history. That Jewish ritual and the German world of legend stand next to one another, equally valued, corresponded to Heine's personal experience and that of his acculturated German-Jewish contemporaries. Heine linked Jewish and German history (this was, as we have seen, one of the central problems of the emerging Jewish historiography) not on the plane of abstract determinations of essence, but through the creation of a common mnemonic realm determined by the topography of the Rhineland landscape. For the Jews also this landscape functioned as "beloved Heimat," but the memories which they associated with the sites and castles, with the mountains and ruins of the Rhein valley, were different: they were stamped by the persecutions and expulsions of the Middle Ages. Heine transformed the Rhine, the central symbol of the rising German nationalism of his time, into the unimpeachable witness to the misdeeds perpetrated against the Jews and into the warm-hearted source of consolation for their suffering. Landscape and memory were linked. Bacherach, which in Heine's characterization lies beneath the beautiful Rhine region "like a fearful legend of olden times," (1: 461) is such a site of memory. In this topographic manner, Heine sought to make present, and, one could almost say, to inscribe in the national memory of Germans the specific experience of Jewish oppression.

To sum up thus far, we might say that the theme "memory" determines in a multiplicity of ways the composition and content of the first chapter of the *Rabbi*. We can distinguish concretely three levels of time, each of them linked by "memory." These are (1) the plane of biblical history, more concretely, the Exodus out of Egypt, which sets the paradigm for all time to follow; (2) the level of narrated time (the Germany of the late Middle Ages), in which experienced history (the flight out of Bacherach) is understood as a return of the biblical paradigm; and finally (3) the level of present time (the beginning of the nineteenth century), which is linked with the other two through the appearance of memories of childhood. This last is a secondary memory, a memory of a memory so to speak, held fast in the moment of its disappearance. A unity of biblical paradigm and present is no longer (as it was in the Middle Ages) immediately given, but is artificially reproduced through a romanticizing view of history. Through it, a modern Jew alienated from his faith might preserve a "Jewish identity," as Judaism is not understood as a religious teaching, but as a community forged of memory and suffering.

How, then, do the second and third chapters of the story jibe with the preceding argument? The sudden change in style, from the romantically-endowed evocation of the strength of medieval Jewish faith presented in the first chapter, to the second chapter and its prevailing satirical and caricatured representation of Jewish ghetto figures, has preoccupied critics for a long time.[40] One possibility would be to see the two chapters as yoked together in the relation of thesis and antithesis, and to invoke for the purposes of explanation Heine's later formulation (in the *Börne Memorial*) of Judaism's "double-face." Following Hegel, Heine had described there the contradiction between the "ideal" and the "common" as a characteristic of Judaism: "What a strange phenomenon, what glaring contrasts! While you find among these people every possible caricature of vulgarity, you also find the purest ideals of humanity among them" (4: 119).

Heine's satiric representation of medieval ghetto life is doubtless influenced by his sharp and often sarcastic critique of Jewish conditions in the present, as we find them in his letters of the time. It would nevertheless be misleading to read the caricatured treatment of Jewish figures simply as the product of personal resentment. A more precise reading shows that the theme so central to the first chapter returns also in the second and third. Also Frankfurt, and especially its ghetto, is a site of Jewish memory. The memories linked to the city are nevertheless only negative: it is a "dreadful monument of the Middle Ages" (1: 486). Heine became even clearer in the corresponding representation of the Frankfurt ghetto described in the *Börne Memorial*: "The houses of this street gazed at me, as if they wished to relate to me their miserable memories, stories, which one knows well but would rather not, would rather forget altogether" (4: 22). Different than in Bacherach, where the hate from beyond only deepened the Jews' religiosity and fear of God, in the Frankfurt ghetto the destructive, deforming effects of the long history of oppression surface in the Jews themselves. The Jews live, so the narrator, "under pressure and in fear, and more in the memories of earlier times of distress than in the present day" (1: 479). As a consequence of this centuries-old pressure, the Jews were traumatized, "crippled in body and soul" (1: 486), as the narrator terms it. Nasenstern and Jäkel the Fool embody the qualities induced by trauma: fear and foolishness. Nasenstern senses danger everywhere, even where none resides. "I am really afraid" is a sentence he repeats constantly. The experience of persecution and oppression has deformed his character. In his case, an "elevation" and transcending of one's own suffering through the memory of the biblical paradigm of redemption is not possible. Even in the Bible he finds only the origin of his fear and cowardice, and no hope, as becomes clear in one commentary which effects an ironic counter-caricature of the first chapter's tone of grandeur:

> "Yes I have fear" replied Nasenstern, sighing. "I know that fear runs in my blood, and I had it from my late mother"—"Ay, Ay," interrupted Jäkel, "and your mother had it from her father, and he from his, and so all ancestors one from the other, back to the forefather who marched with King Saul against the Philistines, and was the first to run away." (1: 483)

The ghetto-figures of the second chapter—Nasenstern, Jäkel the Fool, Schnapper-Elle—are depicted throughout with sweet, sympathetic qualities. Their shortcomings (fear, cowardice, foolishness, an obsession with splendor, talkativeness) are explained away on the basis of the unnatural, barbaric conditions of their environment, and of the long experience of oppression and isolation. On the other hand, the threats that define their everyday life also occasion a certain form of joy. Humor, especially jokes and self-irony, serve as strategies of survival and lend the ghetto-scene, despite its withered appearance, a cheerful expression.

In the third chapter Heine finally has the Spanish knight Don Isaak Abarbanel appear in the Frankfurt ghetto. He is a Jewish renegade, converted to the Catholic faith, but in truth a heathen, to whom the "dry and joyless Hebrews" are as objectionable as the "gloomy self-tormenting Nazarenes" (1: 498). Without concern for historical precision, Heine transposes here onto this figure his own hedonistic ideal of life, stamped by the philosophy of Saint Simon. Abarbanel remains wholly distanced from the Jewish religion, as is revealed in the dialogue with his study-partner Rabbi Abraham. Even in the time under King David, during the very flowering of Jewish history, Abarbanel speculates that he would not have been able to endure life among the Jews, and would have emigrated either to Phoenicia or Babylonia, "where the joys of life sparkled in the temple of the gods" (1: 498). The single link to his Jewish heritage which he retains and which compels him to seek out the kitchen of the Schnapper-Elle in the Frankfurt ghetto, is his special fondness for Jewish food. It is the "pleasant tasting memories" of the past that entice him to the "tent of Jacob" (1: 498). Whereas in the first chapter the memories of childhood concern the Jewish ritual of the Seder evening, in this case memory is fully secularized. Neither the images of the Haggada nor the songs of the prayer service, but rather the "carp with brown raisin-sauce which my aunt knew how to prepare so edifyingly for Friday evening" or the "steamed mutton with garlic and horse-radish" (1: 499) constitute the object of a memory suffused with yearning. The relation to the Jewish past is thus for Abarbanel, despite his transgressions, at hand throughout, but it is no longer simply given as a matter of fate. Rather, it is defined autonomously on the basis of his own, new life maxim. What drives him to seek out contact with Jews is neither the content of the Jewish religion nor the solidarity of a community of fate, but purely the desire for pleasure.

IV

To conclude, I would like to draw out some of the implications of the preceding observations on the *Rabbi* for the broader theme of "Heine's contested identities":

1. Heine's novel-fragment *The Rabbi of Bacherach* is a noteworthy and wholly original attempt to represent and render vital the Jewish past in the modern world. At a time in which a traditional, religiously-influenced Jewish group memory had lost some of its binding power, and in which scientific, source-critical historiography introduced a new era in the relation of Jews to their past, Heine sought in the historical novel an alternative form of representation, which allowed him to produce an immediate, emotion-laden link between past and present. The medium of this historical representation is memory. It evokes images from the past, but provides no (meaningfully-ordered) process of history (that the plot of the tale exhibits countless inconsistencies can be ascribed not least to this predominance of static memories [*Erinnerungsbilder*]). Memory displays Jewish life directly—in all its concreteness, color, sensuality, and contradiction —without reducing this complexity to abstract, philosophical determinations of essence, as was the case in the historiography of the time. For the reader of the nineteenth century, Jewish collective memory is no longer self-understood, but is first activated by memories of childhood (as in that of the Passover ritual) and by the topography of the sites of memory (like the Rhine landscape or the houses of the Frankfurt ghetto). Through the linking-up of personal and collective memory, of historical event and traditional, Jewish "national memory," an identity-bestowing unity of past and present arises, a unity that was characteristic for traditional Jewish collective memory, but which was no longer posited in the same way by the emerging Jewish historiography. In his pathbreaking work *Zakhor: Jewish History and Jewish Memory*, Yosef Hayim Yerushalmi sharply differentiated some years ago between traditional, Jewish group memory and modern historiography, and bemoaned the relative irrelevance of scientific historiography to a contemporary Jewish historical consciousness:

> Memory and modern historiography stand, by their very nature, in radically different relations to the past. The latter represents, not an attempt at a restoration of memory, but a truly new kind of recollection. ... With unprecedented energy it continually recreates an ever more detailed past whose shapes and textures memory does not recognize. (p. 94)

And he continues:

> It would appear that even where Jews [today] do not reject history out of hand, they are not prepared to confront it directly, but seem to await a new, metahistorical myth, for which the novel provides at least a temporary modern surrogate. (p. 98)

Yerushalmi does not mention Heine in this context, but it should be clear from what I have said thus far that Heine's novel-fragment fits precisely in this context. It represents—in clear distinction from the form and content of the emerging modern historiography—a first and wholly independent attempt towards the literary reproduction of Jewish collective memory in modernity.

2. The concept of remembering not only determines in a multitude of ways the composition and style of the *Rabbi*; memory is itself repeatedly thematized. Heine delineates in the three chapters of the *Rabbi* completely different relations between the Jews and their past. For Rabbi Abraham and his wife Sara, memory is defined by a pre-given biblical structure of bondage and redemption, of exile and homecoming. That they might yoke together their experiences with the biblical paradigm enables them to apprehend their faith as meaningful, and thus to preserve it, even in times of suffering. This is not the case, however, with the satirically depicted ghetto-figures of the second chapter. They are represented as men marked and traumatized by their past. An accommodation of a religious ideal to the reality of past and present experiences of persecution is possible for them only through the medium of self-critique and self-irony. And for the renegade Abarbanel, finally, Jewish history no longer retains any direct, existential meaning. He believes—through a rational valuation of its content—to have loosed himself fully from it, and pays tribute only to the memories of his favorite kosher dishes from childhood. These discrepant forms of memory and the correspondingly differentiated forms of Jewish identity they imply exist side by side in the *Rabbi*, a state of affairs attributable not least to the novel-fragment's unusually long and complicated history of composition.

3. What might now be derived from all this for the question of Heine's relation to the Jewish past and to his Jewish identity? Four theses suggest themselves:

a. Heine's relation to Judaism is not determined by a vitally-mediating, unbroken continuum of tradition, but by a rupture in tradition, and in this respect might be termed specifically modern. It is the search of the already acculturated Jews for their historical roots and their existential position in the present that unleashes Heine's preoccupation with Jewish history.
b. In clear opposition to the rationalizing and "objectivizing" tendencies of the emerging "Science of Judaism," Heine's approach to Jewish history is marked by his subjectivity. Memories of childhood and personal feelings—such as the oft-cited "Judenschmerz," the hate directed against Christian persecutors of Jews, pride in the grandeur of the Jewish religion, but also self-hate and self-irony—determine his image of the Jewish past and could be called the foundational elements of his Jewish self-understanding.
c. Heine's relation to Judaism is defined by this structure of personal memory and feeling, and not so much in theological-dogmatic terms or in terms of a theoretical worldview. For this reason he could feel in a certain way still a "Jew," even after his conversion to Protestantism or following his development into a radical Saint-Simonian, and especially when he found himself in situations compatible with his "Jewish" structure of memory and emotion.
d. Heine's life and his "contested identities" are not to be described, as Goethe might have done, in the categories proper to a *Bildungsroman*, in which one stage of identity follows another with necessity and so results in a meaningful "history." Here again, the model of memory (*Gedächtnis*) seems to be more adequate: it preserves multiplicitous and often contradictory memories (*Erinnerungen*) and identities and anchors them in consciousness, where they might be activated and actualized at a given time. Heine's so-called "Return to Judaism" at the end of his life would hold no great surprise if one were to begin from the presupposition that his own life too did not follow the ordered principles of teleological historiography, but—like memory—expressed the clutter, contradictions, and simultaneity of his own various identities.

Notes

1. Translated from the German by Benjamin Lazier. I am grateful to the Bonwit-Heine Endowment for providing the funds for the translation.

2. Yosef Hayim Yerushalmi, *Zakhor. Jewish History and Jewish Memory* (New York, 1989); Jan Assmann, *Das kulturelle Gedächtnis. Schrift, Erinnerung und politische Identität in den frühen Hochkulturen* (München, 1992); Amos Funkenstein, *Perceptions of Jewish History* (Berkeley, 1993).

3. See Jacob Neusner, "Paradigmatic Versus Historical Thinking: The Case of Rabbinic Judaism", *History and Theory* 36 (1997), pp. 353-377.

4. Norbert Glatzer, *Untersuchungen zur Geschichtslehre der Tannaiten. Ein Beitrag zur Religionsgeschichte der ersten zwei nachchristlichen Jahrhunderte* (Berlin, 1933), pp. 34-41.

5. Robert Chazan, "Representation of Events in the Middle Ages," *Essays in Jewish Historiography*, ed. Ada Rapoport-Albert (Middletown, 1988), pp. 40-55, here p. 45.

6. Maimonides, *Commentary to Mishna Sanhedrin*, 10:1, quoted in Yerushalmi, *Zakhor*, p. 33.

7. See, for example, Deuteronomy 9:7, 9:27, 32:7; see also Jan Assmann, "Die Katastrophe des Vergessens. Das Deuteronomium als Paradigma kultureller Mnemotechnik," *Mnemosyne. Formen und Funktionen der kulturellen Erinnerung*, ed. Aleida Assmann and Dietrich Hart (Frankfurt/M., 1991), pp. 337-355.

8. Yerushalmi, *Zakhor*, p. 44.

9. Mishnah *Pesahim* 10:5, quoted in Yerushalmi, *Zakhor*, p. 45.

10. Assmann, *Das kulturelle Gedächtnis*, p. 76.

11. Ibid., p. 213.

12. See Yerushalmi, *Zakhor*, pp. 45-52.

13. For the "modernization" of Jewish historical consciousness see Richard Schaeffler, "Die Wissenschaft des Judentums in ihrer Beziehung zur allgemeinen Geistesgeschichte im Deutschland des 19. Jahrhunderts," *Wissenschaft des Judentums. Anfänge der Judaistik in Europa*, ed. Julius Carlebach (Darmstadt 1992), pp. 113-131; Michael A. Meyer, "The Emergence of [Modern] Jewish Historiography. Motives and Motifs," *Essays in Jewish Historiography*, pp. 160 - 175; Ismar Schorsch, *From Text to Context. The Turn to History in Modern Judaism* (Hanover and London, 1994); Ernst Schulin, *Arbeit an der Geschichte. Etappen der Historisierung auf dem Weg zur Moderne* (Frankfurt/Main, New York, 1997), pp. 114-163.

14. Reinhart Koselleck, "Geschichte, Historie" (V. Die Herausbildung des modernen Geschichtsbegriffs), *Geschichtliche Grundbegriffe* vol. 2 (Stuttgart, 3rd ed. 1994), pp. 647-691.

15. Yerushalmi, *Zakhor*, p. 86.

16. See Christhard Hoffmann, *Juden und Judentum im Werk deutscher Althistoriker des 19. und 20. Jahrhunderts* (Leiden, 1988), pp. 11-27.

17. Isaak Markus Jost, *Allgemeine Geschichte des Israelitischen Volkes* (Berlin, 1832), p. 5.

18. For the Culturverein, see: Heinz Mosche Graupe, *Die Entstehung des modernen Judentums. Geistesgeschichte der deutschen Juden 1650-1942*. 2nd ed. (Hamburg, 1977), pp. 180-199; Nathan Rotenstreich, *Tradition and Reality. The Impact of History on Modern Jewish Thought* (New York, 1972); Sinai Ucko, "Geistesgeschichtliche Grundlagen der Wissenschaft des Judentums," *Wissenschaft des Judentums im deutschen Sprachbereich. Ein Querschnitt*, ed. Kurt Wilhelm. Vol. 1 (Tübingen, 1967), pp. 315-352; Nahum N. Glatzer, "The Beginnings of Modern Jewish Studies," *Studies in Nineteenth-Century Jewish Intellectual History*, ed. Alexander Altmann (Cambridge, Mass., 1964), pp. 27-45; Schorsch, *From Text to Context*, pp. 205-232; Michael A. Meyer, *The Origins of the Modern Jew. Jewish Identity and European Culture in Germany*, 1749-1824 (Detroit, 1967), pp. 144-182.

19. Schorsch, *From Text to Context*, p. 210.

20. Meyer, *Origins*, pp. 144 ff.

21. See Immanuel Wolf, “Ueber den Begriff einer Wissenschaft des Judenthums”, *Zeitschrift für die Wissenschaft des Judenthums* 1 (Berlin, 1822), pp. 1-24, here p. 24.

22. In Leopold Zunz, *Gesammelte Schriften*, vol. 1 (Berlin 1875), pp. 1-31.

23. For Zunz see Max Wiener, *Jüdische Religion im Zeitalter der Emanzipation* (Berlin 1933), pp. 175-187; Fritz Bamberger, “Zunz’s Conception of History. A Study of the Philosophic Elements in Early Science of Judaism,” *Proceedings of the American Academy for Jewish Research* 11(1941), pp. 1-25; Leopold Zunz. *Jude-Deutscher-Europäer. Ein jüdisches Gelehrtenschicksal des 19. Jahrhunderts in Briefen an Freunde*, ed. Nahum N. Glatzer (Tübingen, 1964), esp. pp. 3-72; Leon Wieseltier, “‘Etwas über die jüdische Historik’: Leopold Zunz and the Inception of Modern Jewish Historiography,” *History and Theory* 20 (1981), pp. 135-149; Schorsch, From Text to Context, pp. 233-254.

24. Wieseltier, *History and Theory* 20 (1981), p. 148.

25. Georg Friedrich Hegel, *Die Vernunft in der Geschichte*, ed. Johannes Hoffmeister. 5th ed. (Hamburg 1955), pp. 25, 28.

26. See Nathan Rotenstreich, “Hegel’s Image of Judaism,” *Jewish Social Studies* 15 (1953), pp. 33-52; Ucko, “Geistesgeschichtliche Grundlagen,” p. 351.

27. Ucko, “Geistesgeschichtliche Grundlagen,” p. 347.

28. Quoted in Meyer, *Origins*, p. 168.

29. Meyer, *Origins*, p. 173.

30. Abraham Geiger, *Allgemeine Einleitung in die Wissenschaft des Judenthums*, ed. Ludwig Geiger (Berlin, 1875), pp. 29-30.

31. Wiener, *Jüdische Religion*, p. 179; Arje Berger, *Gemeinschaft und Gesellschaft in der Geistesgeschichte des Judentums. Beitrag zu einer Kulturpsychologie des Judentums* (Berlin, 1936), p. 7 ff.

32. Leopold Zunz, "Ueber die in den hebräisch-jüdischen Schriften vorkommenden hispanischen Ortsnamen", *Zeitschrift für die Wissenschaft des Judenthums* 1(1822), pp. 114-176, here pp. 115-16.

33. For Heine's approach to Jewish history see: Ludwig Rosenthal, *Heinrich Heine als Jude* (Frankfurt/M., 1973). S.S. Prawer, *Heine's Jewish Comedy. A Study of his Portraits of Jews and Judaism* (Oxford, 1983).

34. Ucko, "Geistesgeschichtliche Grundlagen," p. 331.

35. For Heine's ideas of history in general see for example: Susanne Zantop, "Verschiedenartige Geschichtsschreibung: Heine und Ranke," *Heine-Jahrbuch* 23 (1984), pp. 42-68; Klaus Briegleb, "Abgesang auf die Geschichte? Heines jüdisch-poetische Hegelrezeption," *Heinrich Heine, Ästhetisch-politische Profile*, ed. Gerhard Höhn (Frankfurt/M., 1991), pp. 17-37; Gerhard Höhn, "'Blutrosen' der Freiheit. Heinrich Heines Geschichtsdenken," in ibid., pp. 176-194.

36. For Heine's *Rabbi of Bacherach* see: Rainer Feldmann, *"Der Rabbi von Bacherach". Geschichtsverständnis, Jude und Judentum im Romanfragment Heinrich Heines* (Paderborn, 1984); Gerhard Höhn, *Heine-Handbuch. Zeit. Person. Werk* (Stuttgart, 1987), pp. 359-376; Manfred Windfuhr, "Kommentar," *Düsseldorfer Heine-Ausgabe* (*DHA*), vol. 5 (Hamburg, 1994), pp. 498-624; Jost Hermand, "Zweierlei Geschichtsauffassung. Heines Rabbi von Bacherach," in ibid., *Judentum und deutsche Kultur. Beispiele einer schmerzhaften Symbiose* (Köln-Weimar-Wien, 1996), pp. 40-50; Barbara Bauer, "Nicht alle Hebräer sind dürr und freudlos. Heinrich Heines Ideen zur Reform des Judentums in der Erzählung 'Der Rabbi von Bacherach'," *Heine-Jahrbuch* 35 (1996), pp. 23-54.

37. The English translation is taken from Heinrich Heine, *Jewish Stories and Hebrew Melodies* (New York, 1987), pp. 19-80.

38. See Windfuhr, *DHA* V, pp. 534 ff.

39. See Windfuhr, *DHA* V, p. 522-529.

40. See Manfred Windfuhr, "'Der Rabbi von Bacherach'. Zur Genese und Produktionsästhetik des zweiten Kapitels," *Heine-Jahrbuch* 28 (1989), pp. 88-117.

Heine's "Hebrew Melodies": A Politics and Poetics of Diaspora

Bluma Goldstein

Heinrich Heine's "Hebrew Melodies," whose three long poems comprise the third and final part of *Romancero* (1851), has long been scanned by critics for evidence of alterations in his views of religion and affiliation with Judaism. Thus, either the overall meaning(s) and structure of the text are identified and assessed by referring to religious and psychological changes resulting from Heine's reaction to the debilitating illness that confined him to what he called his "mattress-grave"; or the poetic text becomes the evidential source for ascertaining revisions to his religious orientation. As interesting and informative as interpretations may be which rely heavily on biographical data to document the writer's ideational and attitudinal developments or their literary representations, they often leave important aspects and issues of the poems uncharted and the reading of the whole unsettled. There are, however, approaches and alternate discourses recently explored within cultural studies, in general, and Jewish studies, in particular, that might contextualize this poetry in ways better able to accommodate some of the more unyielding portions of these complex and diverse individual poems and to illuminate the larger ideological and aesthetic significance of the overall text. This essay means to probe the "Hebrew Melodies" for the poetic articulation of the connection between a new understanding of diasporic life and the construction of Jewish identity by situating the text within two different, yet interrelated frameworks: namely, the "orientalization" of Eastern European Jewry and glorification of medieval Sephardi culture by early nineteenth-century European Jews, especially German Jews; and a more nuanced, differentiated account of diaspora and exile that explores the viability of a truly integrative relationship between subdominant and dominant cultures. Interpreted within these contexts, the "Hebrew Melodies" may be read variously as a critique—especially apparent in the opening and closing poems—of the devastating consequences of an oppressive exilic life; and as a very exciting effort, in the central poem, "Jehuda ben Halevy,"[1] to conceptualize a productive positive diaspora that is not simply exile within a poetic structure that reflects and constructs that imagined reality.

The three poems of this text are all concerned with Jewish life and culture within a diaspora that is more or less associated with Spain and with Spanish, Islamic, and Christian culture on Spanish soil. Even the initial poem, "Princess Sabbath," which makes only minor reference to Spain in the mistaken identification of Jehuda ben Halevy as the author of a poem that has become part of the Sabbath liturgy, nevertheless grounds the transcendent move from weekday to Sabbath in a tale of transformation from the "Arabian Nights," known only in its Moslem version. Although the final poem, "Disputation," apparently takes place in late fourteenth-century Christian Spain before the Spanish Inquisition was firmly entrenched but nonetheless perilous for the Jewish population, there is a reference to the Moors, to whom—along with the Jews—King Pedro speaks with civility. The central poem, "Jehuda ben Halevy," which is clearly the most interesting and powerful of the three, follows an intricate and complex trajectory between the contemporary narrator-poet and the Sephardi cultural environment of Jehuda ben Halevy, between the ancient and medieval Mediterranean world and nineteenth-century Berlin and Paris, between a thriving Jewish diasporic life in twelfth-century Islamic Spain and a degraded one in contemporary Europe. This is, of course, not the first time that the significance of Spain and the shifting interaction of its Christian, Moorish, and Jewish populations have appeared in Heine's writings—one thinks of two "Almansor" texts (drama and later poem), the unfinished novel "The Rabbi of Bacharach," or the poem "Donna Clara," among others—but the "Hebrew Melodies" seems to be uniquely directed toward both articulating a critique of the disabilities of Jewish exilic life and reconstructing an historically grounded diasporic alternative.

During the period of emancipation and modernization in Europe—particularly in France—Jews of the Middle East and the Maghreb (North Africa), who were generally perceived as the "antithesis of 'civilization,'"[2] were referred to as "orientals"; and sometime during the eighteenth century the term "oriental" (*orientalisch* or *asiatisch*) began to be used negatively by Germans to designate the non-European origins, archaic practices, "impure" language, and primitive living conditions of the German Jewish population.[3] By the end of the eighteenth and the beginning of the nineteenth century, however, there was another major shift in the term's usage: almost solely applied to the Eastern European Jew, the *Ostjude*, it circulated in the discourse of acculturated German Jews, eager to separate themselves from the Polish Jewish population on their border, who were perceived as lacking the language, education, and refinements necessary for participation in modern Western society. Steven Aschheim, who identifies the "modern" Jew as well as the *Ostjude* as products of Enlightenment thinking, regards the stereotype of the orientalized Eastern

European Jew as a "convenient foil upon which German Jews could externalize and displace 'negative' Jewish characteristics."[4] By thus identifying the *Ostjude* as an unacceptable "other," German Jews could both distinguish themselves from their brethren to the East, who maintained archaic "oriental" practices, and adopt for themselves a position equal to German nationals. Although the term "orientalization" may seem dispensable here, I would argue that situating the problems facing German Jews during the period of emancipation within a broad horizon of European hegemonic thinking calls into question the parochial character of this so-called "Jewish problem." This was not a "Jewish problem," but a European problem of modernity. Edward Said has noted that Orientalism has little to do with the reality of the Orient, but everything to do with Western strategies to construct and reinforce Occidental superiority over Oriental backwardness.[5] Not unlike the Europeans, but of course on a far smaller scale, German Jews, who tried to distance themselves from *Ostjuden* by subjecting them to what Virginia Dominguez has called "the orientalizing and primitivizing Eurocentric gaze,"[6] sought to control the discourse applied to Jews and to claim a position of superiority over their Eastern co-religionists and of equality with Germans.

Heine wrote the "Hebrew Melodies" during the period of Western European Jewry's struggle for emancipation, and although his choice of Sephardi culture in medieval Spain was certainly logical and felicitous, it was probably not a merely random or personal one. Rather, it represented an interest of some considerable political and social importance to the larger community of acculturated German Jews seeking emancipation. Indeed, this interest in the culture of the classical Islamic world in medieval Spain and the Jewish participation in it represents a positive aspect of Orientalism, that is, an exemplary model of religious, social, and cultural tolerance that also functions as a critique of intolerant "orientalized" East European Orthodoxy. In "The Myth of Sephardic Supremacy," the historian Ismar Schorsch notes that since the sixteenth century progressive Ashkenazi Jews had deemed the rich Sephardi legacy of biblical exegesis, grammatical research, and philosophical inquiry as providing appropriate models to replace Ashkenazi Judaism's rigid, insular educational system, which was devoted almost exclusively to the study of the Talmud. But it was not until the Enlightenment and the intensified opposition to Polish Jewry by German Jews seeking political emancipation that Jewish intellectuals turned to Spain for historical exemplars of the benefits of equality and a secular education for Jews.[7] It was of course not fortuitous in the late eighteenth and early nineteenth century—when many German Jews were trying to demonstrate their readiness, even their inherent capacity, for participation as equals in the body politic—that they sought simultaneously to distance themselves from Eastern European (primarily Polish) Jewry and to propagate a myth of a "Golden Age" of culture in twelfth-century Spain. After all, a nineteenth-century Jew could witness in medieval Spain a period of European history when Jews actively contributed to a vibrant culture and flourishing intellectual life that benefited the entire population because they enjoyed social and political equality; a German, on the other hand, might discover, in the ameliorative effects of cultural openness and symbiosis, reasons enough to support emancipation for their Jewish population.

Hebrew Melodies[8]

The juxtaposition of the titles "Hebrew Melodies" and *Romancero* suggests dissimilarity and variance between the cycle of poems and the volume in which it appears, but tensions among discrepant aspects of the texts may be precisely what these titles are meant to reflect. *Romancero,* which refers to Spanish collections of romances, ballads, and legendary tales, had gained a certain popularity in mid nineteenth-century Spain and France giving rise to many romancero anthologies featuring a broad array of chivalric adventure tales. Heine's *Romancero,* traversing as it does vast periods of time and many continents; a multitude of cultures, histories, and legends and utilizing various genres and poetic configurations, presents a kind of discursive textual diaspora, a conception only underscored by the title of the final poetic cycle "Hebrew Melodies," taken from a cycle of poems largely about the biblical figures and events written in 1815 by one of Heine's favorite writers, Lord Byron. Although critics are no doubt correct to note little connection between the two collections of poetry, Heine's adoption of the title may nevertheless have a significant aesthetic function, namely, to emphasize the textuality, especially the poetic textuality of his work; to identify himself with an admired iconoclastic, ironic, subversive writer—he often spoke of Byron as his "cousin"—who was, however, a nobleman, English, and a Christian as critical of religion as Heine was; and perhaps also to highlight the nexus between language and music, between the ancient Hebrew and modern languages (German and English). Such multiple interactions suggest a kind of textual diaspora, which I hope to demonstrate is reflected in the poems in complex ways.

By comparing the transition from weekday to Sabbath with fables from the *Arabian Nights* about all too brief transformations of bewitched princes into their original princely form, the opening verses of the first of the "Hebrew Melodies," "Princess Sabbath,"[9] may be questioning the likelihood that a struggling impoverished Jew could actually experience a pure joyous spirituality even one day a week. Yet if this reference to fairy tales also functions to position the poet-narrator as an outsider to Jewish religiosity who, in "singing his song," is relying on extraneous texts to explain and communicate the divided existence of an unassimilated Jew, then it may be that the poem has less to do with the Sabbath celebration itself than with the significance of the narrator's intervention into matters of Jewish religious observance. Once the prominence of the narrator's perspective is recognized, two large textual issues are foregrounded: on the one hand, the system of values and strategies through which his own social environment as well as that of Jewish piety are represented and critiqued, perhaps at the expense of what some critics have understood as the poem's concern with the "poetry of Judaism," the tragic division in Jewish life, or with empathy for Jewish religion and its practices;[10] and, on the other, the issue of the ability of an outsider, here probably a non-traditional Jew, to sing this song of the Sabbath—a problem which haunts the "Jehuda ben Halevy" poem as the question of whether the exile from Zion is able to sing Zion's song ("How shall we sing the Lord's song in a strange land?" the psalmist of Psalm 137 asks). In addition, read from the point of view of the narrator, those errors in the text which are usually attributed to Heine's inadequate knowledge of Jewish culture or to a deliberate move to maintain meter or enhance reader recognition,[11] may better be understood as a way of identifying the narrator as the one who possesses a flawed knowledge of things Jewish. Indeed, the narrator's treatment of the three texts he cites—the *Arabian Nights*, the Sabbath song "Lekha dodi likras kalla" ("Come, beloved, the bride awaits you"), and Schiller's "An die Freude" ("Ode to Joy")—characterizes him as a rather cultured cosmopolitan writer who, by situating the sacredness of the Sabbath within a rather wide horizon of folk and high literary culture, can portray and perhaps even honor the Sabbath, but also deride certain aspects of Jewish life and ritual.

Since it is impossible here to analyze the poem in depth, let me explore a segment of about ten consecutive verses in which the narrator shifts the focus from the sanctity of the Sabbath service to a rather broad critique of Jewish diasporic life. "Princess Sabbath" is divided roughly into two parts: the Sabbath eve service in the synagogue, where the traditional liturgical song “Lekha dodi likras kalla” welcomes the arrival of the Sabbath; and in the home, where, after the luxury of the Sabbath meal, the final ritual, the “havdala” (“the separation” [here between sacred and secular]) service, ushers out the Sabbath and the poem. The segment under consideration here, which forms the bridge between synagogue and home, begins, once the atmosphere of piety in the synagogue is depicted, with a portrayal of the cantor, which, given the unpleasant description of his preciosity, vanity, and pomposity, may very well coincide with the Reform movement’s attack on the “oriental” characteristics of the traditional cantorial performance.[12]

> Dapper little man who shoulders
> His little black cloak coquettishly.
>
> To display how white his hand is,
> He fidgets with his neck, oddly
> Index finger pressed to the temple,
> Thumb reposing on the throat.
>
> He hums to himself very softly,
> Until finally loudly exulting
> He raises his voice and sings:
> Lekha dodi likras kalla!
>
> Lekha dodi likras kalla!
> Come, beloved, already there awaits you
> The bride who for you unveils
> Her blushing face! (6/I: 126; D 652)[13]

Written by Solomon Halevy Alkabets, a sixteenth-century kabbalist and mystical poet, the esoteric poem “Lekha dodi likras kalla,” whose meaning is considered obscure even by religious scholars, has nevertheless been incorporated into the liturgy and is known by almost every ordinary observant Jew. Given the citation of its opening line in the original Hebrew and the narrator’s obvious knowledge of the text’s allegorical content, his reference to the song, which depicts the mystical union of the nation Israel as Prince and the Princess Sabbath, as a “charming nuptial verse” (“hübsches Hochzeitscarmen”) confronts the poem’s exclusively religious significance with a possible secular literary reading. Indeed, this move to connect the sacred and the profane is supported by his incorrect attribution of authorship to "the great / highly celebrated minnesinger / Don Jehuda ben Halevy", that is, not to Jehuda ben Halevy as religious poet and scholar, but to "Don Jehuda" the courtly bard. Indeed the meaning of the name Jehuda ben Halevy—Jehuda, son of the Levite—may have an important aesthetic function in mediating between the secular and the sacred or religious. After all, the Levites had the function of reciting or intoning the psalms and hymns in the Temple (the *mizmor* [sung poem] recited in the synagogue today is preceded by a statement indicating that this was a song "which the Levites used to recite in the Temple").[14] Being cast as a singer who is not a Levite, but *descended* from one underscores Jehuda ben Halevy's complex identity as troubadour and minnesinger, on the one hand, and Jew and rabbi, on the other. The introduction of alternative secular cultural perspectives into the discussion of traditional practices in Jewish life allows the narrator to challenge and yet augment the religious significance of the Sabbath.

The critique of traditional Jewish life subtly, but significantly pervades this entire segment. Observe, for example, the narrator's curious preoccupation with silence, the silence that, in this text, prevails in the synagogue and also emerges as a primary attribute of the Princess Sabbath, who is referred to several times as "the silent Princess" ("die stille Fürstin") and "personified stillness" ("die personifizierte Ruhe"). His interest in silence is probably neither merely arbitrary nor idiosyncratic, directed as it is at highlighting what is commonly regarded as an abhorrent trait often associated with Jews, namely, their propensity for argumentation and polemics, an issue that appears marginally in the "Jehuda ben Halevy" poem and is the agonizing subject of the final poem, "Disputation." The narrator's aversion to intellectuality was already alluded to early in this poem in the transformation of the miserable "weekday" Jew from a "dog with doggish ideas" into the Sabbath Jew as a "human being with human feelings". This shift from "doggish ideas" to "human feelings" may seem innocent, but its importance is exposed in the narrator's admiration for the silent princess who, he notes, is surely more beautiful than the Queen of Sheba and definitely not the intolerable person that the clever "Ethiopian bluestocking" is. After all, "The Princess Sabbath, who / Is indeed personified/ Stillness, loathes all / Polemics and debates" (6/I: 127; D 653). What seems to be merely a discussion of the attributes of the Sabbath is in fact an attack on what was perceived as the stereotypical behavior of the Jews, but an attack that may also have a larger, perhaps constructive agenda. For just as the narrator can, by identifying the author of one of the most recognized and recondite religious texts in the liturgy as a great minnesinger, locate within Jewish history and traditional culture an opportunity for an alternate, more secular and modern conception of Jewish life; so too may it be possible to uncover in the silent, but profoundly spiritual union of the nation Israel with the Sabbath an aspect of Jewish tradition that might serve as a model for a different mode of social interaction that could be more productive or acceptable in the modern world.

What is intimated in "Princess Sabbath"—the possibility of integrating substantive aspects of Jewish tradition and secular culture into an alternative diasporic life in which the modern Jew (and poet) could thrive as Jew and European—is developed more explicitly during the course of the long "Jehuda ben Halevy" poem. Although the narrator-poet of "Jehuda ben Halevy" seems to amble rather effortlessly through a very varied, complex text replete with digressions that spans thousands of years, widely separated geographical areas, different cultures, religions, and genres, the poem nevertheless has a surprising coherence, the coherence perhaps associated with an extensive diaspora in time and space that nonetheless secures identity amid great variation. This sense of coherence may in fact issue from the relationship between the text's explicit interest in the dynamics of exile and diaspora, which is depicted, on the one hand, in the poem's extensive temporal and spatial journeys of people, as well as of objects, texts, stories, and ideas; and, on the other, in the diasporic poet's role as traverser of the often uncharted border terrain between multiple cultures and linguistic groups, between diverse social and discursive constructs. So vast a territory cannot, of course, be covered in this essay, but it may be possible to survey the area.

The importance of exilic existence cannot be overlooked in "Jehuda ben Halevy," given the fact that the first two parts of this four-part poem commence with paraphrases of and allusions to Psalm 137, often identified as the "great Psalm of exile."[15] The poem opens with the Psalm's fifth and sixth verses in which, although the psalmist speaks from the predicament of exile, the actual subject is not exile, but the connection between memory, precipitated to be sure by separation from origins, and the possibility (or impossibility) of singing and writing should memory cease:

> Dry with thirst, longingly may my tongue cleave
> To my palate, and let my right hand
> Wither, should I ever forget

You, Jerusalem— (6/I: 129; D 655)

Had the first verses of the Psalm, which in the Luther Bible is titled "Wehklage der Gefangenen zu Babel" ("Lamentation of the Prisoners in Babylon"), been cited here,[16] attention would certainly have been drawn to a cessation of creativity that exile had brought about, to the recognition that loss of the homeland behooves the exiles, in the psalm's words, to "hang our harps upon the willows." But verses five and six articulate a possibility other than silence, for it is precisely the condition of absence of homeland and center of meaning and the memory of their presence in the past that gives rise to the poet's creativity, that activates the poet's voice and hand when harps are silenced. The narrator-poet of "Jehuda ben Halevy" may be in exile, but it becomes clear from the first verse, which cites the Psalm, and the next five that he is not exiled from Zion, but from Jehuda Halevy. These six verses comprise an introduction to the entire poem and function as an overture to the immediately ensuing extended biography of the medieval Sephardi poet. Indeed, the narrator seems able to venture into the substance of this poem, which in part consists of constructing the monumental Spanish diaspora poet, only after he has struggled with the "dream-figures / phantoms" and "ghosts" that occupied his mind to recollect the figure of Jehuda ben Halevy, whom he finally recognizes not by definite physical characteristics, but rather by an ephemeral "enigmatic smile / Of those beautifully rhyming lips, / Which are found in poets only." (6/I: 131; D 655). This narrator-poet is himself obsessed not with Jerusalem, as his Jehuda ben Halevy was, but with remembering the renowned Jehuda ben Halevy.

Cast here as an important scholar of Bible and Talmud, a leader of the nation Israel "In the wasteland of exile" ("In der Wüste des Exils" [6/I: 134; D 659]), and a poet who, though writing in Hebrew and Arabic, could match or surpass any European courtly poet, Jehuda ben Halevy is clearly a central figure in this text, but, the title of the poem notwithstanding, he is not the only—or perhaps even the main—protagonist. It is, after all, the narrator-poet who takes great pains not only to reconstruct the life story of Jehuda ben Halevy from his birth to his death and even thereafter to heaven, but also, in fine modernist fashion, constantly to reveal the intricacies of the complex construction that houses the Sephardi poet, yet not only him. There are other bards (Ibn Esra, Gabirol, and Rudello), other lives and deaths; there are the wandering pearls that go traveling East to West into the diaspora from the treasury of Darius, King of Persia and transferred by the initial largesse of Alexander the Great to, among others, Queen Atossa, the courtesan Thais, Cleopatra, the Moors of Spain, its Catholic royalty, to their final resting place on the neck of Baroness Solomon, Baron Rothschild's wife; and the beautiful cask—it once held the pearls, but in it Alexander stored the works of his favorite poet, Homer—and the narrator's fantasy that, had he possession of the cask and did poverty not force him to sell it, in it he would store "the poems of our great Rabbi— / Of Jehuda ben Halevy", which the narrator sees as pearls that emanated from a profound beautiful soul (6/I: 146; D 668);[17] and then there is the search for the origin of the name "Schlemihl," who figures here as the forefather of both Jew and poet, a search that takes the narrator to Berlin where the baptized Jew Hitzig unlocks the secret of the origin, which even Adelbert Chamisso, the author of the famed *Peter Schlemihl's Wondrous Story*, did not know, and from thence to the Bible and Talmud, to Greece and the God Apollo; and of course there is more, much more, including a critique of French and probably European education which makes no mention of these great Spanish Jewish poets. By constructing an unfinished tapestry—the poem is a fragment—of disparate aspects of life in which everything and everyone, including the Jews of course, move about and disperse, and by making apparent the complex structure of the routes he has designed, this narrator-poet has created for himself, under the title "Jehuda ben Halevy," the role of poet-protagonist in charge of the world.

But if Jehuda ben Halevy is not the protagonist of the poem bearing his name, what then is his function in the text? Has the narrator merely colonized this extraordinary figure of the "Golden Age of Spain" in order to create his own *ars poetica*? Or is Jehuda Halevy actually central to this work, perhaps indeed its center, as much of a center for the narrator-poet as homeland, Zion, or Jerusalem may be for an uprooted or dispersed people? I would argue that, without a doubt, the latter is the case. In this text, Jehuda ben Halevy is presented as having generally a dual function for the narrator-poet: on the one hand, he is a rabbi with a formidable Jewish education for whom Jerusalem provides but one site of religious and national identity; on the other, he is a quintessential representative of productive diasporic life for which this narrator longs. He is, after all, presented as the renowned Jewish scholar and philosopher; the poet admired in both the Jewish and European cultural communities; the Spaniard able to write in Hebrew and Arabic using complex Spanish, Arabic, French, and Jewish literary forms and genres; the Jew who, in this poem at least, was not driven by miseries of exile to venture to Jerusalem,[18] but rather by stories of its decimation; a person who, by integrating into his life and work the complexities of the cultures around him, provided the dominant society with a marvelous creative oeuvre. Surely if, in this poem, the troubadour and minnesinger's proverbial "object of desire," namely the lady, could be replaced by Jerusalem, as it is for Jehuda ben Halevy, then, for this Jewish narrator-poet awash in the diaspora, the lady and Jerusalem could also be replaced by this world-renowned and untroubled Sephardi troubadour and rabbi. Of course, having inherited the ill luck of a double "Schlemihldom" as poet and Jew and having finally reached his beloved Jehuda Halevy, this narrator-poet might best take heed that he not die at that poet's feet as his Jehuda died at the ruins in Jerusalem.[19] One wonders whether he considered that when he left the poem a fragment.

This text's intense preoccupation with an integrative diasporic life represented by Jehuda ben Halevy seems not to denote a detached intellectual interest on the part of the narrator, but rather to derive from painful experiences of exile—his own and the age-old one of the Jewish people—and of homelessness, depicted in the poem by the attention accorded the continual wanderings of people and things through time and space. If the narrator-poet's yearning for the paragon of Sephardi culture he finds in Islamic Spain is indeed rooted in the anguish of exile and homelessness, then exploring some of the specific ways in which exile and homelessness are communicated may illuminate not only their effects on the narrator as person, poet, and Jew, but also the conceptual difference between exile and diaspora represented in the poem.

Because of the limitations of this paper and the length of the poem (four parts, 224 verses), let me focus on the first nine verses of part two, which first elaborate on the detrimental effects of exile. While part one opened with verses five and six of Psalm 137, which noted the importance of memory for exiles who write or sing about the homeland, the second part, commencing as it does with a reference to the Psalm's very recognizable opening lines about grief and silenced song—"By the rivers of Babylon, there we sat down, yea, we wept, when we remembered Zion. We hanged our harps upon the willows in the midst thereof." (Psalm 137: 1-2)—foregrounds the pain of exile and the harm it engenders. Furthermore, just as the first six verses of part one comprise a preface to the biography of Jehuda ben Halevy's formative years, so too do the first nine verses of part two function as a preamble to a discussion of the Sephardic poet's creative activity and yearning for Jerusalem. Occupied with the pain and anger that exilic life caused the narrator and the Jewish people, these nine verses encompass a series of discursive journeys that bespeak broad cultural and social despair: from the lamentations of Babylonian exiles to the anguish of the contemporary narrator, who struggles with his "west-easterly dark spleen" ("westöstlich dunkler Spleen"); from the elegiac rhetoric of the biblical passage to the idiom of the folk, of home and hearth; from the ailing narrator's miserable condition, which is comparable to Job's, to the dream of a mythological Pegasus waiting to carry him aloft and back to the "great poet" Jehuda ben Halevy. The scope and power of these exchanges and transitions reverberate in the first four verses of the prelude:

By the waters of Babylon sat
We and cried, our harps
Leaned against the weeping willows—
Do you still know the old song?

Do you still know the old tune,
Which at the start so elegiacally
Wimpers and hums, like a kettle,
Which is boiling on the hearth?

Long already, millennia long
Has it boiled in me. A dark woe!
And time licks my wound,
As the dog did Job's ulcers.

Thank you, dog, for your spittle—
But that can only coolingly soothe—
Only death can heal me,
But, alas, I am immortal! (6/I: 135-6; D 659-60)

Although the immortality alluded to here seems to refer specifically to the narrator, it becomes clear, within the context of the references to the Babylonian exile, the silenced harps, and a millennia-long exilic condition, that it applies as well to the Jewish people and poets, whose Pegasus-flights can recover and resuscitate the literary production of great poets such as Jehuda ben Halevy. Thus, the Jew, the poet, and the ailing individual—designations all applicable to the narrator—may each suffer from exile, but they can also hope to live beyond their mortal lives. Indeed, the narrator's reconstruction of Jehuda Halevy's creative life as Jew and multitalented, heterogeneous poet and scholar, which comprises the substance of part two of the poem, not only attests to the possibility of transcendence and immortality, but also suggests that an integrative diasporic life may very well be able to ameliorate or even overcome the grief and paralysis of exilic existence. Witness, for example, how the narrator's involvement with the "Golden Age in Spain" seems to provide him with a model not only for transcending his own physical and existential suffering detailed in the preamble, but for transforming it, within a poetic text and through its construction, into an alternative positive conception of diaspora.

The activity of the narrator-poet, who delights in the creative construction of a text, comes to an end in the closing lines of "Jehuda ben Halevy" and seems to have disappeared completely from the final poem of the "Hebrew Melodies," entitled "Disputation." Set in fourteenth-century, Christian Spain, the poem depicts a public debate about whether the Christian or Israelite God is the true one. Although fictional, this disputation between the Capuchin monk Friar Jose and Rabbi Juda of Navarre is certainly reminiscent of a famous debate that took place in Barcelona is 1263 between Rabbi Moses ben Nachman, known also as Nachmanides or Ramban, and a learned baptised Jew, Friar Paolo. Debates like these were very serious encounters, but not because of their subject matter. Since they were in fact generally staged for the express purpose of converting Jews, who could therefore hardly be expected to win, a loss meant that the losing debater and a group of his co-religionists would be forced to convert or be severely punished.

Since the details of this disputation are hardly difficult to grasp because of the commonplace dogmas and cliches exchanged by the parties, let me concentrate on an issue more difficult to assess, the relationship of this final poem to the earlier ones. This may bring us closer to an understanding of the aesthetic and ideological contours of the "Hebrew Melodies" and return us to a central focus of this essay, that is, the problematics and poetics of diaspora. Critics, especially (but not exclusively) those primarily interested in Heine's relation to Jews and Judaism, have registered dismay at the "Disputation" text because it seems to countermand what is regarded as the significance of the first two poems: as one critic put it, "Heine's reawakened love for the tradition of the people from which he descends, for Jewish practices and Jewish poetry."[20] Prawer even thinks that because

"*Prinzessin Sabbat* and *Jehuda ben Halevy* had both been paeans to the spirit of the Jewish faith," Heine felt obligated to reaffirm "the tartness of his unsweetened imagination and the refusal of his free-ranging intellect to be fettered by orthodxies of *any* kind."[21] While Sammons' insight that the poem "is an attempt to expose the vulgarity of zealous religious faith where it is not ennobled by poetic imagination"[22] is closer to my own, the implication of some of his language is disquieting. It is not, it seems to me, the "vulgarity" of absolutely rigid religious positions or their articulation that is at stake in this poem, but the social and cultural conditions they represent and reproduce; and I rather doubt that the crass and vicious dogmatic views presented by monk and rabbi could be ennobled or dignified, even by "poetic imagination."

A striking feature of this final poem of the "Hebrew Melodies" is, as already mentioned, the absence of an identifiable, interactive narrator, which seems here to be connected with a substantive change in the social and cultural environment represented in "Jehuda ben Halevy." There the narrator, who had the flexibility and creativity to weave together temporally, geographically, and ideologically diverse cultures, clearly identified with the dynamic diasporic situation in which the major figures represented—Jehuda Halevy, Gabirol, Ibn Esra—integrated substantial aspects of several cultures (Christian troubadour poetry, Moslem poetic forms, Jewish midrashic tradition) into their lives and work. This kind of interactive possibility is absent in "Disputation," where the parties, representing immutable positions, do not seek common ground or insight into their opponent's views, but rather to gain ascendency for their own fixed ideas. The intellectual and cultural immobility that reigns in this text is also reflected in the stationary scene presented in the poem: in an auditorium in Toledo, a royal audience and their servants sit and listen, the disputants argue, and Queen Donna Blanka casts the final judgment—"That both of them alike stink." (6/I: 172; D 688). Neither the transformation realized in "Princess Sabbath" nor the continual movement of people and things, of temporal position and geographical location, of genre and idea in "Jehuda ben Halevy" is to be found in "Disputation," whose opaque narrator is also so completely absorbed into the narrative that no comment on this grim yet grotesquely bombastic paralysis is even possible. Both the structure and the subject matter of this poem suggest that when religion becomes institutionalized and completely dogmatic, cultural exchange, perhaps culture itself is obliterated; and the individual is either confined to fixed roles—rabbi or monk—or disappears completely, as does the narrator, in an anonymous authoritative script without agent or author.

One may well wonder whether any remnant of the creative cultural vitality represented in the "Jehuda ben Halevy" poem remains after "Disputation," which marks the end of both the "Hebrew Melodies" and *Romancero*. In my reading of the "Hebrew Melodies," it is precisely the grim moral vacuity, intellectual stagnation, and the absence of individuality and creativity so conspicuous in "Disputation" that prompts the reader to revisit that earlier Golden Age, be it myth and or reality, that stirred the modern poet to construct such a marvelously complex and multivalent cultural document as "Jehuda ben Halevy." Thus, despite, or perhaps because of, the bleak and foreboding social and ideological circumstances portrayed in "Disputation," that Golden Age lives on.

Indeed, negative images of diasporic life and identity haunt all three poems, whether it is the miserable situation of the weekday Jew in "Princess Sabbath" and his insulation within traditional ritual; or the impoverishment of the narrator-poet in "Jehuda ben Halevy," who still hears "the old song," "the old melody" of Babylonian exile stirring in him: "Long already, millennia long / Has it boiled in me. A dark woe! / And time licks my wound, / As the dog did Job's ulcers." (6/I: 135; D 659); or the Rabbi and Jews of "Disputation," who, threatened with death or loss of identity, are forced to defend the exclusivity of their traditional religious beliefs and practices, despite the fact that the defense itself would most likely lead to conversion or death. But the "Hebrew Melodies" as a whole is addressing the possibility of another model of diaspora. Daniel and Jonathan Boyarin have noted that "[d]iaspora culture and identity allows (and has historically allowed in the best circumstances, such as Muslim Spain), for a complex continuation of Jewish cultural creativity and identity at the same time that the same people fully participate in the common cultural life of their surroundings."[23] The Boyarins' conception of diasporic cultural identity is a disaggregated one that is being continually constructed anew when circumstances and conditions demand, an identity protected only by interaction with other cultures. James Clifford underscores the importance in diaspora cultures of the social interaction among groups and of the construction of communities that allow for the active intersection of different cultures: "Diaspora discourse articulates, or bends together, both roots *and* routes to construct ... alternate public spheres, forms of community consciousness and solidarity that maintain identifications outside the national time/space in order to live inside, with a difference. Diaspora cultures are non separatist, though they may have separatist or irredentist moments."[24] It is precisely the possibility of interactive cultures and communities that informs the environment of "Jehuda ben Halevy"; and it is their complete impossibility that is critiqued in "Disputation."

The impetus to the plethora of recent discussions of diaspora (rather than exile) was probably the burgeoning interest in postcolonial and multicultural studies and the enormous increase in the transnational circulation of peoples, goods, and information. The focus on diaspora theory, discourse, and identity has been particularly helpful in distinguishing diaspora as an interactive integration of dominant and subdominant cultures from exile understood as a tragic situation of forced homelessness and an anguished longing to return to the homeland, the center of national identity. Of course, each position—diaspora or exile—presupposes an identity very different from the other: the former would construe distinctiveness through connection and coexistence; the latter likely to insist on the necessity of uniqueness, separatism, and sovereignty. Understood in this context, the "Hebrew Melodies" seems invested in establishing the importance of an integrative diaspora that promotes interactive dialogue across multiple borders—cultural and social, temporal and geographical—and in developing a poetics that communicates that possibility. It accomplishes this in two ways: negatively in "Disputation," by depicting the menacing effects of absolutist thinking and practice in a completely polarized society; and positively in "Jehuda ben Halevy," by portraying not only the rich creativity of Sephardi culture in medieval Spain, but especially the imaginative narrator-poet who, using a variety of poetic techniques and genres, ingeniously constructs the connections among multiple cultures across vast areas of space and time, from the Middle East to the European west, from biblical and Hellenistic times through the Middle Ages to the nineteenth century. A challenging performative enactment of the politics and poetics of diaspora.

Notes

1. The poet's name is actually Jehuda ben Samuel Halevy, which means Jehuda son of Samuel the Levite. One cannot normally abreviate the name as Jehuda ben Halevy, which means Jehuda, son of the Levite. The implications of Heine's designation will be discussed later.

2. Daniel Schroeter, "Orientalism and the Jews of the Mediterranean," *Journal of Mediterranean Studies* 2.2 (1994), pp. 184-96, here p. 189.

3. Paul Mendes-Flohr, "Orientalism, the *Ostjuden* and Jewish Self-Affirmation," *Studies in Contemporary Jewry* I, ed. Jonathan Frankel (Bloomington, 1984), pp. 96-139, here p. 100.

4. Steven Aschheim, "The Eastern European Jew and German Jewish identity," *Studies in Contemporary Jewry* I, ed. Jonathan Frankel (Bloomington, 1984), pp. 3-25, here p. 7; see also his *Brothers and Strangers: The East European Jew in German and German Jewish Consciousness 1800-1923* (Madison, 1983), especially Chapter 1.

5. Edward W. Said, *Orientalism* (New York, 1978), pp. 1-28.

6. Virginia R. Dominguez, "Questioning Jews," *American Ethnologist* 20.3 (1993), pp. 618-624, here p. 622.

7. Ismar Schorsch, "The Myth of Sephardic Supremacy," *Leo Baeck Institute Year Book* 34 (1989), pp. 47-66, here esp. pp. 47-53. See also pp. 57-66 for a discussion of the many works about medieval Sephardi philosophy, poetry, and culture written in Germany during the first half of the eighteenth century.

8. Heine's title was taken from Lord Byron's 1815 poem cycle, "Hebrew Melodies," which is largely concerned with biblical figures and events; and although there is, as most critics have noted, little substantive connection between Heine's poems and those of Lord Byron, the allusion to Byron's title, especially in the tension with the title *Romancero*—which refers to Spanish collections of romances, ballads, and legendary tales—may have an important aesthetic and ideological function. The intersection between medieval chivalric culture and religious biblical tradition, between different geographical and temporal arenas, and between ancient Hebrew and

modern languages (German and English) hints at the idea of diasporic culture explored in Heine's poems.

9. The Sabbath in traditional Judaism is often referred to as Queen, not Princess; and it is God (traditionally the King) who sends the Queen Sabbath to Israel as a bride. Since the narrator in "Princess Sabbath" compares this mythology about the Sabbath transformation of Israel to *Arabian Nights'* fables of enchanted princes who are returned for a spell to their former princely selves, it seems appropriate for Israel to be figured as Prince and the Sabbath bride as Princess.

10. See S. S. Prawer, *Heine's Jewish Comedy: A Study of His Portraits of Jews and Judaism* (Oxford, 1983), pp. 554-561; Jeffrey L. Sammons, *Heinrich Heine, The Elusive Poet* (New Haven, 1969), pp. 387-89; Hartmut Kircher, *Heinrich Heine und das Judentum* (Bonn, 1973), pp. 266-70; see also Israel Tabak, *Judaic Lore in Heine: The Heritage of a Poet* (Baltimore, 1948), pp. 156-61 and Ludwig Rosenthal, *Heinrich Heine als Jude* (Frankfurt/Main, 1973), pp. 89, 292-95 for Heine's sources and for a discussion of the significance of references to Jewish history and the practices and traditions of Judaism.

11. For example, Sander L. Gilman, *Inscribing the Other* (Lincoln, 1991), pp. 132-33, states that in this poem Jehuda ben Halevy was identified as the author of the famous Sabbath song *because* readers would associate him with the "Golden Age," whereas that would not be the case with the actual author, Solomon Halevy Alkabets; Prawer, *Heine's Jewish Comedy,* p. 797, n. 10: "Heine seems to have chosen the form 'Jehuda ben Halevy' for reasons of euphony." The aesthetic significance of this designation will be discussed later.

12. Mendes-Flohr, "Orientalism," p. 100.

13. Parenthetical references in the form of "D" followed by a number refer to page numbers of the English translation in Heinrich Heine, *The Complete Poems of Heinrich Heine: A Modern English Version,* trans. by Hal Draper (Boston, 1982).

14. I am indebted to Chana Kronfield for this information on the function of the Levites in Temple and synagogue.

15. The importance of this Psalm for Heine has been discussed in different contexts in two very fine articles: Inge Rippmann, "'Wir saßen an den Wassern Babylons': Eine Annäherung an Heinrich Heines *Denkschrift über Ludwig Börne,"* *Heine-Jahrbuch* 34 (1995), pp. 25-47, is largely concerned with the relationship between Heine's experience of exile and homesickness in Paris, and his sense of linguistic isolation as a German writer. It seems to me, however, that Heine's reference to verses five and six in "Jehuda ben Halevy" is less about homage to Zion, as Rippmann maintains (pp. 30-31), than about the importance of memory for writing. Ruth Wolf, "Versuch über 'Jehuda ben Halevy,'" *Heine-Jahrbuch* 18 (1979), pp. 84-98, is more concerned with the importance of the Psalm for Heine (he speaks of the Psalm in a letter to Moser in 1826 in relation to his unhappiness about his conversion the previous year) than its function in the poem.

16. The first two verses are cited at the beginning of part two of the poem; I shall return to their significance.

17. Michael Sachs, *Die religiöse Poesie der Juden in Spanien* (Berlin, 1845), p. 287. There is an interesting reference to pearls in a passage about Jehuda Halevy's works which Sachs quotes from a poem by Rabbi Judah ben Solomon Alcharisi: "The song which the Levite Jehuda sang is like a magnificent diadem twined about the head of the community, like a string of pearls it holds its neck surrounded." (Translation is mine.) Heine was very much indebted to Sachs' work for his knowledge of medieval Spanish Jewish poetry and culture. See Rosenthal, *Heinrich Heine*, pp. 290-96.

18. Sachs, *Die religiöse Poesie*, pp. 300-01, comments that Jehuda Halevy was not driven to go to Jerusalem by an oppressive situation, but by "a clear pure loving yearning, which expressed itself sometimes in childlike simplicity, sometimes in glowing inwardness." (Translation is mine.)

19. Sachs, *Die religiöse Poesie*, p. 291 notes that there is evidence that Jehuda Halevy did not, as legend had it, die when he entered Jerusalem, but most likely *en route* from Egypt to Palestine. Heine, however, adopts the legendary narrative in the poem.

20. Kircher, *Heinrich Heine*, p. 280.

21. Prawer, *Heine's Jewish Comedy*, p. 599. Emphasis in the original.

22. Sammons, *Heinrich Heine*, p. 395.

23. Daniel Boyarin and Jonathan Boyarin, "Diaspora: Generation and the Ground of Jewish Identity," *Critical Inquiry* 19, no. 4 (1993), pp. 693-724, here pp. 720-21.

24. James Clifford, *Routes: Travel and Translation in the Late Twentieth Century* (Cambridge, 1997), p. 251.

Confessions of an Apostate: Heine's Conversion and Its Psychic Displacement

Robert C. Holub

I

Heine often wrote about himself, but the nature of these self-references is not always autobiographical. Heine's first-person comments have a variety of different statuses: some do indeed impart information relating to Heine and his life, but many others are included to create an effect. If we want to be less charitable to Heine, then we could simply state that Heine sometimes lies about himself, but we would want to note that his lies are hardly ever without a purpose. When Heine calls himself the first man of the century, for example, he does not literally mean that he was born on January 1, 1800, and although his birthday and his remarks about it are still the source of some confusion, we understand that in this case his comment is meant to convey the coincidence of his approximate date of birth and his claim of preeminence in the nineteenth century. Similarly, when in *Ideas. The Book of Le Grand* he has Napoleon appear in his native Düsseldorf in the middle of a beautiful summer day, when we know that the French leader in fact visited Düsseldorf in 1811 at the beginning of the "sad month of November"—as it is called in his famous mock epic, *Germany. A Winter's Tale*—we recognize that Heine rearranges the calender slightly to celebrate the emancipatory aspects of the French occupation. I could enumerate further, since the inaccuracies and exaggerations in Heine's works are sufficiently abundant, but I think my point is already rather obvious. Heine is an unreliable reporter about Heine. And because Heine's statements about himself in his writings are so often hyperbolic, fictionalized, or simply contrary to fact, it is difficult to gather accurate biographical information from him simply by taking him at his word.

Heine is even more unreliable about himself when he is dealing with matters that were very close to him personally and about which he had conflicting emotions. In these cases he seems less in control of his writing; instead a kind of psychic pressure relating to an uncomfortable biographical fact or event seems to exert a distorting influence on his writing, resulting in displacements, false attributions, and related confusions. One of the issues that caused him the most psychic distress was his Judaism in general and specifically his conversion from Judaism to the Protestant faith. It occurred, as we know, in June of 1825 shortly before Heine completed his doctoral degree in jurisprudence at the University of Göttingen, and although Heine later characterized it in a famous *bon mot* as his "entrance ticket to European culture" (6/I: 622), we must suspect that it had a great impact on him. Conversion, of course, was not so unusual for German Jews in precisely the early years of the restoration, and we often hear the undoubtedly correct observation that many assimilated Jews, having already become integrated into German society, converted to Protestantism in order to facilitate professional life.[1] The Napoleonic Code, which had brought some degree of emancipation to the Jews of Germany, especially in those areas under the direct jurisdiction of the French, had been negated by restoration authorities, and Jews who had ambitions to enter the German civil service, which encompassed, of course, a large number of professional positions from university professor to doctors at hospitals, found themselves faced with a choice of professional proscription or conversion. In light of this alternative, many of Germany's intellectually enlightened Jews—I cite the names of Eduard Gans, Ludwig Börne, and Heinrich Marx (the father of Karl Marx) by way of example—opted for a formal conversion to a belief to which they adhered in name only. Although there were some cases in which the converted Jew genuinely embraced his new religion, Heine's conversion was certainly of the insincere variety since we have no record of him attending church, and no evidence whatsoever that he believed in a Christian God. If he embraced anything in Protestantism, it was, as he suggested in later writings, the protest that he later associated with Luther's defiance of the Catholic hierarchy.

Despite his own witty remarks about his baptism, we should not believe that he took his conversion lightly. Psychologically the conversion was an action that took a heavy toll. Perhaps most importantly it signaled for Heine the end of the German-Jewish synthesis that he had tried to perpetuate during the early 1820s. Heine experienced the impossibility of this synthesis clearly and painfully in the third decade of his life, which was also the first decade of his career as a writer.[2] Indeed, this period, and in particular his stay in Berlin from March of 1821 until July of 1823, is decisive for an understanding of the role the Jewish heritage played in Heine's life and works since it includes important events and experiences for the young Jewish man who wished to become a celebrated German writer. The most important of these is probably Heine's acquaintance with other young Jewish intellectuals in the *Association for the Culture and Scholarship of the Jews* (*Verein für Cultur und Wissenschaft der Juden*), an organization Heine joined in August of 1822. Until his association with members of the *Verein* we have scant evidence about Heine's own feelings toward his co-religionists and about his knowledge of the traditions, practices, and history of Judaism.[3] Most of what we do possess, including his personal correspondence, does not indicate that the young Heine had an avid interest in Jewish affairs. At Bonn and Göttingen he evidently did not seek out Jewish friends or organizations; he appears instead to have led a rather typical German student existence, although it is quite possible that his expulsion from a nationalist student club (*Burschenschaft*) in Göttingen at the end of December in 1820 was related to his religious heritage: Heine preferred to claim that he violated the chastity oath, but we know already that Heine does not always tell us the entire truth about his own life. In any case, during his stays in Bonn and Göttingen, he does not appear to have hidden his religious affiliation, but he also does not seem to have emphasized his Jewishness in his dealings with friends and acquaintances. Indeed, his main interests before he arrived in Berlin in March of 1821 were related to romantic poetry, to the theoretical and poetic insights of his teacher at Bonn, August Wilhelm Schlegel, and to a progressive strand of German nationalism, which was commonplace for the liberal young men of his era.

It appears that before his arrival in Berlin the tension inherent in the existence of a German poet with a Jewish heritage was either not felt or not particularly urgent for Heine. In Berlin, however, Heine could not avoid a confrontation any longer, even though one could argue that his initial experiences in Berlin actually affirmed the compatibility of Germanness and Jewishness under enlightened, modern Prussian conditions. The two most important circles he frequented could be viewed as illustrations of the harmonious co-existence of Jewish and German life. In the salon of Rahel von Varnhagen, a former Jewess married to the retired Prussian diplomat Varnhagen von Ense, Heine encountered not only a successful German-Jewish symbiosis embodied in the host and hostess, but also a social forum for important intellectuals who were both Jewish and gentile. Even more decisive for Heine's development was his association with the *Verein*. Heine had gained entrance to Rahel's salon a few months after he arrived in the Prussian capital, and approximately a year later he first made the acquaintance of Eduard Gans, who had presided over the *Verein* since March of 1821. Heine himself became a member on 4 August. Although he left for Poland shortly thereafter, upon his return he was a fairly regular participant at the meetings of the *Verein* and its affiliated scholarly institute until he left Berlin the following May. From the letters Heine wrote to

Moses Moser, his closest friend in the *Verein*, after his departure from the Prussian capital, it is apparent that he retained an interest in it until its dissolution in 1824. Significant about the *Verein* was that it did not emphasize a separatist Jewish identity outside of Germanness, but that it sought to bring Judaism into the framework of modern European thought. The *Verein* was an openly assimilationist organization; the guiding spirit behind it believed in and propagated the compatibility of Judaism and contemporary Germany. If there still existed tensions between Jews and Germans—at least on an intellectual level—then the problem was just as likely to result from Jewish backwardness as German intolerance. And as predominantly enlightened Hegelians, the members of the *Verein* appeared to envision a future in which cultural differences might be further sublated and an even more harmonious state of affairs might be attained.

Although Heine's stay in Berlin obviously introduced him to many examples of an apparently successful Jewish-German synthesis, it simultaneously exposed him to several situations in which he could have easily doubted the ultimate efficacy of remaining Jewish in a predominantly Christian social order. It is not apparent whether Heine considered relinquishing his connections to his Jewish heritage before he arrived in Berlin, but certainly one of the results of his experiences in the Prussian capital was the recognition of conversion as a potential, practical, and acceptable means of integration. Indeed, conversion was an option that was being preached to Jews from a number of angles. Christian Friedrich Rühs, for example, a professor of history in Berlin who died shortly before Heine's arrival, refuted the enlightenment tendency toward tolerance for the Jews, insisting that if Jews wanted to be full members of a Christian state, they would have to convert to the Christian religion. Rühs' views were not unchallenged, but his opinions were sufficiently popular and representative that they attracted much support as well.[4] While Heine could ignore or oppose reactionary positions such as Rühs', it was more difficult for him to avoid the support that conversion received inside the Jewish community itself. Although earlier estimates of mass conversion have been revised someone in recent years, it still appears that a significant number of Jews converted to Protestantism, especially in the 1820s and 1830s, and in particular in urban centers like Berlin.[5] We may not be dealing with the phenomenon of "mass baptisms," which Heinrich Graetz thought he could deduce from the statistics,[6] but Deborah Hertz could recently assert with confidence that we can speak of a "conversion wave" in Berlin of the third and fourth decade of the nineteenth century.[7] What made this "wave" particularly important for Heine was that it encompassed many prominent members of the Jewish community.[8] Four of the six children of Moses Mendelssohn eventually left the religion of their illustrious father, and Leah Salomon, the granddaughter of Daniel Itzig, and Abraham Mendelssohn had their own children baptized, among them the seven-year old Felix, in 1816, six years before their own conversion.[9] Heine was undoubtedly familiar with these conversions, as well as the baptisms that had taken place or were contemplated within his closest circle of friends. Rahel Levin, after all, along with her brothers, had abandoned her orthodox Jewish roots before Heine made their acquaintance, and Eduard Gans, well before his baptism in 1825, had been in a struggle with the Prussian state focussing on conversion and the possibility of obtaining an academic position. The irony, therefore, of Heine's intensive introduction to the German-Jewish synthesis was that it simultaneously legitimated conversion as the next logical step toward full integration in the Christian state.

It is thus not surprising that at the same time that Heine was becoming acquainted with paradigms of German-Jewish integration, he also appears to have suffered his most severe crisis of identity with regard to his status as a German poet of Jewish heritage. Reacting to the climate created by the anti-Jewish writings of Rühs and Jakob Friedrich Fries, who likewise insisted on the incompatibility of Jews and German intellectual life, and possibly also to the defections from the Jewish community around him, Heine went through a period during which he emphasizes the utter incongruity of the German-Jewish synthesis. Writing to Christian Sethe in April of 1822 he expresses his disgust for everything associated with Germany: "Everything German is repulsive to me, and unfortunately you are a German. Everything German affects me like an emetic. The German language rips my ears apart. My own poems disgust me sometimes, when I see that they are written in German" (HSA 20: 50). This attitude represents a decisive change from his previous identification of himself not only as a German writer, but as a writer in the German national tradition; from this point in time onward, we have to consider Heine cured of his youthful flirtation with Germanness, at least of the nationalist variety. A letter from the following February, written to Moritz Embden, indicates clearly that his allegiances to the nationalist cause were severely damaged, and that he must now differentiate between progressive and nationalist sentiments. Although he believes he belongs to the radicals according to the English and to the Carbonari according to the Italians, in Germany he cannot identify himself with the "demagogues" (the group he feels corresponds to these foreign radicals) since a victory of this revolutionary group would mean that the necks of a few thousand Jews would be severed (HSA 20: 70). For a time he appears to accept his own disenfranchisement from a German identity. Writing to Moser in May of 1823, he calls himself a "a Jewish poet" and states that he prefers speaking with him "in our national images," by which he means, of course, the images of the Jewish nation (HSA 20: 87). In two other letters he cites anti-Jewish writings as ironic confirmation that he is not a German. As is so often the case, the irony reveals two levels: on one Heine is obviously pointing to the absurdity of such Judeophobic nonsense. But on another level Heine is wounded, alienated from the nationalist feelings he had previously embraced. In March of 1824 he writes in a similarly ironic tone to Rudolf Christiani— prefiguring Caput XI of *Germany. A Winter's Tale*. He speaks first about the misfortune of Arminius' victory, which has caused him to learn Latin as a foreign language, and he continues:

> I do not want to write any further; a patriotic German could surprise me and thrust a dagger into my un-German heart with the pathetic cry: Die infamous lackey of tyrants and traitor to the Fatherland! But I would then reach for the *Nibelungenlied* lying next to me and hold it as a shield against the Don Quixote from Jena, and the dagger would fall from his hands, and he would fold them in prayer, saying: O sancta Chrimhilda, Brunhilde et Uhta ora pro nobis!

But in this letter he also reveals how difficult it will be for him to discard his Germanness:

> I know that I am the most German of all creatures; I know only too well that German is to me what water is to a fish, that I cannot escape this element so important for my life. . . .I love things German even more than anything else in the world; I derive my pleasure and happiness from them; my heart is an archive of German feeling, just as my two books are an archive of German songs. (HSA 20: 148)

Clearly Heine was going through an identity crisis forced on him by a bifurcation in an existence he had previously considered relatively unproblematic. With some degree of certainty we can maintain that during the early 1820s Heine came to recognize that one could not be simply a German-Jewish writer; the conflict between the problematic halves of this artificial synthesis would have to be resolved, and when they were, there would inevitably be a loss.

His writings from this period are a reflection of this dichotomous existence. In his public persona Heine remained primarily a German romantic poet during the first half of the 1820s. Despite his membership in the *Verein* and his increasing familiarity with Jewish culture and tradition—to a degree that probably exceeded anything he had experienced in his early years—this knowledge of and identification with Judaism remained largely confined to the private sphere. Although he had touched on the topic of religious discrimination in his play *Almansor*, which he began at Bonn and finished during his first stay in Göttingen, it is significant that he does not thematize directly the fate of the Jews in Spain, but rather uses the Moslems, who were persecuted at the same time as the Jews, as a cipher for the plight of the Jews in modern Europe.[10] Indeed, mention of Jews and the Jewish question in Germany are fairly infrequent in his published works. In the second of his *Letters from Berlin*, dated 22 March 1822, Heine mentions the new, refurbished project of Jewish conversion, but he claims he does not want to describe it in detail because "the Jews are really too sad a topic" (2: 36). By the time he composes his report *On Poland*, he had already been involved in the *Verein*, and it is not surprising to find a preoccupation with his co-religionists. In Heine's analysis of Polish society, the Jews occupy a separate class between the nobility and the peasants, a sort of "third estate," to which he devotes a great deal of attention. He shows sympathy with the Jewish plight and concern with their future; and it is interesting and consistent with the remarks cited from his correspondence that at one point he contrasts Polish Jewry favorably with the more assimilated German Jews with whom he has obviously had more contact and affinities. But in the large poetic production of his early years we find very few traces of Jews and Judaism.[11] For the reading public Heine, even after his baptism, remained H. Heine, the witty German romantic poet of unrequited love:

> I am a German poet
> In Germany well known;
> Name the greatest names and
> You're sure to name my own.

And that which ails me, little one,
Makes many Germans moan;
Name the greatest sorrows—
You're sure to name my own. (1: 115)[12]

At the same time that these words appeared in print, Heine was privately disavowing his Germanness and proclaiming his identity as a Jewish writer. Eventually Heine defiantly reasserts his Germanness even in his correspondence. In June of 1824 he includes the following, irony-laden sentence in a letter to Moser: "Oh how we Germans have perfected ourselves!" (HSA 20: 168). And similarly he writes to Friederike Robert almost a year later that there are people in India who have suffered and endured even more than "we Germans have" (HSA 20: 198). But his only real Jewish work of these years of his identity crisis, *The Rabbi von Bacherach*, remained fragmentary and would be published only a decade and a half later during the Damascus crisis.

The identity Heine eventually embraced was therefore filled with contradictions that should not be glossed over in the easy formula German-Jewish writer. After 1825 Heine became a Protestant, and although he was never an adherent to the Protestant religion in anything more than name, it would be inaccurate to call him a simply a German Jew: his disavowal of Judaism was forced upon him to a certain degree, but there were also reasons for his conversion that had to do with a commonly held notion that Protestantism was the most progressive religion of the time. In any case, we should exercise caution in applying the label German-Jewish to Heine (or to any writer who has converted), lest we fall into the same camp inhabited by a certain breed of racist who contends that Jewishness is located in the blood or some other unalterable part of a person's being or upbringing. With regard to Heine and his identity, we can probably state the following with some degree of certainty: He identified with Germany and evidenced German pride, but he abhorred narrow German nationalism and unreflective patriotism. And he remained a former Jew, whose uneasiness with his own conversion and concern with his quondam co-religionists never finds resolution in his writings—or in his own thoughts. When during the course of the nineteenth century Heine's identity crisis, which marked of course simultaneously a number of social crises in German life, became resolved in an ex post facto German-Jewish synthesis, he became known primarily as the composer of a romantic poetry, in which there are few overt traces of his actual personal conflicts or ethnic heritage. The *Book of*

Songs became one of the most popular lyric collections in the world, and the poems in it were set to music by major and minor composers of all religious backgrounds. Significantly, the single transparently "Jewish" poem in the style of his early verse is included in no public collection of verse by H. Heine, but instead appears in one of the letters written to Moser and is conceived as a private, future dedication to his friend in connection with the *Rabbi* project:

Burst out in loud lamenting,
O somber martyr-song
That's lain so unrelenting
On burning hearts so long!

It pierces through ears and vision,
And so into heart and brain;
I've conjured up with precision
The thousand years of pain.

They weep, little men and big powers,
Even lords with frigid eyes,
The women weep, and the flowers,
The stars weep up in the skies.

And all of the tears are flowing
South, quiet and unified,
They're flowing together, and going
To pour into Jordan's tide. (1: 271)[13]

Immediately after writing these poignant lyrics, Heine reminds his friend "that the verses I just wrote are worth very little and were made merely for my own amusement" (HSA 20: 178). We may want to dispute this self-deprecating evaluation or consider it a rare moment of "Jewish" modesty in contrast to the versified "German" boasting cited above. It is nonetheless clear that the poem evidences formal continuities as well as content-related ruptures with his early verse. The rhyme scheme, strophic form, and even some of the figurative language are similar to those we find in the *Book of Songs*. But the narrative persona for this poem is not a longing German lover obsessed with a woman who has spurned his advances, leaving him pining away for her, but a suffering Jew, identifying with a persecuted people. Here the "I" is not looking inward at his sorrow, bewailing his personal fate as part of the German Fatherland, but reflecting on a tradition of anguish and pain that a Jewish collective has experienced. It is not Heine's individual tears alone that will flow into the Jordan river, but the tears of the entire Jewish community on earth. What is significant about this poem, therefore, is that, exceptionally, the speaker in not H. Heine, German poet, and certainly not the baptized German-Jewish writer Heinrich Heine, but most definitely Harry Heine, the German poet of Jewish origins.

II

Considering his identity crisis in the early 1820s, we should not be surprised to find Heine's conversion a source of psychic disruption. Indeed, in his writings one of the central ways Heine dealt with this issue was through the technique of displacement. In employing displacement, Heine did not simply take his own thoughts and feelings and project them onto other people or onto characters in his works. Rather displacement functioned, I believe, in ways of which Heine himself may not have been totally aware. The most famous example of such displacement is probably Heine's poem "To an Apostate," which scholars presume was written about Eduard Gans, the leader of the previously mentioned *Association for the Culture and Scholarship of the Jews*, to which Heine had also belonged when he was in Berlin in the early 1820s. Heine's poem castigates his unnamed apostate for betraying his own youthful ardor, selling out to social pressures, and hypocritically embracing a faith that he had recently despised. It closes with a strophe that blames erudition, or at least the exposure to conservative thought for the renegade's actions:

Oh, the holy spark of youth—
Oh, how fast it's by the board!
In cold blood you have, in truth,
Made a deal with the good Lord.

To the cross you crawled your way
That you scorned with scorn profound,
Cross that, just the other day,
You would trample to the ground.

You read Schlegel, Haller, Burke,

Whom reaction keeps in vogue—
Once you did a hero's work,
Now you're nothing but a rogue. (1: 266)[14]

Unusual about the list of reactionaries is that Heine otherwise does not associate them with Gans. Obviously Friedrich Schlegel and Karl Ludwig von Haller may have been included because of their own conversions; both men left the Protestant faith for Catholicism, Schlegel in 1808, Haller—with much fanfare—in 1820. Edmund Burke is oddly out of place in this group, having undergone no religious conversion; he belongs with Schlegel and Haller only as a fellow conservative thinker, a feature that Gans does not share. In any case, the grouping is odd because of their dissimilarity with Gans on political issues and reflects Heine's momentary anger with his friend more than any true political affinities. But more germane for our concerns is the obvious and frequently remarked displacement of self-accusation and self-betrayal onto a third party. Gans had done the same thing in October of 1825 that Heine had done several months earlier: he had abandoned the religious tradition of his youth, and, like Heine, we presume he had done so without any real religious conviction and for precisely the same practical reasons that are usually attributed to Heine.[15]

Let me cite one further example of Heine's technique of displacement as it relates to his more immediate attempt to cope with his own conversion. In chapter XV of *Ideas. Book Le Grand*, written at about the time that Heine became a Protestant, the narrator relates a different and humorous sort of conversion, from the party of the fools to the party of the reasonable ones. The text is obviously not an allegory in which Jews and Christians line up precisely with fools and reasonable ones; Heine's displacement in this case, and in most cases, does not operate with one-to-one correspondences. Rather this passage repeats themes and sentiments that are bound up in Heine's religious conversion and refracts them in various ways. At the outset the reasonable ones are said to have been at war with the fools for 5588 years, a clear reference to the date according to Jewish calender. At another point, Heine relates the hatred of the fools for him:

> I, poor thing, am especially hated by them (the fools); they assert that I originally was one of them, that I am an apostate, a deserter who has broken the holiest ties, that I am now even a spy who secretly reveals what they, the

> fools, have garnered together for the purpose of exposing them to the laughter of my new associates, and that I am so stupid that I do not recognize that the latter are all the while laughing at me and will never regard me as one of their own. And about this the fools are perfectly right. (2: 298)

Here Heine repeats the reproaches or imagined reproaches a converted Jew would have suffered from his old co-religionists, as well as the suspicions Heine himself harbored about many of his new co-religionists. The resentment toward a traitor, which Heine himself expressed in his poem about Gans, the inability to become a Christian despite one's profession of a change in faith, the furtive ridicule a convert experiences from those who do not truly accept him—all of these motifs, which are sentiments expressed privately in Heine's correspondence, are contained in the passage from *Ideas* in distorted and displaced form. At this point in his life Heine was unable to speak about his conversion openly; indeed, he refers to it infrequently even in his correspondence with his most intimate friends. But in a displaced fashion his status as an apostate finds its way nonetheless into his published writings.[16]

Heine's self-doubt about his conversion appears to have diminished noticeably in the 1830s, perhaps because in Paris he was no longer confronted with the ambiguous position of a German Jew. Initially in France he seems to have identified himself and to have been identified simply as a German writer, and it was not until 1840 and the Damascus crisis that we find Heine again taking up Jewish concerns with any intensity. In this context conversion again becomes a theme. It is noticeable in the *Ludwig Markus Recollections*, where Heine argues against conversion, insisting instead that the Jews must emancipate themselves and in this way integrate into German Christian society. But conversion is also a topic in *Ludwig Börne: A Memorial* in a typically Heinesque manner. In the heavily fictionalized meeting between Heine and Börne in book one Heine places the following sentiments into Börne's mouth:

> Baptism is now the order of the day for rich Jews, and the gospels that have been preached in vain to the poor of Judea are now *in floribus* with the rich. But since embracing it is only self-delusion, if not an outright lie, and hypocritical Christianity sometimes contrasts very

> sharply with old Adam, these people expose themselves in a dubious fashion to jokes and ridicule. Or do you think that inner nature can be changed entirely through baptism? Do you think that you can transform lice into fleas if you pour water on them? (4: 31)

This passage, written long after both Börne and Heine had chosen to change their putatively "parasitic" nature by leaving the religion of their birth, is projected backward into a time when both were still Jewish. It is quite possible, of course, that Börne may have uttered something like this to Heine at some point. But one must suspect, again, that Heine is projecting his own feelings onto the person purportedly accompanying him through the Frankfurt ghetto. A half year after his conversion Heine recognized that baptism was a futile concession to the Christian world. "I am now hated by Christian and Jew," Heine reports to Moser six months after his conversion. "I regret that I had myself baptized; I don't think that things have been better for me since then; quite the contrary, since then I have had nothing but misfortune" (HSA 20: 234).[17] And approximately a year after his baptism he writes of the "torture of his personal relations (the Jew that can never be washed off)" (HSA 20: 265). The difference between his private comments in 1826 and his public remarks in the Börne *Memorial* are considerable, however. In the 1820s Heine is bitter; his conversion has not brought him the opportunities that he desired. He has abandoned his heritage without apparent gain. In 1840 he is less concerned with his own status as an apostate; secure in his adherence to no positive religion, he appears neither to regret his baptism, nor accept its religious consequences. As he makes clear in the *Memorial*, he belongs to the Hellenes, not to any species of Nazarene.

That Heine had difficulties in the psychological processing of his conversion is further evidenced by a conversation reported by Alexandre Weill. Responding to the question of why he converted, Heine evidently answered in a rather strange manner. He spoke of his return from visits to Italy and England, and that he felt no strong sentiments for his religious heritage. He then brings up his appointment to edit a German journal and states that as a Jew he could not possibly assume that position. He then cites Börne as a similar example since Börne likewise could not have edited *Die Wage* without having himself baptized.[18] The reason Heine gives for his conversion is thus one of employment, but the time line he has established is well off the mark. Heine's sojourn in London occurred from

April until June of 1827; his short-lived editorship of the *Neue Allgemeine Politische Annalen*, the only journal to which he could have possibly referred in his conversation with Weill, began in January of 1828 (and lasted less than a year); he travels to Italy only in August of the same year. If Weill's report is at all accurate, then Heine's recollection is faulty here, as it so often was in connection with this important and traumatic event. His conversion in June of 1825 happened before his European trips and well before he could have conceived of becoming the editor of a political journal.

A meaningful public discussion of his conversion does not occur until the appearance of *Confessions* in 1854. As many commentators have noticed, Heine's entire attitude toward Judaism undergoes a rather substantial revision during the final decade of his life. Although, as I stated earlier, Heine had occasionally shown sympathy for the Jewish cause in the 1820s, his early work, in particular his poetry, exhibits almost no hints of Heine's heritage. In the *Travel Pictures* there are numerous references to Jews and Jewish themes, many of them quite deprecatory to converted Jews, but Heine most often distances himself from his religious and cultural origins, writing of the Jews as if he did not belong to them—which, strictly speaking, after June 28, 1825, he did not. In the 1830s we find an even greater endeavor to dissociate himself from Judaism. In response to a description of him as an "israélite" he claims that he is not a member of the Israelite religion, and adds that he has never set foot in a synagogue, while reaffirming in no uncertain terms his Lutheran affiliation (5: 19). Only in the 1840s, perhaps as a result of the Damascus crisis, does Heine again allow the public to glimpse his Jewish origins, for example, in the sincere homage to Ludwig Markus, and in the dubious tribute to Ludwig Börne. In the Mattress Grave (*Matraztengruft*) he is more candid still. A published remark in the *Augsburg Gazette* contains the following remark:

> In the meantime, I confess it freely, there is a great transformation that has affected me: I am no longer a divine biped; I am no longer the 'freest German after Goethe,' as Ruge called me in healthier days; I am no longer the great pagan Nr. 2, whom one compares with Dionysus wreathed in vine leaves, while one gave my colleague Nr. 1 the title of Jupiter of the Great Dutchy of Weimar; I am no longer a satiated Hellene who enjoys life while smiling condescendingly on the melancholy

> Nazarenes—now I am only a poor Jew, sick to death, an emaciated image of wretchedness, an unhappy man. (5: 109)

Here we find an openness toward his former Judaism that goes well beyond anything he had written publicly during the previous three decades. In most remarks from his last years Heine, of course, still refrains from identifying himself as a Jew—or he is at least ambiguous—and in this passage it is almost surely done for its dramatic effect. But it is evident in nearly all of his late writings that he has altered fundamentally his perspective toward Jews and Judaism, now finding them a past that he no longer wishes to deny, a fate from which he no longer feels it necessary to flee.

In this context Heine is able to write in a more forthright fashion about his conversion in 1825. Answering questions putatively posed about his current religious beliefs, Heine asserts in his *Confessions* that with regard to Lutheranism, his status remains unchanged. He characterizes his own conversion as one undertaken in a lukewarm, official fashion, and maintains that "if I remain a member of the evangelical faith at all, it is because it does not embarrass me now in the least, just as it never embarrassed me very much earlier" (6/I: 482). He continues by claiming that during his stay in Berlin he would have declared himself independent of any organized religion, as some of his friends had done, if the absence of an identifiable confession had not been a reason for denying residence in Prussia and its capital. This explanation is odd. His conversion, as we know, did not occur while he was in Berlin, but during his second stay in Göttingen, shortly before the completion of his law degree and several years removed from his sojourn in the Prussian capital. And certainly we have no evidence that any of his acquaintances abandoned religion entirely and officially, which, according to Jacob Toury, was a practical impossibility before 1848.[19] He continues in the *Confessions* to write about his conversion by posing, and then circumventing, the question of whether he has become a believing Protestant. He claims that in former years he appreciated Protestantism because of its association with freedom of thought and German philosophy, which begins with the reformation. Now, however, he reveres Protestantism for rediscovering and disseminating the Bible. But after praising the reformation for the rediscovery of the Hebrew texts and for translating the Old Testament from its original language into a modern idiom, he turns to an extended discussion of the Jews as prototypical democrats and eventually builds his tribute to a climax in a veritable *laudatio* to Moses as a socialist revolutionary. In other words, he addresses the question of his Protestantism by writing about Judaism.[20]

What is going on in this unusual passage? Why do we again have mysterious remarks concerning Heine's conversion? Why does Heine appear to be avoiding the issue once again? My hunch is that Heine's discussion of religion and religious conversion in the *Confessions* has something to do with a displacement involving his more recent and less official conversion. The fact that Heine so easily slips from his conversion in 1825 to his later change of beliefs indicates that they were closely associated in his mind. But what is unusual about his later conversion is the way it is repeatedly characterized in his writings both public and private. More than anything else Heine depicts his religious transformation in the Mattress Grave as a rejection of Hegel and a renewal of former beliefs. The insistence on a renewal has led some commentators to believe Heine embraced something akin to Judaism, although Heine insists that his God is a personal one. By renewal it seems obvious that Heine simply means that he again harbors a conviction that God, as a Supreme Being, exists. The rejection of Hegel, however, is more difficult to explain. It is true of course that Heine writes about Hegel in his earlier works with considerable respect and admiration, as well as occasionally with some humor. We know that Friedrich Engels later considered Heine's *Religion and Philosophy in Germany* to be the first work of a left Hegelian. And Heine tells us after the fact that he himself composed a two-volume book on Hegel that he consigned to the fires after he rejected Hegelian philosophy. But there is no strong indication of an avid adherence to Hegel, or even a deep understanding of Hegel at any place in Heine's writings from the 1820s to the 1840s. Hegel is conspicuous by his marginality in *Religion and Philosophy in Germany*, where he is called "the greatest philosopher that Germany has produced since Leibniz," but also cited for his support of the Prussian state and the Protestant church. And the famous line in the poem "Doctrine," which equates drumming people out of an inactive lethargy and kissing young salesgirls with Hegelian philosophy is more easily conceived as a vast and ironic oversimplification than as a validation of one of the most eminent minds of the nineteenth century.

The association of Hegel with Heine's late renewal of faith makes sense—at least psychic sense—if we view it in terms of displacement. We know, for example, that the real Hegelian convert among the members of the *Verein* was Eduard Gans, and certainly his embracing of Protestantism can be conceived more easily as a rejection of Judaism for Hegelianism than Heine's. That Hegel is not on the list of authors the apostate read in Heine's poem covers up the one genuine ideological influence Heine could have associated with his friend, and perhaps the one intellectual influence that really mattered in Gans's conversion. But there is another Hegelian convert that could have affected Heine's anti-Hegelian crusade and his depiction of conversion in the *Confessions*. I am thinking of Karl Marx, another former Jew whose Hegelianism led him precisely to the type of atheism Heine decries so vociferously. It was the left-Hegelian socialists and communists, after all, who relinquished all religious belief, and who were banned from Germany because of their political and religious views. In his late reflection on his conversion in 1825, Heine may have been projecting forward into the 1840s. And in citing the heritage of Judaism in such a pronounced fashion when he should have been discussing Lutheranism, Heine may have been identifying with the religious roots he shared with the more apparent Hegelian converts Eduard Gans and Karl Marx.

This explanation for the discrepancies in Heine's text is of course highly speculative; there is no way to offer a secure proof since we are dealing with Heine's psychic economy, which was neither precise nor consistent. I could mount more evidence for the associations I have found, but no textual evidence would be definitive. Indeed, my more general contention is that the autobiographical oddities in Heine's works, especially the strange claims and bizarre statements he sometimes makes, can often be accounted for by the ways in which particularly sensitive issues in his personal life played themselves out in his writings. Conversion was obviously one issue that Heine had trouble confronting or processing mentally. The transition from a German poet of Jewish origins to a converted Lutheran poet with oppositional and pantheistic convictions was a difficult one. In the 1820s we therefore find Heine avoiding the topic of his own baptism, while simultaneously heaping ridicule or scorn on others who had done exactly what he did not want to promulgate in public. Only in his death-bed writings, when another conversion had taken place, is he able to speak about his 1825 conversion a bit more openly. But even then he apparently confuses his own conversion with that of others, confounding his beliefs with theirs, displacing his own views with those that were not quite his own. The confusion and displacement of Heine's autobiographical writings makes them of dubious value for facts and actual occurrences, but it makes them invaluable if we hope to understand the complex workings of Heine's mind.

Notes

1. Jacob Katz, in *Jewish Emancipation and Self-Emancipation* (Philadelphia, 1986), notes that there were three main reasons for conversion: religious conviction, material gain, and ideological belief (pp. 37-38). Guido Kisch in *Judentaufen* (Berlin, 1973) tends to agree with this evaluation and points out that few converts embraced Christianity out of religious conviction.

2. For an analysis of the role of Judaism in Heine's early years, see Jürgen Voigt, *O Deutschland, meine ferne Liebe . . .: Der junge Heinrich Heine zwischen Nationalromantik und Judentum* (Bonn, 1993).

3. Some writers, for example Israel Tabak in *Judaic Lore in Heine: The Heritage of a Poet* (Baltimore, 1948), have placed a great deal of emphasis on what they assume Heine must have experienced as a child and young man of Jewish heritage. But the evidence of a thorough-going preoccupation with Judaism is simply missing or indirect at best. Ruth L. Jacobi in *Heinrich Heines jüdisches Erbe* (Bonn, 1978) is probably more accurate when she claims that Heine had only a superficial knowledge of Hebrew and Jewish customs from his parents' home (p. 55).

4. For a brief review of the debates around emancipation in the early nineteenth century, see David Sorkin, *The Transformation of German Jewry 1780-1840* (New York, 1987), pp. 13-40.

5. See Jacob Toury, *Soziale und Politische Geschichte der Juden in Deutschland 1847-1871: Zwischen Revolution, Reaktion und Emanzipation* (Düsseldorf, 1977), esp. pp. 51-68.

6. For a statistical analysis of conversions in Berlin, see Peter Honigmann, "Jewish Conversions—A Measure of Assimilation? A Discussion of the Berlin Secession Statistics of 1770-1941," *Leo Baeck Institute Yearbook* 34 (1989), pp. 3-39.

7. Deborah Hertz, "Why Did the Christian Gentleman Assault the Jüdischer Elegant?: Four Conversion Stories from Berlin, 1816-1825," *Leo Baeck Institute Year Book* (1995), pp. 85-106.

8. Deborah Hertz in "Seductive Conversions in Berlin, 1770-1809," *Jewish Apostasy in the Modern World*, ed. Todd M. Endelman (New York, 1987), pp. 48-82, points to the significant number of "elites" who converted (pp. 59-62). It is also interesting to note that the number of women who converted outnumbered men in the eighteenth century, but that during the time of Heine's conversion, more men than women were baptized from the Jewish community.

9. See Hertz, "Why did the Christian Gentleman," pp. 91-95.

10. Similar to Michael Beer, who selected an Indian setting for his *Paria*. See Jacob Katz, "Rezeption jüdischer Autoren durch deutsche Kritik und deutsches Publikum," *Bulletin des Leo Baeck Instituts* 75 (1986), pp. 41-53.

11. The most obvious exception is the poem "Donna Clara," in which the knight with whom Donna Clara falls in love turns out to be the son of a rabbi.

12. Translation by Hal Draper, *The Complete Poems of Heinrich Heine: A Modern English Version* (Boston, 1982), p. 82.

13. Translation by Draper, p. 285.

14. Translation by Draper, p. 286.

15. In a letter to Moser from 19 December 1825, Heine indicates the similarity between his conversion and Gans' when he refers to the stealing of silver spoons (HSA 20: 227). Two factors that Heine may have believed distinguished his conversion from Gans' are mentioned by Heine occasionally. Heine claims that Gans actively sought to persuade other Jews to convert, and Gans had more responsibility to remain Jewish because of his leadership role in the *Verein*.

16. For a discussion of other works relating to his conversion, as well as of the baptism itself, see Ludwig Rosenthal, *Heinrich Heine als Jude* (Frankfurt/Main, 1973), pp. 218-253.

17. Other Jews obviously felt the same way. See Voigt, pp. 10-11.

18. Cited in Rosenthal, p. 234. The passage Rosenthal cites is not cited in its entirety in the *Begegnungen mit Heine*.

19. "Praktisch bestand bis 1848 in keinem deutschen Lande die Möglichkeit, aus der jüdischen Gemeinde auszuscheiden, ohne gleichzeitig einer anderen konfessionellen Gemeinschaft beizutreten" (p. 61).

20. The most extensive treatment of Heine's Judaism, S. S. Prawer's *Heine's Jewish Comedy: A Study of his Portraits of Jews and Judaism* (Oxford, 1983), does not focus on the strange way in which Heine's conversion was thematized in the *Confessions*.

"Keine Systematie": Heine in Berlin and the Origin of the Urban Gaze

Hinrich C. Seeba

Few critics commenting on contested identities and the modern crisis of identity formation can avoid quoting Heinrich Heine's ironically pompous dictum in *The Baths of Lucca* (1829) that "the great schism of the world" ("der große Weltriß") runs through the middle of his heart (2: 405). Claiming to be the center of the world and therefore more torn apart than anybody, Heine paradoxically restored the post-romantic craze of subjectivity, being torn ("Zerrissenheit"), to the more objective realm of contradiction ("Widerspruch"), which to him means both the logical contradiction and the oppositional, if not dialectical, discourse. What I will present on the following pages is meant as a response to a claim made by Gerhard Wolf in his collection of Heine texts, *Heine in Berlin* (1980), that all documents of the time Heine spent in Berlin from 1821 to 1823 point mainly to his state of being torn apart both inside and outside,[1] as if his writing on Berlin were nothing but an early expression of his own personal contradictions. I will try to show instead how already in Berlin Heine, using the contradictions of urban experience, began to construct an oppositional discourse by shifting the burden of contested identities from his psyche to the city. Implicitly, my talk will be as much about the identity of Berlin as a city in transition as about Heine's identity as an aspiring political writer who as early as 1822 encodes his emerging agenda in the crafty construction of a poetic argument. In the attempt to reconstruct the rhetorical buildup I will start where, I believe, Heine eventually takes his urban discourse: the promise of culinary pleasure.

The Cheeseboard, a social-minded cooperative in Berkeley's so-called gourmet ghetto, has a staggered price list for senior citizens, with a blackboard telling the rare customers over 100 years of age: "What you see is what you get," indicating that they will get for free anything they want. It wouldn't be Berkeley if even this innocent promise did not carry some intellectually and socially redeeming message. In a socialist utopia seeing is validated as an act of taking possession without having to pay for it—and not just for the centenarians. Against the background of mythological and metaphorical references to the possessive gaze, from the Medusa's petrifying eyes to the magic phrase of a devouring glance, obsessive fixation may either turn into a feeding frenzy or mellow to what Nicholas Green has called, with regard to urban perception, the "consuming gaze."[2]

A cheerfully attentive outlook that takes in the sights of the city to live on and to get strength from the urban energy, the consuming gaze is contrasted with the pessimist's "environmentalist eye," which sees nothing but the pollution of the city and the ensuing potential for disease, both physical and moral. It is between heavenly Jerusalem and Armageddon, no less, that the mythical battle for the redemptive interaction of "seeing" and "having" takes shape in the city, as if the utopian dream, in which the rules of capitalism are suspended, consisted of seeing, devouring, swallowing up the commodities of urban life without having to pay the price for it.

The gaze without the intent—or the means—to buy is, of course, another, more mundane kind of disinterested pleasure, which Kant had put at the center of his aesthetics. It is, in fact, the etymological quintessence of aesthetics, as the Greek verb *aisthanomai* means the process of seeing, perception, and contemplation without partaking in the action observed. As the mode of the *vita contemplativa* the gaze has always been seen in opposition to the *vita activa* and thus been defined as detached. Such binary oppositions, however, are much too simple to account for the critical involvement of the viewer, however inactive he or she may appear. The consuming urban gaze, as I will try to demonstrate with regard to Heine, is not without its interest in changing the underlying social structure of what the *flâneur* perceives as merely visual dynamics.

The *flâneur* has come to represent the crisis of modernity in an urban attitude that seems only to record, rather than control, the explosion of sensual stimuli tearing at the city dweller's identity. Casually watching and contemplating significant details, the *flâneur* often flaunts his or her individuality by aimlessly strolling through the city, by enjoying the sights and sounds of the hustle of an emerging metropolis, be it Paris in the past or Berlin, possibly, in the future. As Paris and Berlin are the two places most often mentioned in discussions of the urban gaze, writers such as Walter Benjamin who lived in both cities to observe the accelerating changes in the cityscape have become celebrated witnesses—and critics—of the metonymic construction of urban space. Ever since the Italian architect Aldo Rossi published *The Architecture of the City* in 1966,[3] the interest, both historical and current, in urban renewal has surged. While Paris in the age of the self-proclaimed "artiste démolisseur" Georges-Eugène Haussmann, at least in Benjamin's perceptive view, was the undisputed "capital of the nineteenth century,"[4] Berlin in a grandiose scheme of construction and reconstruction is now preparing to become the capital of the twenty-first century. At least, city planners, not known for their modesty, hope for this outcome. Not unlike Paris after 1859, Berlin after 1989 has been a city in transition, desperately trying to reinvent itself, literally to build a new identity and marking time by advertising the largest "construction site" (*Baustelle*) of the world as "viewing site" (*Schaustelle Berlin*), with tour buses taking visitors from one unruly construction site to another. A major tourist attraction, Berlin's reconstruction zone has become a sideshow as if it were arranged by a "showman" (*Schausteller*) in a country fair. The unintended pun confirms the circus-like display of showing and viewing itself in this unparalleled urban spectacle. The desperate call of Berlin's Lord Mayor, Ernst Reuter, during the Berlin Blockade of 1949, "peoples of the world, look at this city," has been answered in an entirely unexpected way. The whole nation, it seems, if not the world is fixated on Berlin in an urban gaze that, for lack of a finished product to look at, has become self-referential. The eyes of the spectators are turned inward to look at their own act of viewing as a truly "constructivist" gesture. In the best postmodern manner, the process of viewing the building process is both concentrated and displayed in the red *Infobox*, a visual anchor in the vast sea of construction where there once was the most traveled square of the world, Potsdamer Platz. In a sense, the constructivist urban gaze, which has to first create what it wants to see as its own object, meets the requirements of Friedrich Schlegel's transcendental poetry in that it represents the act of producing as well as the actual product,[5] thus evoking the city of the mind in a kind of urban poetics, as Italo Calvino invented it in his *Le città invisibili* (1972), where Kublai Khan has Marco Polo tell him stories about the imagined cities of his empire: "Your gaze scans the streets as if they were written pages."[6] The urban gaze creates a narrative as if the city were a chapter in a book: "Tell me another city."[7]

No wonder that there is a booming interest in, to give but two recent titles of urban poetics, *Reading Berlin* and *The Imagined Metropolis*[8]—Berlin as it once was, or rather, as it was perceived by those who first invented and "read" it in their initial gaze. Reading the city like a text was first propagated, with regard to Paris, by Ludwig Börne ("Paris can be called an open book, strolling through the streets means reading.")[9] and applied to Berlin a century later in Franz Hessel's *Spazieren in Berlin* (1929): "Strolling is a kind of reading the street, with faces, exhibits, display windows, terraces of cafés, street cars, cars, trees becoming equitable letters that combine to make up the words, sentences and pages of an ever new book."[10] There is a uniform understanding that the city as the site (and the text) of modernity may have been discovered theoretically by Georg Simmel in his famous essay of 1903, "The Metropolis and Intellectual Life", but that the true philosopher of the modern city was Walter Benjamin. While Simmel defined urban identity individually by the intensity of nervous energy and collectively by protective indifference conditioned by monetary exchange,[11] Benjamin came to be seen as the paragon of a melancholy chronicler of urban experience forever lost. Moving back and forth between Berlin and Paris, Benjamin had written both *A Berlin Childhood* (1938) and *Paris, Capital of the Nineteenth Century* as the centerpiece of his posthumous *Passagenwerk* and thus was the ideal intellectual to conceptualize in urban vignettes the complexity of living in the city.

But the critical concentration on Benjamin has eclipsed two other *flâneurs* who preceded him in learning their vocation in Berlin and in transferring it to their exile in Paris. One is Franz Hessel, on whom the role of Jules in Truffaut's classic film *Jules et Jim* is modeled,[12] the influential editor of the Rowohlt Verlag from 1919 to 1933 and Benjamin's mentor, whose city walks through Berlin represent, in the words of Benjamin's review, remembering by strolling.[13] And the other *flâneur* is, of course, Heinrich Heine, who lived in Berlin from 1821 to 1823. Long before Benjamin, Hessel and Siegfried Kracauer Heine, too, lived in exile in Paris, recalling the Berlin of his youth as if to admit, to modify Catharina Valente's hit song of the Fifties, "Das hab ich in—Berlin gelernt" ("I learned that—in Berlin"). Heine, the first famous German exile in Paris and one of the first *flâneurs* ever, would have to be seen in his many street scenes as equally indebted to Berlin. It was, indeed, Heine, as I intend to show, who started the urban gaze with which Benjamin and, only recently, also Hessel have been credited. But Heine not only preceded the others by a full century, but also superseded them in his determination to turn the urban spectacle into a political lesson.

Heine clearly belongs at the beginning of the tradition of ocularcentric explorations of the emerging metropolis which, strangely enough, Benjamin himself has traced to the year of Heine's *Letters from Berlin*, 1822, without even mentioning Heine. Instead, Benjamin welcomes E.T.A. Hoffmann's last narrative, *Des Vetters Eckfenster* (1822), as "one of the first attempts to grasp the street scene of a bigger city."[14] As Hoffmann used the protagonist's view from the window to introduce the principles of gazing,[15] this narrative can, indeed, be considered a seminal text in the history of the fictionalized urban gaze. More surprising is the fact that the parallel urban text by Heine, published in the same year and advancing a similar concept of the interaction of gazing ("Schauen") and writing ("Schreiben"), has been widely overlooked. Brushed aside by Max Brod as nonsense,[16] Heine's early urban text was even hidden in the footnotes of Ernst Elster's authoritative edition of Heine's works.[17] Had he known Heine's *Letters from Berlin*, Benjamin could have made a stronger case for his interest in the representation of the masses of people milling in the streets, or in Hoffmann's case, in a market square, the Gendarmenmarkt in Berlin. Comparing Hoffmann's street scenes to E. A. Poe's famous *Man of the Crowd* (1845), he complained that Hoffmann failed to record the uncanny of urban experience.[18] But even if Poe can be credited with introducing the new type of a city dweller without traits who "refuses to live alone"[19] and who is obsessed with the anonymity of the urban crowd, Heine eventually gave the uncanny lure of the city a social edge by emphasizing "the uncanny contrast" between the crowd and the city's window displays. The social contradiction of "seeing" and "having" inspired his urban fantasy. Going far beyond Poe's clandestine and eventually failing pursuit of mystery in the throngs of London's busy streets, Heine openly gleaned from this contrast, and perhaps even enhanced, the uncanny potential for social revolt and political revolution he sensed while walking the equally busy boulevards of Paris.

Almost a century before the strolling spectators of the urban crowd made their celebrated comeback in the streets of Berlin and Paris, Heine, who came to Berlin the very year Baudelaire was born, developed nothing less than a social theory of the *flâneur* from his musings about the window display of elegant shops in Paris during Christmas in 1841: "The sight of them can offer the leisurely stroller the most pleasant pastime," Heine ponders in *Lutetia* (1854), lulling the unsuspecting reader with the appearance of a merely entertaining gaze, one which may help the "flaneur", this unfocused gentleman of leisure, kill time. But Heine continues on a more serious, almost devious note: "if his mind is not quite empty, he may sometimes get ideas when he views behind the shining glass panels the colorful array of luxury and art items and possibly takes a glance also at the people standing next to him." As the viewing itself becomes thematic, with the viewer taking the place of the luxury items on display, the occasional thoughts take off in an alarming direction. For through such seemingly innocent associations, called "Assoziation der Ideen" (2: 10) already in Heine's first urban text, *Letters from Berlin*, the leisurely stroller turns out to be an observant social critic drawing some ominous conclusions from the juxtapositions he carefully staged. He highlights the contrast between luxury commodities and those who cannot afford them to emphasize the point he wants to make: In the social reality of the city "seeing" certainly does not mean "having" and, in the end, the "have-nots" will no longer be content with just "seeing" what is not meant for their consumption: "The faces of these people are so hideously serious and pained, so impatient and threatening that they contrast uncannily with the objects at which they stare. We begin to fear that these people might suddenly start swinging their balled fists and reduce to pitiful ruins all the colorful, noisy toys of this elegant world, and this elegant world itself along with them." Here the social critic becomes a prophet projecting the revolutionary potential of a consuming gaze without consumption: "Someone who is no great politician, but, rather, a common flaneur who concerns himself with the expressions of people in the street, will be firmly convinced that sooner or later the whole bourgeois comedy in France, and its parliamentary stars and extras along with it, will end terribly amidst hisses, and it will be followed by a piece called the communist regime!" (5: 373).

Whether or not we agree with Heine's prophetic view that the communist regime will be an imperative, "genuine tragedy," however short-lived, we can only marvel at the rhetorical construction of his argument centered on the ominous social "contrast": Gradually the *flâneur*'s leisurely gaze at the promise of material bliss is questioned by the gaping eyes of less fortunate people, who some day will realize the reasons for their exclusion from the spectacle of leisure; then they will smash much more than just the glass of the display windows keeping them outside for the time being. The urban gaze, whose temporal mode is the present, has become a foreboding look into the future, to the last act of the "bourgeois comedy" (*Bürgerkomödie*) and its "terrible end amidst hisses." Against the background of similar stagings of apocalyptic visions of revolution,[20] Heine's "flaneur" clearly sheds the image of a detached observer to become the partisan prophet of most spectacular scenes in the drama of politics.

The vision of Heine's "flaneur,"—considering Heine's qualifier: if he is not empty-minded and not lacking social conscience—is much stronger than the cautiously utopian outlook into an uncertain future that marks the last sentence of the most famous account of a modern *flâneur*, Siegfried Kracauer's *Abschied von der Lindenpassage* (1930): "What role was there left for a passage in a society which itself is nothing but a passage?"[21] However vaguely formulated in playing on the homonym of *passage* for both "galleria" and "historical change," the rhetorical question points in a similar direction as Heine's prophecy. For Kracauer the dismantling—or, rather, modernist refurbishing—of Berlin's notorious gallery between Unter den Linden and Friedrichstraße, the former Kaiserpassage, anticipates the passing of the bourgeois society he both desires and fears; for as the sanctuary of an alternate culture which is not accepted in standard society, the window displays of this passage question the very norms of this society: "Thus the passage through the bourgeois world criticized this very world in a way that every true flaneur understood."[22] What Kracauer invokes as historical change is at the same time mourned as a future loss: "The time of the passages has passed."[23] There is an obvious melancholy permeating the musings of the *flâneur* as Kracauer or, for that matter, Walter Benjamin perceived him.

But even if Heine's urban gaze, with its revolutionary zeal, lacks the gloom so typical of the modern *flâneur*, it comes as a surprise that Heine, who explicitly counts himself among the "genuine flaneurs" (5: 376), does not figure prominently, if at all, in the recent surge of studies in urban culture. From most of the recent collections of urban studies dealing with the textual construction of the city, especially Berlin, from Helmuth Kühn's *Preußen. Dein Spree-Athen* (1981), Klaus Scherpe's *Unwirklichkeit der Städte* (1988), Heidrun Suhr's *Berlin: Culture and Metropolis* (1990), Tilo Schabert's *Die Welt der Stadt* (1990) to Katharina von Ankum's *Women in the Metropolis* (1997) Heine's name is strikingly absent or, as in the latter, mentioned only as a gendered backdrop to the even more suppressed "female flanerie."[24] Even after Jost Hermand had tried in 1969 to rescue from oblivion Heine's more obvious and, considering the times, rather daring political insinuations,[25] Klaus Hermsdorf, writing on Heine's *Letters from Berlin* in 1987 from the perspective of the GDR, surprisingly restored the conventional notion that this text is nothing but a trivial, even dubious "Chronique scandaleuse" of the cultural life in the capital.[26] But even where Heine's anecdotal musings on Berlin's culture were recognized, his ingenious street scenes, as Klaus Briegleb remarked in 1986, have gone largely unnoticed: "Heine's street scenes have found only fleeting interest among literary scholars." Yet these street scenes, Briegleb continues, "permeate his writings as a real and imagined site, a narrative space, in which the observer encounters the reality of the cities. Düsseldorf, Hamburg, Berlin, London, Munich, Lucca, Paris—in their streets we can read their world of signs, join in the observation and be absorbed in a dramaturgy of signs."[27] Briegleb implies not only that Heine "reads" the text of the city streets, as Börne and Hessel did, but also that he constructs his reading—in my view in a dramaturgy of political action.

Therefore, it seems appropriate to look at the semiotic significance of Heine's first street scenes, when he adopted for the first of his *Letters from Berlin* the fictional role of a Berlin city guide to captivate the attention of the presumably provincial readers of the *Rheinisch-westfälischer Anzeiger*, where his letters were published. These readers were considered disadvantaged and in need of some cultural tutoring, because it was only seven years earlier that their Western province had become part of the Prussian territory and thus subject to Berlin, the new and rapidly expanding capital. Allusions to the present situation are obvious—and intentional: Taken over by the Prussians, the "Wessies" of the 1820's in Bonn, Cologne and Düsseldorf had to learn quickly the ways of the "Ossis" of the time; Heine's role as a correspondent from the new capital Berlin was to narrow the information gap between West and East and to familiarize the people in the new provinces with Berlin's emerging claim to a metropolis which in Karl Friedrich Schinkel's classicist masterplan was only beginning to take shape. Schinkel's *Neue Wache* was completed in 1818, his *Schauspielhaus am Gendarmenmarkt* in 1821, his *Schloßbrücke* in 1823, his *Torhäuser am Leipziger Platz* in 1824 and his *Altes Museum* in 1828. When Heine came to Berlin in 1821, Berlin was as much a construction zone as it is today, with Schinkel being the equivalent of today's Josef Paul Kleihues; an earlier "Schaustelle Berlin" commanded an urban gaze to grasp the rapid changes of a city in the process of reinventing itself as the capital of recently united and vastly enlarged Prussia: "I saw the new stock market... Unter den Linden, the construction sites through which Wilhelmstraße is being extended are moving forward rapidly. Terrific colonnades are springing up. During these days also the foundation stone of the new bridge was set" (2: 59). With construction going on everywhere, Berlin was—as it is today—a site of constant upheaval when Heine arrived in 1821 to inspect and to use it as a backdrop for his own aspirations.

After his third and last visit to Berlin in 1829 Heine confessed in *Journey from Munich to Genoa* (1830) that it is mainly for political reasons, i.e. in the pursuit of a particular political interest, that he celebrates or denigrates a city, adding, however, that Berliners cannot be bribed with literary praise because they don't care too much about a visitor's reaction to their city: "No city has less local pride than Berlin" (2:

316-17). Thus ironically relieved of the consequences if he were to denounce Berlin, Heine can pursue his political interest by projecting onto the Berliners the fact that he himself does not care much about this non-city:

> Berlin is not a city, it only provides the place where a lot of people, among them many cultured people, gather even though they don't care at all about the place. One truly needs several bottles of poetry to see in Berlin anything but dead houses and Berliners. Here it is difficult to see spirits. The city contains so little antiquity and is quite new; and yet, this new is already so old, so wilted and dead. For the city emerged, as mentioned before, not from the convictions of the masses, but of individuals." (2: 317)

Considering Benjamin's praise for E.T.A. Hoffmann for introducing to the urban gaze the notion of "masses," we cannot easily overlook Heine's emphasis on "a lot of people" ("eine Menge Menschen") and "conviction of the masses" ("Gesinnung der Masse"), especially since the latter, the mindset of the dynamic urban masses, is seen in striking contrast to the stagnant architecture that is a relic of the Prussian ruler, Frederick II. For the sake of contrastive argument Heine conveniently overlooked the more recent building boom he was witnessing in his time. The older and unattractive row houses in what is appropriately called Friedrichstadt constituted a better contrast than the splendid public buildings, most of them by Schinkel, going up in the 1820's. Already in Berlin Heine's carefully constructed argument alludes to the "uncanny contrast" that he would later stage in Paris as part of his more outspoken social agenda.

Before Heine's arrival, Berlin was an unlikely place for the kind of awe we have become accustomed to associate with the urban gaze. Rahel Levin Varnhagen complained already in 1793: "Is it possible for a decent person to accept that Berlin presents itself as the world?"[28]; and Madame de Staël was similarly unimpressed during her visit to Berlin in 1804: "This is a country which does not inspire fantasy, the society is lined up in a Prussian way."[29] Only in her later recollection of the Berlin visit in *De l'Allemande* (1813) did Madame de Staël acknowledge that the active social and intellectual life had made Berlin "the true capital of the new, the enlightened Germany."[30] But what a century later became an asset of modernity, was seen by Madame de Staël as an uninspiring lack of history: "Berlin is a big city with wide, straight streets and built quite regularly. As most of it is newly built, there are few traces of older times." If there is anything attractive about Berlin, it does not offer itself to visual pleasure: "Berlin, this very modern city, as beautiful as it might be, does not produce a festive, serious effect; it is shaped neither by the history of the country nor by the character of the population."[31]

Heine, of course, was so familiar with this lackluster report on Berlin that some of his own observations seem to be taken almost verbatim from Madame de Staël's famous book on Germany. But he gives the notion of unimaginative rows of uniform houses, this topos of contemporary travel accounts of Berlin, an ironic twist. He turns it into an indictment of the autocratic rule that does not adequately represent the masses living under the king's jurisdiction: "The foreigner who travels through the city sees only the expansive, uniform houses, the long, wide streets, which form rows and are, for the most part, built according to the will of a single individual" (2: 317). If the visitor to Berlin needs to be drunk from poetic fantasy to see more than "dead houses," the singular ruler who built the unvarying row houses according to the rule of Prussian uniformity ("nach der Schnur"), is relegated to the figurative realm of death where even the newest buildings seem dead or by-gone ("abgestorben") as Heine wants any political system to appear that is unrepresentative of the emerging urban masses. This "uncanny contrast" between the king of the past and the masses of the future could spur some radical energy. As Heine writes "mainly for political reasons," even when the rhetorical construction of his argument only faintly suggests his agenda, it is not merely playful caution if he wants to defer his more candid writing on Berlin to his prospective exile from Germany: "What I presently think about the intellectual Berlin," he writes on May 4, 1823 in a letter to Julius M. Schottky, a folklorist and professor of German in Posen, "I am not allowed to have printed; but you will read it some time when I am no longer in Germany" (HSA 20: 84). Yet we know, of course, that Heine did write and publish on Berlin long before he left Germany. In fact at the time when he wrote this letter, he had just published his *Letters from Berlin*. Should we, then, assume that this epistolary probe of urban space does not reflect Heine's critical thoughts on Berlin because such remarks might not have been publishable? What, then, is the disguise he chose to advance his subversive and, as we know from his later assertions, potentially revolutionary ideas about Berlin?

At the outset he defines the *Letters from Berlin* as a text that includes its own unwritten countertext: "Upon receiving your letter I immediately got out paper and pen and am already - writing. There is no shortage of notes, and the only question is: What shouldn't I write? i.e., what does the public know already, what leaves it indifferent, and what is it not permitted to know?" (2: 9). In delineating the well-known, the tedious, and the forbidden as subjects not to be covered, it becomes clear that writing is as much about what is not written as about what is. Underscoring the opposition of "writing" and "*not* writing," Heine makes the former an oppositional form of the latter. But he goes one step further: Just as his writing suggests the unwritten, the new mode in which he does write is negatively defined by what it is not: "Just do not demand of me any kind of system, because that is the angel of death for all correspondence" (2: 10). Rather than merely advancing, as has been generally assumed,[32] the new style of casual journalistic prose for which Heine was to become famous and scolded by Karl Kraus,[33] this exclusionary remark draws the reader's attention precisely to what seems to be excluded, i.e. to the systematic construction of unwritten thoughts in a political agenda that would be strangled by the censors. The rhetorical dialectics of Heine's argument promise the "public" an implicit answer to the central question: "what is it not permitted to know."

Therefore, it is important to understand how Heine both poses and handles the fictional questions that remain better unanswered so as not to provoke the unnamed authorities, but that at the same time must be raised to question this very authority. He invents an urban dialog with a visitor who needs to be taken on a fantasy tour of Berlin, and includes a fictional exchange of questions assumed and answers suppressed: "I see you asking already: Why isn't the post office on Poststraße and the black eagle on Königstraße?" (2: 10). What, on the surface, seems like a fairly harmless inquiry about the location of hotels requires an answer that just may involve, we suspect, a political taboo and therefore is pointedly avoided: "I will answer this question at another time; but now I want to walk through the city, and invite you to keep me company" (2: 10). In deferring the answer to some other time, as he deferred his true thoughts on Berlin to his prospective exile, Heine keeps us guessing as to what the unwritten implications are, clearly assigning the casual city walk the place of the potentially risky answer. Only as a critical *flâneur*, who reads the city as a text, will Heine inscribe the urban space with the answer the public is not supposed to know.

While the cognitive, the rational, the systematic probe is suppressed because it may lead to dangerous conclusions, it is supplanted with another mode of critical perception. The phrase "I see you asking already" is very unusual and rather revealing: It is the first time in this text, so replete with references to the urban gaze, that the word "see" (*sehen*) is used. Taking the place of "hearing," "seeing" is introduced as a more sensual alternative to rational perception. Where systematic questioning is banned, the impressionistic gaze of the *flâneur* suggests the unwritten answer. The urban stroll turns out to be a political venture in disguise. In this light the programmatic statement "association of ideas shall always prevail" appears as a displaced call for exactly what Heine purports to reject, namely "systemic thought" ("Systematie"), i.e. the focused organization of thoughts that will logically lead to daring consequences. In a warped chronology, the prophet of social upheaval Heine strives to be emerges from the kind of *flâneur* Heine will place in front of the window display on the Boulevard Montmartre almost twenty years later: "if his mind is not quite empty, he may sometimes get ideas." What sometimes comes to mind, in deceiving nonchalance, as "association of ideas" turns out to be, in the end, the focal point of a gaze that is not at all detached, be it a revolution in *Lutetia* on the one hand or the less radical sensualism in *Letters from Berlin* on the other. Tracing the sequence of displacements, we have found, I believe, the origin of Heine's urban gaze: seeing what is not written and what must not be questioned as an oppositional act that defies censure.

As a *flâneur* boasting his critical gaze, Heine benefitted from—and contributed to—the emerging visual interest in the recently upgraded capital, which was in the process of becoming an urban spectacle to marvel at when Heine came to Berlin in 1821.[34] While other cities were represented in their medieval quaintness, Berlin was the only place in Germany where aspiring artists of the 1820s concentrated on contemporary buildings gracing spacious new boulevards and plazas. Featuring the brand-new architecture of classicist *Spree-Athen*, these splendid representations of urban development dwarfed scattered groups of minute men and women of society in elegant Biedermeier attire, who probably gathered only to inspect and admire the grandiose public buildings. After the first panorama of Berlin, painted by Johann Friedrich Tielker, was shown in 1802, the panorama craze started in earnest in 1808 when Schinkel joined Wilhelm Gropius, a producer of masks and himself a puppeteer, to paint so-called "optic-perspectival panoramas" ("optisch-perspektivische Schaubilder") of Berlin and other cities, which subsequently were staged during the Christmas season in the display windows of shops and coffee houses.[35] The first printed *Panorama vom Königlichen Schloß bis zum Brandenburger*

Tor, a visual strip of the architectural façades Unter den Linden just ten centimeters high but almost eight meters long, was advertised by the art dealer Jacobi (address: Unter den Linden 35) in all newspapers of Berlin on November 18, 1820.[36] Such displays proved so popular that Carl Wilhelm Gropius, Wilhelm's son who, starting in 1820, painted Schinkel's set designs for the new Royal Theater on the Gendarmenmarkt, opened a separate diorama building in 1827, five years after the famous Diorama by Daguerre and Bouton in Paris. This building, complete with an art shop and a book store featuring only *Berolinensia*, marked the early commercialization of the "Schaustelle Berlin." Dramatically staged, the urban gaze became a marketable perspective represented by painters such as Carl Gropius (1793-1870), Wilhelm Brücke (1800-1874), Johann Heinrich Hintze (1800-1861), Friedrich Wilhelm Klose (1804-1874) and, most of all, by Eduard Gaertner (1801-1877). Gaertner's many street scenes include *Unter den Linden* (1853), one version of which was exhibited in the *Galerie der Romantik* of Schloß Charlottenburg and another in the *Sammlung Oskar Reinhart* in Winterthur. Gaertner left the Königliche Porzellan-Manufaktur in 1821, where he had learned the art of painting city scenes on porcelain in so-called *Veduten*, to become the best known genre painter of Berlin. He, like Heine, would take the visitor by his hand and guide him through the sites of recently completed construction, especially along the boulevard Unter den Linden.

But unlike the genre painters who cultivated the urban gaze to propagate the emerging metropolis as a site of spectacular new buildings, Heine was much too shrewd to be so easily co-opted in what today would be called a public relations project. In his fictional guided tour of Berlin Heine seems to retrace the famous panorama of 1820, but the visual tour de force he imposes on his fictional companion takes them beyond the usual tourist attractions: "Follow me... Look around... Look up... But look... Just look... If you want to feast your eyes, look at the pictures... Or if you would see... Look at the beautiful buildings... Here to the right you can see something new... Notice there... Notice... Notice..." (2: 10-20). Constantly feeding the hungry urban gaze, Heine takes the visitor on a walking tour from the Royal Castle to the Brandenburg Gate and back, now in a rented carriage, to the real destination, the Café Royal, thus setting up an ironic balance between the aesthetic and the culinary pleasures. It is among the tempting dishes of this coffee house that the urban gaze reveals the city's sensual underbelly: Disregarding luminaries such as Friedrich August Wolf and E. T. A. Hoffmann, who are holding court in the Café Royal, Heine remarks: "But of what concern are all these gentlemen to me? I am hungry. Garcon, la charte! Look at all these magnificent dishes!" (2: 20). Thus summoned for the last time during the guided city tour, the urban gaze turns out to be, indeed, a "consuming gaze" one which overcomes the spatial difference between subject and object, swallowing up the distinction of "seeing" and "having." In sharp contrast to the spectators on the Boulevard Montmartre, Heine clearly belongs to the fortunate few who can have what he sees, without losing sight of those who may not.

Even more so than E. T. A. Hoffmann in the same year or E. A. Poe twenty years later, Heine takes notice of the danger the emerging urban masses might pose to the individual: "But I see that you are being pushed from all sides. On this bridge there is an eternal crowd" (2: 11). Using the new concept for uncontrollable urban crowds, he even mentions "the turbulent masses" populating the open-air stock market (2: 12),[37] which ironically is located directly next to the cathedral and thus an urban marker of a historic paradigm shift from the transcendental to the monetary exchange. Already at the beginning of his tour even before he turns to the nearby Royal Castle, Heine directs the gaze of his companion to an elegant street, "where one department store boarders on another, and the colorful, luminous exhibited wares are almost blinding" (2: 11). Heine thus foregrounds the more conventional city tour of the imposing architectural sites by focusing the urban gaze on the brilliant display of commodities in department stores—exactly forty years before the advent of bigger *grands magazins* like Bon Marché in Paris: "Here the ocularcentric spectacle of desire," Martin Jay commented on the department stores in the 1860s, "was removed from the aristocratic court and given its bourgeois equivalent in the massive sheet glass windows displaying a wealth of commodities to be coveted and, if money allowed, consumed."[38] The name of this street, where the truly consuming gaze engages in unroyal commerce so far removed from the aristocratic court nearby, is of all names, "Königstraße," the very street to which Heine had just drawn our attention only to frustrate it.

It is in this ironic name of the commercial kingdom that we may find the deeply hidden answer to the question Heine had pushed aside when he started the walking tour instead of engaging in a debate about street names and proper locations: "I see you asking already: Why isn't the post office on Poststraße and the black eagle on Königstraße?" Now we know that the Schwarze Adler, Heine's cheap hotel at Poststraße 30 (as it is listed in the *Adreß-Kalender* of 1826), does not belong in the elegant "great magnificent street" named after the king in general, any king, even if it is no longer a Hohenzollern; for who nowadays but the customer of the many department stores located in the Königstraße is "king" here? The twilight of the monarch—the "individual" who had outlined the blueprint of Berlin with its uniform houses—is anticipated by the masses who would try to fill their needs in the department stores and, if they can't, eventually turn their anger against the king. The inappropriate naming carries its own irony—as in the example Heine cites explicitly: "We are standing on the 'Long Bridge.' Bemused, you ask: 'But it is not very long?' It is irony, my dear sir" (2: 10). As the *Lange Brücke* is not long and the *Lustgarten* nothing but an empty square without any trace of pleasure (*Lust*) ("Dear Lord! Don't you see that it is irony again?"), the Königstraße, we can infer from Heine's instruction, is no longer royal; it has become bourgeois. It is a business street no longer reserved for the king for whom the black eagle stands as Prussia's national symbol. To Heine, as he later concedes in Caput III of *Germany, A Winter's Tale* (1844), the black eagle is "so deeply hated" that he wants it shot in a revolutionary act: "Whoever shoots the bird for me / Will win the offering / Of crown and scepter. Trumpets will blow, / We'll cry, 'Long live the King!'" (4: 583). If anyone can be king if he is only willing to kill and replace the black eagle, the Königstraße will eventually turn into the republican staging area for the last act of the "bourgeois comedy," as it did in November 1918. What Heine calls irony is a contradiction he places into the object itself, thus hiding his own ironic effort to let the visual sites reveal their own paradox, i.e. the contrast between name and significance, between word and meaning. It is the same "uncanny contrast" from which he expects the social energy for political change to unfold, the contrast between "seeing" the luxurious "displays of commodities" and "having" the means to obtain the merchandise on display. Only if the masses, we are to assume, can afford the consuming gaze that pulled Heine with his companion, the imagined addressee and reader of his fictional letters, into the elegant eatery Unter den Linden, on the corner of Charlottenstraße, where E. T. A. Hoffmann lived and died the same year, can Heine's *flâneur* be as carefree as his more detached successors, who were careful enough—or too bourgeois—not to predict or even urge a "communist regime."

But, then, let's not get our hopes up. We may have to reach the age of one hundred to feed our own consuming gaze and to get for free what we see in Berkeley's gourmet ghetto. Obviously, the nostalgic, mourning gesture sported by this century's *flâneurs* in their fragmented, but highly individualized gaze has prevailed over the more daring, carefully orchestrated and potentially collective agenda of the nineteenth century's first *flâneur*, Heinrich Heine in Berlin. At the same time that he demanded "no systemic thought," he started engaging in a very systematic buildup of a poetic argument based on images, metaphors, allusions and anecdotal scenes, of an urban "dramaturgy of signs" that leaves little doubt about the intended signified. But if the "systematic thought" Heine invoked by denying it failed on the political stage of our time, thus breaking the ground for Berlin's urban wasteland to become another "Schaustelle Berlin," we can only conclude by saying with Heine: "It is irony, my dear sir!"

Notes

1. Gerhard Wolf, "Heine in Berlin,"*Und grüß mich nicht Unter den Linden. Heine in Berlin. Gedichte und Prosa*, ed. Gerhard Wolf (Berlin, 1980), pp. 275-301:"die Zerrissenheit seines äußeren und inneren Befindens in diesem *großen Krähwinkel*" (p. 287).

2. Nicholas Green, *The Spectacle of Nature: Landscape and Bourgeois Culture in Nineteenth-Century France* (Manchester, 1990), p. 66.

3. Aldo Rossi, *The Architecture of the City* (Cambridge, Mass., 1982).

4. Walter Benjamin, "Paris, die Hauptstadt des XIX. Jahrhunderts," *Das Passagen-Werk*, ed. Rolf Tiedemann, 2 vols. (Frankfurt/Main, 1983), pp. 45-59.

5. Friedrich Schlegel, "Athenäums-Fragment 238," *Kritische Schriften*, ed. Wolfdietrich Rasch (Munich, ^{2}1964), p. 53: "auch das Produzierende mit dem Produkt."

6. Italo Calvino, *Invisible Cities*, trans. William Weaver (San Diego, 1974), p. 14.

7. Ibid., p. 85.

8. Peter Fritsche, *Reading Berlin 1900* (Cambridge, Mass., 1996), p. 1: "In an age of urban mass literacy, the city as a place and the city as text defined each other in mutually constitutive ways. The crush of people and welter of things in the modern city revised ways of reading and writing, and these representational acts, in turn, constructed a second-hand metropolis which gave a narrative to the concrete one and choreographed its encounters." Michael Bienert, *Die eingebildete Metropole. Berlin im Feuilleton der Weimarer Republik* (Stuttgart, 1992).

9. Ludwig Börne, "Der Greve-Platz [Schilderungen aus Paris, 1822-24]," *Sämtliche Schriften*, ed. Inge and Peter Rippmann, vol. 2 (Düsseldorf, 1964), pp. 34-39, here p. 34.

10. Franz Hessel, *Ein Flaneur in Berlin* (Berlin, 1984) p. 145.

11. Georg Simmel, "Die Großstädte und das Geistesleben," *Gesamtausgabe*, ed. Otthein Rammstedt, vol. 7/I, *Aufsätze und Abhandlungen 1901-1908* (Frankfurt/Main, 1995), pp. 116-131, here p. 116.

12. Cf. Manfred Flügge, *Gesprungene Liebe. Die wahre Geschichte zu "Jules und Jim"* (Berlin, 1993). The film was based on a real-life ménage à trois between Hessel (1880-1942), his wife Helen Grund (1886-1982) and his friend Henri-Pierre Roché (who wrote the story).

13. Walter Benjamin, "Die Wiederkehr des Flaneurs," *Gesammelte Schriften*, ed. Rolf Tiedemann and Hermann Schweppenhäuser, vol. 3, *Kritiken und Rezensionen*, ed. Hella Tiedemann-Bartels (Frankfurt/Main, 1991), pp. 194-199: "ein Memorieren im Schlendern, ein Buch, für das Erinnerung nicht die Quelle, sondern die Muse war," p. 194. On Hessel cf. Jörg Plath, *Liebhaber der Großstadt. Ästhetische Konzeptionen im Werk Franz Hessels* (Paderborn, 1994); Michael Opitz and Jörg Plath, eds., *Genieße froh, was du nicht hast. Der Flaneur Franz Hessel* (Würzburg, 1997).

14. Walter Benjamin, "Über einige Motive bei Baudelaire [1939]," *Schriften*, vol. 1 (Frankfurt/Main, 1955), p. 446.

15. E. T. A. Hoffmann, "Des Vetters Eckfenster," *Späte Werke* (Stuttgart, n.d.), pp. 597-622: "die Primizien der Kunst zu schauen," p. 600.

16. Max Brod, *Heinrich Heine* (Amsterdam, 1935), p. 134: "Klatsch und Quatsch."

17. *Heinrich Heines Sämtliche Werke*, ed. Ernst Elster, vol. 7 (Leipzig, [1890]), pp. 560-597.

18. Benjamin, p. 446: "das Unheimliche herauszustellen, das andere Physiognomen der großen Stadt gespürt haben."

19. Edgar Allan Poe, "The Man of the Crowd," *The Works of Edgar Allan Poe* (New York, 1857), vol. 2, *Poems and Tales*, pp. 398-407, here p. 406.

20. "Es wird ein Stück aufgeführt werden in Deutschland, wogegen die französische Revolution nur wie eine harmlose Idylle erscheinen möchte" (3: 640).

21. Siegfried Kracauer, "Abschied von der Lindenpassage," *Der verbotene Blick. Beobachtungen, Analysen, Kritiken*, ed. Johanna Rosenberg (Leipzig, 1992), pp. 49-55, here p. 55. Cf. Michael Schaper, *Der gläserne Himmel. Die Passagen des 19. Jahrhunderts als Sujet der Literatur* (Frankfurt/Main, 1988), pp. 205 ff.

22. Ibid., p. 55.

23. Ibid., p. 50: "Die Zeit der Passagen ist abgelaufen."

24. Anke Gleber, "Female Flanerie and the *Symphony of the City*," *Women in the Metropolis: Gender and Modernity in Weimar Culture*, ed. Katharina von Ankum (Berkeley, 1997), pp. 67-88, here pp. 67-68.

25. Jost Hermand, "Heines 'Briefe aus Berlin'. Politische Tendenz und feuilletonistische Form," *Gestaltungsgeschichte und Gesellschaftsgeschichte. Literatur-, Kunst- und Musikwissenschaftliche Studien*, ed. Helmut Kreuzer (Stuttgart, 1969), pp. 284-305.

26. Klaus Hermsdorf, *Literarisches Leben in Berlin. Aufklärer und Romantiker* (Berlin, 1987), p. 348.

27. Klaus Briegleb, *Opfer Heine. Versuche über Schriftzüge der Revolution* (Frankfurt/Main, 1986), p. 154.

28. Rahel Levin Varnhagen, *Gesammelte Werke*, ed. Konrad Feilchenfeldt, Uwe Schweikert and Rahel E. Steiner (Munich, 1983), vol. 7/1, p. 12.

29. Madame de Staël in a letter to Goethe, March 1804, quoted from Monika Bosse, "Nachwort," Anne Germaine de Staël, *Über Deutschland*, ed. Monika Bosse (Frankfurt/Main, 1985), p. 840.

30. de Staël, *Über Deutschland*, p. 110.

31. Ibid., p. 107.

32. In addition to the article mentioned above by Jost Hermand, cf. Klaus Pabel's chapter on "*Briefe aus Berlin*: Das Assoziationsprinzip als literarische Strategie zur Darstellung der partikularisierten Gesellschaft and zur Überwindung der Zensur" in *Heines "Reisebilder". Ästhetisches*

Bedürfnis and politisches Interesse am Ende der Kunstperiode (Munich, 1977), pp. 52-73); or, more recently on the epistolary form, Elke Frederiksen, "Heinrich Heine and Rahel Levin Varnhagen. Zur Beziehung and Differenz zweier Autoren im frühen 19. Jahrhundert," *Heine-Jahrbuch* 29 (1990), pp. 9-38.

33. Karl Kraus, "Heine and die Folgen," *Ausgewählte Werke*, ed. Dietrich Simon (Munich, n.d.), vol. 1, pp. 290-312.

34. Cf. Sybille Gramlich, "Königliches Spree-Athen. Berlin im Biedermeier," *Stadtbilder. Berlin in der Malerei vom 17. Jahrhundert bis zur Gegenwart* (Berlin, 1987), pp. 95-172, here p. 108-9.

35. Cf. Stephan Oettermann, *Das Panorama. Die Geschichte eines Massenmediums* (Frankfurt/Main, 1980). For contemporary reactions to the "Schaubilder" cf. Mario Zadow, *Karl Friedrich Schinkel* (Berlin, 1980), pp. 51-56.

36. Cf. another "Lindenpanorama" from around 1847, with references to the first one from 1820, in *Panorama der Straße Unter den Linden*, ed. Winfried Löschburg (Hanau, 1987).

37. Cf. Karl Riha, "Menschen in Massen. Ein spezifisches Großstadtsujet and seine Herausforderung an die Literatur," *Die Welt der Stadt*, ed. Tilo Schabert (Munich, 1990), pp. 117-143.

38. Martin Jay, *Downcast Eyes: The Denigration of Vision in Twentieth-Century French Thought* (Berkeley, 1993), p. 120.

Columbus, Humboldt, Heine, or the Rediscovery of Europe

Susanne Zantop

> Since the great era of Columbus and da Gama, when one part, one side of the planet became aware of the other, the fluid element, the sea, has made possible the ubiquity of one kind of civilization (the West-European). From all of the fixed continent's contours into the undifferentiated lands flow a different morality, a different faith, a different way of life. The South Sea islands are already Protestant hamlets; one sea-born battalion, a single battleship changes the fate of Chili. . .
> (Alexander von Humboldt to Varnhagen von Ense, 17 May 1837).[1]

In recent years, Heine criticism has increasingly focused on Heine's "identity."[2] The International Heine Congress in Düsseldorf in May 1997 was no exception. While many participants lamented as one-sided the "political" interpretations of Heine in the sixties and seventies and demanded a more balanced assessment of his contribution instead, a surprisingly uniform group now focused on an "ethnic" Heine. As the *Neue Rheinische Zeitung* put it: "Entdeckt: Heine als Jude" (5/29/97)—Discovered: Heine as Jew. The focus on Heine as a Jewish writer was underscored by the wall painting that decorated the main lecture hall at the conference: a huge illustration of the Rabbi von Bacharach fragment, with the fateful Seder as its centerpiece. Of course, I do not want to suggest that the question of Heine's Judaism is irrelevant. On the contrary, the nuanced discussions in this volume prove how productive a focus on Heine's Jewish origins or on Judaic discourses can be. What bothered me in the presentations and in much of the critical literature on the topic, however, was my sense that "identity" is understood as something essential and unified; something that one is born with or that one acquires, and that one therefore "owns"; something that can then be investigated and pinned down. What seemed to be lacking was an understanding that has begun to undermine traditional identity politics, at least in the United States: namely, that identities are multiple and in process; that they are historical and positional, and depend as much on the context as on the individual; that identities can be imposed from the outside or claimed by the individual in response to outside pressures, in opposition to or in solidarity with particular groups; that ethnic or even biological identity has a performative quality; and that identity is not just destiny, but a utopia; for that one-ness with oneself, that self-sameness implied by the term, is more of an unattainable goal than a reality. Reflections on the nature of identity are all the more important in the case of Heine. Not only is his preoccupation with multiple, often conflicting identities a central aspect of his work, but his struggle with identities can become for us a vehicle for addressing larger theoretical issues. Reflections on the historicity of identity and self-identification are indispensable, for example, if one looks at an identity Heine claims and problematizes throughout his writings: that of the European.

Today, the label "European" has mostly positive connotations. Not so much in the United States, where Eurocentrism has become increasingly suspect, as in Europe itself, where it is used to signal transcendence of narrow national categories and interests, in favor of a larger, better whole. To be a "great European" ("großer Europäer") like Adenauer or de Gaulle, or to support the idea of a unified Europe, means to abandon the nationalist legacies of the past, to overcome economic egotism, militaristic jingoism, or exclusionary conceptions of national identity. More often than not, this enthusiastic rhetoric of transnational friendship and cooperation adopted by both the right and the left obliterates the attitudes and actions that fueled the "idea of Europe" in the past, that is, the colonialist-imperialist expansion that accompanied the emergence of a *European* consciousness in the first place. And yet this legacy reverberates not just in the concept of the Good European, as Robert Holub has recently pointed out,[3] but also for example in the slogan "fortress Europe." For to define oneself as a "European" not only signals the transcendence of national boundaries, but demarcates the boundaries between "us" and "them," Europe and the "rest of the world."

Profoundly aware of the problematic historical legacy of Europe and closely attuned to questions of conquest, colonialism, and acculturation of dominated peoples, Heine himself occupies ambivalent, shifting positions vis-à-vis the blessings of Europe. His ruminations about Europe and America in *Ludwig Börne: A Memorial* or "Vitzliputzli"—to name just two of the texts in which this topic appears prominently—can be better understood, if we read them in the context of nineteenth-century Occidentalism, that is, European attempts at and fantasies about re-discovering the New World. In this context, Heine's most important contemporary is undoubtedly another "great European," Alexander von Humboldt. In an implicit dialogue with Humboldt, Heine negotiates his own position with respect to Europe and a "European" identity.

* * *

> To the great Alexandros the last greetings of the dying Heine.
> (Heine's note to Alexander von Humboldt, scribbled on a calling card in February 1856; HSA 23: 482)
> The pencilled lines of the dying Heine are a precious keepsake for me, and they will be honorably stowed away in its envelope inscribed by Your Excellency's hand. (Varnhagen to Alexander von Humboldt, 14 March 1856)[4]

Heine's connections to Humboldt are somewhat tenuous. In fact, both men seem to have moved in opposite directions, geographically and socially: while the writer, having been rejected from public office in Prussia, set up residence in Paris in 1831, the explorer was called from Paris to Berlin in 1827, in order to serve the Prussian King as Chamberlain. They did meet socially during Humboldt's many visits to Paris, where he had been made a member of the Académie des sciences morales et politiques and served as Prussian emissary—for example in the salon of Nanette Valentin, in the bookstore of Heideloff and Campe, or at the house of Privy Councillor Koreff.[5] Yet throughout their contacts and despite certain political affinities, their relationship appears to have been distant, marred by mutual reservations, distrust, and feelings of rejection. "Humboldt will be there now; since I'm no friend of his (I avoided him as much as I could), I hope he won't talk badly about me" (HSA 21: 37), Heine writes to Varnhagen von Ense in Berlin, in 1832. This cool relationship did not improve when the sick Heine solicited Humboldt's help in obtaining a travel permit for Berlin and Humboldt half-heartedly—and unsuccessfully—complied.[6] To Heine, Humboldt seems to have owned everything that he, Heine, was struggling in vain to attain: social status, recognition in Germany, and access to office. As Heine confesses to Varnhagen in 1843: "To tell you the truth: as much as I think of his power, as little I think of his will to help me" (HSA: 22: 76). Veiled references to Humboldt's "ascents"—of the Chimborazo (2: 114; 6/I: 417) or to an official post in Prussia—attest to Heine's anxiety and ambivalence over social climbing.[7] If Heine envied or regretted Humboldt's collusion with power, with the detested Prussian state, Humboldt rejected Heine's character. To him, Heine embodied the immoral *bohémien* with elusive politics: "As far as his writings are concerned, they suffer—despite all the brilliance of style—from a strange fragmentation, a broken-ness in execution [*eine Gebrochenheit der Behandlung*]. One cannot speak of morality to begin with, as far as he is concerned; but one can never even be sure about his final stand on anything," Humboldt reportedly stated to Friedrich Althaus in May 1852.[8] It is therefore all the more surprising that Alexander von Humboldt would be the recipient of two of the dying Heine's last messages. A calling card addressed to the explorer, which Philarète Chasles carried with him to Berlin in October 1855, reads: "To the beloved and much celebrated Alexander von Humboldt the great French literary scholar Philarète Chasles transmits many greetings from—Heinrich Heine" (HSA 23: 465). And on yet another calling card, possibly written shortly before his death, Heine again pays homage to his famous contemporary: "To the great Alexandros the last greetings of the dying Heine." (HSA 23: 482). After so much hype—"beloved," "much celebrated," "great"—the simple "Heinrich Heine," dying low down in his "Mattress-Grave," sounds even more pathetic and diminished. Humboldt in turn scribbles on the back of the card: "The last I received from Heine" and sends it on, with other documents, to Varnhagen, who stows the "precious memory" away with other letters to and by Humboldt.[9]

Without a doubt, Heine wanted to bring himself to Humboldt's attention, once again, by inscribing himself literally in Humboldt's memory and the Humboldtian legacy. But why? What had happened in the ten years since their last contact? Why this effusive praise now? What moved the dying Heine to pay belated tribute to someone whom he had considered more of an adversary than an ally? Or is the epithet "great Alexandros" to be read with a grain of salt, as an ironic allusion to another great "conqueror"? And what are we to make of the connection between the "great Alexandros" and the "new Alexander," Frederick William IV? After all, Heine's poem "The New Alexander," which had angered Prussian authorities to such an extent that they had refused him entry in 1846 despite Humboldt's intervention, also made fun of a would-be conqueror by comparing the weak liquor-happy Prussian King to far greater predecessors—both the Macedonian king and, significantly, Louis XIV.[10] As I want to suggest, rather than looking for biographical explanations for Heine's overtures to Alexander von Humboldt, we might explore Heine's imaginary during the last years of his life, the semantic field circumscribed by terms such as "Alexander," "conquest," or "new." In other words, we need to investigate the links between discovery and conquest, colonization and acculturation, between New World and Old, and between Columbus and the Second Discoverer, the "new" Alexander and Alexander von Humboldt. Or, to put it more succinctly, we must explore how Heine locates himself in the discourse of European expansionism. Let me do this by way of another historical detour—after all, we are talking about the age of travel and exploration.

* * *

> Europe never has been a self-evident or natural geographical, cultural, or political division of the world. It is something created, artificial, and elusive.[11]

Most critics agree that the "idea of Europe" emerged and took hold in the fifteenth, sixteenth, and seventeenth centuries, alongside the discovery and colonization of the so-called New World (Hennigsen). The idea was codified during the eighteenth century, when "civilized" Europe defined itself vis-à-vis uncivilized, "savage" America, in an attempt to explain the power differential between the two continents and justify the violent takeover in retrospect as a natural event. The term Europe had, of course, been around for a long time.[12] It had been employed to denote usually hostile polarities between geographic regions—Europe versus Asia in Greek ideology; Europe versus Africa in Roman thought—and to affirm Europe's superiority over the rest of the known world. As such, the idea of Europe contained an element of wishful thinking: to counter, as Timothy Reiss points out, "internal violence and memories of war" which had always torn the continent apart.[13] In the eighteenth-century context of European travel and colonialist expansion, however, the idea of Europe took on a particular urgency. It implied not just the hope for "perpetual peace" in view of local in-fighting, but "the realization of the possibility of global domination"[14] characterized as a "civilizing mission" to which not just Spain but all of (Western) Europe were called. In fact, the Spanish Empire had actually forfeited its claim to colonize and missionize and would now be displaced by technically and morally more advanced nations. In the words of the Ecuadorian critic José Juncosa: *European* thinking emerged to "rationalize the political and economic expansion of the overseas empires at the moment of Spain's irremediable demise."[15]

Significantly, in the minds of eighteenth-century *philosophes*,

Columbus's "discovery" of America had not so much added a fourth continent to the existing three as reconfirmed a dualistic, hierarchical world-view. According to Corneille de Pauw, writer of the *Encyclopédie* entry on "America," the Discovery literally divided the world into two "halves," Europe and America. As he stated in 1768:

> No event in human history is more noteworthy than the Discovery of America. If one goes back from present times to those of the remotest past, no single event can be compared to this one; and it is no doubt a great and awful spectacle to see one half of the globe so much hated by nature that everything there is degenerate or monstrous.[16]

Throughout the eighteenth and into the nineteenth century, the differences between the two halves and their populations would be cast in polar opposites: as strong versus weak, vigorous versus decrepit, civilized versus primitive, young versus old. These binaries served to confirm the physical, moral, and intellectual superiority of either area over the other, depending on the philosophical perspective of the speakers. To Voltaireans like de Pauw, the manly, mature European civilization had proven superior; to Rousseaueans, the natural men of the New World exhibited greater strength and moral vigor than their decadent, effeminate European counterparts. Yet whether they belonged to the Voltairean or the Rousseauean camp, to the denigrators or idealizers of America—Europeans of the Enlightenment saw themselves in a direct and competitive relation to Americans. This did not change much after 1776, when rebellious European settlers, casting off the yoke of British colonialism, assumed the "American" identity, by displacing "Native Americans" both physically and symbolically. After U.S. independence, the imaginary competition between Europe and America just moved further north, so to speak. It remained caught, however, in the same binary structure: now, "decrepit" old Europe saw itself challenged by "young" American states full of vitality; the knowledgeable metropolitan perspective of civilized Europeans clashed with the "provincial," "naive" attitudes of the young barbarians, the prisonhouse of the Old World with the freedom battles of the New, and so forth. The "invention of America," to use Edmundo O'Gorman's phrase, thus corresponded—and continues to correspond—to a simultaneous invention of Europe: America, the one half, was what Europe, the other half, was not.[17] America was less a geographic region to be explored and scrutinized than a concept to be integrated into European systems of meaning. Not having left European soil—which seemed to have been the rule for European philosophers—proved to be an advantage, for they could thus establish their neat divisions and hierarchies without confronting a more complicated reality.

Despite widespread critique of colonial violence on moral grounds, both camps basically agreed that the conquest was inevitable, even natural; that the search for knowledge went hand in hand with territorial and economic expansion; that the "conquest of the intellect" was not to be stopped. As I have shown in *Colonial Fantasies*, this conviction hinged on two fantasies which simultaneously populated the European discourse on America: the fantasy of a natural attraction of "America," embodied by an Indian queen, to the physically, mentally, and morally superior "Europe," embodied by the noble conquistador, an attraction that would result in physical surrender and, in the best of all scenarios, the indissoluble bond of matrimony. This fantasy cast conquest and colonization, that is, political and economic power relations, in terms of a familial bond and made acculturation into an act of voluntary, "natural" subordination and absorption of the "weaker" culture into the "stronger." The second fantasy that undergirded many of the more theoretical reflections on the two worlds saw the "children" of the New World in need of tutelage by a wiser Old World. As preceptor-father, Europe could impart his knowledge, civilize and domesticate, and thus eventually raise America to his own advanced level. Again, the model was a familial one; it proposed that the hierarchy as well as assimilatory processes followed natural laws, and if all went well, that America might be released into adulthood without jeopardizing familial cohesion and loyalties.

The conviction of the inevitability of the conquest could not just be sustained by familial fantasies. It also grounded itself in "reality," that is, in the historical figure of Columbus. Or rather, by the reconfiguration of the historical person, about whom little was known, into Columbus, the myth. As carrier of a divine mission, as executor of a divine will, as non-Spaniard, as a man of deep convictions, but misunderstood and slighted by his contemporaries, Columbus provided an identificatory frame that allowed non-Spaniards to claim him as their own. As a discoverer driven by the thirst for knowledge, he became the focal point of a distinction between exploration and colonization, between "discovery" and "conquest." In stories, epics, and dramas, Columbus was cast as the "good discoverer"—a visionary, hero, genius, searcher, an *Aufklärer* incarnate (Tietz), innocent of colonialism (Schultz), even though he engaged in it and managed to live by it quite nicely, at least for a while.[18] In short, Columbus the traveler, Columbus the explorer served as legitimizing myth for Northern European sallies into "new" territories. And "newness" was a matter of definition.

This is where Alexander von Humboldt enters the picture. If the image of Columbus, throughout the Enlightenment, had oscillated between that of the kind father who cares for his native "children" and that of the Storm and Stress genius pressing ever onward, the intervention of a German "Second Columbus" reconfirmed that image, gave it actuality, presence, potentiality. Humboldt was not only called the Second Discoverer of the New World by Europeans and Americans alike,[19] but he consciously fashioned himself as Columbus's successor. Or rather, he refashioned Columbus in his own image. In his *Personal Narrative of a Journey to the Equinoctial Regions of the New Continent* (1807-1839) Humboldt already draws a positive picture of the traveler Columbus as literal forerunner whose footsteps he retraces. In his much later *Critical Investigation of the History of the Geography of the New Continent* 1836-38) Humboldt carries the identification further by stressing the "extensive scientific knowledge," the skills as observer and painter of nature, and "the decisive will power" of the "Genuese sailor."[20] He pays little attention to the negative aspects of Columbus's personality and actions, his mercantile interests, involvement in the slave trade, and his share in guilt for the massacres of the indigenous. Instead, Humboldt transforms Columbus into the prototypical scientist whose work initiates the history of discoveries that ends in the present of Humboldt's own scientific contribution.

As the titles of the two above-named works suggest, Humboldt upholds the old-new dichotomy introduced by Columbus's Discovery: His travels lead to the equinoctial regions of the "New" World; he critically examines the history of geography of the "new" continent. Like the eighteenth-century philosophers, Humboldt sees the relationship of Old World and New in terms of a civilization and power differential:

> In the Old World the nuances and differences between nations form the main focus of the picture. In the New World, man and his productions disappear, so to speak , in the midst of a wild and outsize [sic!] nature. In the New World the human race has been preserved by a few scarcely civilized tribes, or by the uniform customs and institutions transplanted on to foreign shores by European

colonists.[21]

If the first sentences repeat the conventional Enlightenment dichotomy, confirming European supremacy, the next sentences sound almost apologetic. The differentiation between Old and New Worlds, it now appears, is more guided by Humboldt's need to generate sympathies for his scientific project than by a sense of European superiority: "Facts about the history of our species, different kinds of government and monuments of art affect us far more than descriptions of vast emptinesses destined for plants and wild animals," he says. Yet "[i]f America does not occupy an important place in the history of mankind, and in the revolutions that have shattered the world, it does offer a wide field for a naturalist."[22] In other words, it is natural to be interested in human affairs in Europe where political relationships and cultural differences between the nations matter. In the New World, however, with its few "scarcely civilized tribes," nature and nature observation are called for. Hence, in many of his published writings, the vast landscapes, the abundant vegetation, and the natural wonders of the South American continent take precedence over human achievement. This man-nature, populated-empty, civilized-wild dualism that underlies Humboldt's "views of nature" has led Mary Louise Pratt to suggest that Humboldt had ulterior, if unconscious, intentions; that he, like Columbus, constructed South America as "new," as a "primal world of nature, an unclaimed and timeless space occupied by plants and creatures (some of them human) but not organized by societies and economies; a world whose only history was the one about to begin" in order to justify the civilizing, I. e. colonizing, intervention of the European. Humboldt's *Aspects of Nature*, she claims, "and his viewing stake out a new beginning of history in South America, a new (Northern European) point of origin for a future that starts now, and will rework that 'savage' terrain."[23]

Perhaps here is not the place to engage in Pratt's argument—after all, we are trying to get to Heine—but let me just state that Humboldt's very varied texts themselves do not bear out such a verdict.[24] His gaze does not so much "depopulate" and "dehistoricize" the landscape as point to the result of 300 years of colonial history, which has transformed once populated and cultivated areas into empty territory. Nature, the "jungle," has been able to overwhelm civilization in the New World, he suggests, because European greed, misguided colonial politics, and constant revolutionary upheavals have left the terrain in neglect.[25] Humboldt's direct observations of the workings of the colonial system are acute and attest to his vital interest not just in the unexplored virgin territories or "empty" spaces of a "new" world, but in the abuses perpetrated by European colonizers and the sufferings of the colonized under European rule. In his diaries, Humboldt dwells for pages on end on the "immoral idea" of colonialism which he attacks not just on ethical but on economic, political, and psychological grounds. In private communications to Varnhagen, he laments the pervasive effect of acculturation, the omnipresence of "one kind of civilization, the Western European," which has already transformed the South Sea islands into "Protestant hamlets."[26] If, in his public writings, Humboldt chooses to concentrate on the world of nature, or, as in his *Political Essay on the Kingdom of New Spain*, on a politically more advanced Creole society where decolonization and independence from Europe seem imminent, the decision seems to be guided by purely political considerations. To explore and describe the vast "empty" interiors of South America allows him to avoid political controversy and to concentrate on what the Spanish Crown had allowed him to do and what he liked to do best: the natural sciences and the "new" continent—new to the European scientist, since its interiors had never been explored and mapped scientifically, not even by the Spanish colonizers.[27] By extolling nature, as Ralph Rainer Wuthenow suggests, Humboldt does not so much invite its domestication and exploitation as present an antithesis to "unlimited human brutality" [*unumschränkte Gewaltherrschaft*] and the failings of civil institutions.[28]

Humboldt was, however, not particularly consistent in his critique of foreign intervention in Latin American affairs, since he also maintained his faith in the regenerative forces of the world market. He was optimistic that once peace was established in the colonies, a "new social order" based on local resources and free trade would emerge.[29] His writings about the natural potential of the countries, he hoped, would contribute toward such a peaceful, mutually beneficial development—an opinion that was shared by progressives in Europe as well as in Latin America in the early 1800s and that has, of course, been proven wrong by history.[30]

Pratt, to my mind, has a point when it comes to the instrumentalization of Humboldt's work by others for specifically colonialist purposes. I am thinking not so much of the practical use that was made of his discoveries or the silver trade projects hatched by the Hamburg citizenry on the basis of Humboldt's mining and trade reports.[31] I am thinking more of Humboldt's spiritual legacy and Humboldt the legend. Humboldt's enthusiastic descriptions of natural beauty, his Romantic conception of the explorer, his Goethean belief in the harmony and allure of unspoilt nature, and his unswerving faith in progress through trade may indeed have contributed to reviving a sense of adventure and reactivating the fantasies of seizing virgin territory, sensations that were already figured in the familial fantasies of the eighteenth century. But it was above all his status as a "German" Columbus, as a national idol, that made him an unwitting precursor of German colonialism.

This is precisely how he seems to have been received by nineteenth-century German colonialist advocates: "Unser Welteroberer"—as Goethe had jokingly called him in a letter to Zelter[32]—became precisely that, *our* world conqueror.[33] One of the most popular Humboldt biographies in the nineteenth century, Hermann Klencke's *Alexander von Humboldt. A Biographical Memorial* (1851), for example, serves the avowed purpose of claiming Humboldt for a German national project: "Should we not give proof of our maturity as a nation [*Volksmündigkeit*] by seeking to come as close as possible to him in spirit and pay him the esteem due to him by our insight into his life as a scholar and scientist?" Klencke asks rhetorically.[34] Humboldt, "this scientific Columbus of modern times", this "discoverer of a new scientific and real world",[35] is to Klencke not just the "successor," the *Nachfolger*, of the first Columbus, but he surpasses his model, as he surpasses all models, all geniuses or heroes of history. As this and later texts propose, the identification with Humboldt the Discoverer will lead the German nation to adulthood, to national maturity. Humboldt's Columbian legacy of material and scientific conquests becomes a national endowment bestowed on future generations of Germans. "He has elevated the once small and quiet Prussian capital to become a hotbed of the Cosmic Spirit [*zu einer Pflanzstätte des kosmischen Geistes*]," a pamphlet of 1886, published by the German Colonial Society, reads. His genius "sowed the seeds." "German Science" like Humboldt's discoveries, does not just point the way to "energetic actions in colonial matters," but must continue to serve them and "stand by them."[36] If Columbus, in and through Humboldt's reception, became a German Columbus, then Humboldt, in the reception of his German contemporaries, became a German Alexander. This brings us back to Heine, and to Heine's obsession with Alexanders, conquests, new worlds and old Europe.

* * *

To my enemy's own homeland,
Which goes by the name of Europe,

Will I flee to take my refuge
And begin a new career there.
(Heinrich Heine, "Vitzliputzli"; 6/I: 74)

Throughout his life, but particularly in his late years, Heine exhibited a keen and vital interest in questions of conquest and subjugation, physical as well as spiritual, literal as well as metaphorical. Whether it was the defeat of Poland in the 1830s or the *conquista* of the Americas in the fourteen and fifteen hundreds, whether it was the *reconquista* of Spain by the Catholic Kings or the conquests in the Near and Far East achieved by the Macedonian Alexander around 300 B. C.—they all mattered simultaneously since they were associated in the mind of the poet with questions of physical defeat and cultural survival: his own and that of subjugated peoples within Europe and of nations subjugated by Europe.[37]

Heine's preoccupation with the Americas and with the Humboldtian legacy—not just the person of Humboldt—must be read in this context. There are a number of points where Heine's project departed from Humboldt's. First and foremost, of course, Heine rejected the appropriation of scientific achievement, intellectual conquests, for nationalist or colonialist purposes.[38] But there are also profound differences in perspective. For Heine, too, the contrast Europe-America constitutes one of the basic oppositions of European modernity. But unlike Humboldt, Heine cannot muster any faith in the ultimate harmony of the universe or in universal progress due to free trade and the development of postcolonial civic society. Heine's gaze is thus not only directed outward to assess or lament the ever-receding horizon, the ever greater degree of the "Europeanization" of the world, as Humboldt had done. Heine's occupation with the New World always redirects him back to the Old. Where Humboldt reinvents the "New World" as unspoilt nature, in opposition to the populated, "civilized," bustling Europe, Heine reinvents Europe in opposition to or in analogy with America. Where Humboldt, from the perspective of the disinterested outside observer, remarks on the devastation that Spanish colonialism has wreaked upon the societies of New Spain, Heine experiences colonialism, so to speak, in the flesh. He sees himself right in the middle of the clash between old and new worlds, a clash that to him has geographic as well as historico-political and aesthetic connotations. To Heine, "America" is not "new" but all-too-familiar territory.

According to the critical literature on Heine, Heine's engagement with the New World, that is, the United States, unfolded in three separate phases[39]: the phase of positive identification until 1831, when Heine considers America as an effective counter image to Europe, as the home of the free, as a place where human rights flourish; the phase of increasing skepticism in the 1830s, when Heine polemicizes against American monotony, colorlessness, and petty conformism; and the years from 1840 onward, marked by his attack on slavery, persistent racism, and plebeian egalitarianism, for example in *Ludwig Börne. A Memorial*. If we set the accents somewhat differently, namely by including Europe in the equation early on, the divisions between the three phases become less clear-cut. Thus, in the *Journey from Munich to Genoa* of 1828, where Heine laments the persistence of European feudalism, America is not the promised land, but a large "escape hole" (2: 380), a way out of the "dungeon" Europe. While "all of Europe" is enslaved by Church and feudal aristocracy, America functions not so much as a counter image but as an undefined space with an empty center, a loophole. In other words, although the author is "weary of Europe" (*Europamüde*), the "New World" does not seem to offer any attractions to Europeans other than an imaginary escape into basically abstract freedom.[40] Even though Heine's skepticism regarding America is not yet apparent in this early phase, the seeds of a full-fledged rejection of the American way are already planted.

Heine's obsession with Europe increases during his years of involvement in daily politics, before his forced retirement to the sickbed. In his characterization of Europe in the thirties and forties, Heine borrows freely from eighteenth-century philosophers. His Europe also oscillates between decrepitude—"hoary Europe" (3: 73)—and youth—"poor virgin Europe" (5: 344)—with the only difference that he does not choose one over the other, but conjures up either one of the two, depending on what he wants to point to: Europe's ossified socio-political structures or the political naiveté of the European peoples who have allowed restoration to take over. In either case, the rejuvenating forces do not come from across the Atlantic—Republican rule *à l'Américaine* is in fact "unfitting, undelectable, and unsavory" (3: 87) for old Europe. And as to the maiden Europa—she has already surrendered to the oxen: "Yes, Europa bent to power— / Who could stop an ox? Not she" (6/I: 98).[41] However, while America with its puritanical monotony and rampant materialism does not offer an alternative to old-young Europe, it reflects one aspect of European traditions and attitudes which Heine despises throughout his life and which he circumscribes with the term "Nazarenism" (*Nazarenertum)*. In the thirties and forties, "America" thus serves not as an alternative or an empty space, but as a concave mirror that concentrates the rays and reflects Europe back to itself.

The imaginary overlap between America and Europe becomes particularly evident in *Ludwig Börne*. First, Heine laments the "enslavement" to material goods, that keeps many a revolutionary from sacrificing his life for the cause of freedom (4: 16). Then he associates "Jewish spiritualism," "Nazarene narrowmindedness" and "ascetic Republicanism" with Börne and links all three to England and America. If Europe is a dungeon, Heine proposes, then America is a dungeon too, only that the chains are invisible there. If Europe is ruled by tyrants, so is America—only in America the riff-raff (*Pöbel*) are the tyrants, not the aristocrats. Formal equality in America, finally, is undermined by racism, which to Heine is worse than slavery itself (4: 38). Slavery, however, is not an American phenomenon (as we already know from book one, where Heine had talked about Börne's "enslavement" by material goods). In book three, after a detour to Judaic and Christian spiritualism and the 1830 Revolution, Heine returns to slavery in Europe and Germany, but with a different twist. As Börne—here Heine's mouthpiece—says: "The Germans were always the *ludi magistri* of slavery, and wherever blind obedience had to be battered into the bodies and minds, they chose a German drill master. We have also flooded all of Europe with slavery, and as memorials of this deluge German monarchies are occupying all the thrones of Europe" (4: 70). Heine's diatribes against the puritanism, materialism, republicanism and racism brought by European colonists to America thus reflect back on very similar phenomena in Europe, or in Germany, with the only difference that Europeans have replaced racism with class oppression or anti-Semitism (4: 90). If slavery and "modern puritanism" have enveloped "all of Europe" like a grey dawn, which "precedes a rigid winter" (4: 141), as Heine suggests by way of conclusion, then the differences between the two continents amount to zero.

The association of Europe with America, and American conditions with European conditions, does not function on a synchronic level alone; in the imagination of the poet, the present is always linked to many different levels of the past. Thus, in his polemic against the "Republican form of government" Heine associates current political movements in "our *decrepit* Europe" with conditions in *ancient* Europe, Athens and Sparta, as well as in the *new* American states, in order to reject Republicanism, the "bad kitchen of equality in which the black soup is so poorly cooked" (3: 116).

Likewise his preoccupation with the fate of subjected or assimilated peoples allows him to establish links between the displacement of the natives in the New World and the expulsion of the Moors and Jews in fifteenth-century Spain, between German peasants suffering under feudal lords and Indian Brahmins lamenting the destruction of their world by British colonizers. Heine refuses to juxtapose "us" with "them" and to construct rigid binaries. Nor does he suggest a teleology or a progression towards greater harmony or world peace, as Humboldt did. Instead, he creates a space of interaction, overlap, of mutual refraction, a kind of "middle passage" in which metaphors and realities—of past and present slavery, past and present republicanism, past and present conquest—intersect and are interchanged.

In his late epic poem "Vitzliputzli" Heine thematizes and reenacts this back-and-forth movement between perceptions and realities, between continents, and between present and past that I have outlined.[42] In this tale of conquest and reconquest, Heine debunks once and for all the "euromyths" (Pratt) that had hitherto sustained the relationship between Europe and America and the Humboldtian legacy. The *Prelude* contains a mock first encounter with America in which the poet, posing as a kind of Second Columbus, reinvents the new world in contrast to the old. Heine implicitly alludes to Alexander von Humboldt when the poetic I describes "America's" pristine beauty, *as if* he saw it for the very first time:[43]

> This is America indeed!
> This is a new world, really new!
> Not today's land, which already
> Withers, Europeanized.
>
> This is a new world, really new,
> As it was the day Columbus
> Plucked it sparkling from the ocean.
> Still it shines with sea-fresh colors,
>
> Still it drips with pearls of water
> Which dissolve in bursts of color
> As the sunlight's kisses touch them.
> Oh, how healthy is this world! (6/I: 56)

The confusion of temporal and semantic levels manifests itself in the verbs and terminology Heine chooses. Present (this "is" the new world) and past (as Christoval Kolumbus plucked it from the ocean") coincide in this Humboldtian "view of nature"; the names "Amerika" and "Christoval Kolumbus" (in the German original) locate the poet's voice in post-Discovery, even postcolonial Europe, for "Cathay," or even Columbus's New World, have already been renamed after Amerigo Vespucci, and "Cristóbal Colón," the hispanicized Italian, has already been germanized into Kolumbus with a K. This decidedly *ex posteriori* perspective—this *is emphatically not* the New World as Columbus plucked it from the ocean—is underscored by the comparison of the pristine New World with today's new world which already "withers, Europeanized." Colonial history, I. e., destruction and transformation, have already left their mark, particularly in the language of this Second Columbus for whom everything seems "new" because he wills it to be, and yet everything new "reminds" him of experiences he has already had before. The "new soil," "new flowers," and "new perfumes" which had so enchanted the first discoverers, have already been imported, incorporated into the old world. The apparent health of the new world is seen in contrast to the diseases of the old. History has inscribed itself literally in the body of the monkey, who, at the sight of the foreign intruder, makes the sign of the cross and displays his hairless backside which bears the tricolor black-red-and-gold. Catholic church and German national myths have both left their mark on the body of the animal, which has been civilized, acculturated, hybridicized —somewhere between animal and human, somewhere between old and new. In the mutual gaze of the monkey and the poetic I, the poet thus both reconstructs and erases the difference between old world and new so that the two mirror, refract, "ape" each other, thereby exploding the traditional old-new opposition. The present new world, with its violent clashes and aborted revolutions is no different from the old; the old is no less "savage" than the new.

The second part of "Vitzliputzli" directly addresses the Columbian myth, as it had been propagated by nineteenth-century playwrights[44] and by Humboldt himself. Like his predecessors, Heine separates the "hero," "Messer Christoval Kolumbus" from the villain, "Don Fernando Cortez." The former has given the world a whole new world, Heine says, the latter was but a bandit, who robbed the new world and gave it to Spain. Yet despite attempts to divide the conquest into good discoverer and bad conqueror, in history and in the memory of nations the two names are tied together.[45] Columbus is not just the precursor of Humboldt, but the precursor of Cortés. Heine's summary of the Columbian legacy therefore questions the heroization of Columbus he himself had just undertaken. In typical Heinean fashion, the stanza

> He had not the power to free us
> From our dreary earthly prison,
> But at least he could enlarge it,
> Make the chains a little longer. (6/I: 59)

can be read in more than one way. By enlarging the prison Europe to encompass the New World, and by extending the chains that enslaved Europeans to enslave the peoples on both continents, Columbus has not only expanded "our" horizon, but facilitated global oppression. Hence discovery and conquest are only two sides of the same (gold) coin. In the subsequent recounting of the Spanish betrayal and the Aztec revenge during the conquest of Tenochtitlán, Heine spells out the betrayal, greed and destruction implicit in the colonial experience. Here, the central trope is not mutual refraction but mutual incorporation: While the Spanish conquistadors incorporate more and more foreign territory, Aztec warriors literally incorporate Spanish conquistadors. Instead of a holy alliance, a marriage of Europe and America that earlier writers had fantasized about, Heine exposes conquest and colonization as an unholy communion, in which one cannibalizes and thereby transforms the other.

Heine's critique of the seductive, euphemizing colonial discourse of his forbears and contemporaries is carried even further in the third part of "Vitzliputzli," Vitzliputzli's revenge. Whereas the second part was characterized by a constant shifting of conquest scenario and perspective, from the Spanish to the Mexican and back to the Spanish, now the poet assumes the voice of the vanquished: The dethroned Mexican war-god Huitzilopochtli, transmogrified into the cartoon devil Vitzliputzli, swears that he will in turn "discover" the old world to haunt the colonizers. Again, Heine proves to be a true historian, a prophet looking backward, for Vitzliputzli's prophesy, placed into the sixteenth century, has already become reality in the 300 years since the conquest: by 1851, colonialism has haunted the Spanish colonizers; it has drained their resources, created dependencies, and fomented revolutionary backlashes. Heine is also a seismograph of the present who registers even the minutest socio-political movement: for the cannibalistic orgy and Vitzliputzli's return, which serve as central metaphors for colonial incorporation and corruption, not only address past colonialism and the older familial fantasies of peaceful co-existence, but also anticipate and undermine future competitions for global mastery. In place of the Columbian myth of a clean slate, instead of Humboldt's vision of sublime nature and vast empty spaces, Heine presents images that anticipate the dirty entanglements of neo-colonialist and imperialist interventions. By assuming the perspective of the colonized, and ending the poem with Vitzliputzli's anguished prophesy, Heine underscores the plight of cultures that have been violently subjugated. However, by lending his voice to a bloody War-God, who, through priests and ritual, had repressed his own people, Heine extends his "colonial suspicion" to include any form of domination and control, be it religious, political, or economic.[46]

Allusions to Humboldt are indirect in this conquest poem, and focus mostly on the reception of the Columbian myth as the myth of disinterested "scientific discovery." Discovery, Heine seems to suggest, leads to conquest even if the Discoverer himself pleads innocent. There are always those who will transform the "gift" of knowledge into "booty." In several of his late texts Heine addresses another aspect of European conquest, namely the confluence of eroticism and violence inherent in the term, which had given vent to some of the heterosexual fantasies about America I mentioned earlier and to which Humboldt had unwittingly contributed. This time, Humboldt's namesake Alexander the Great, one of the great "sensualists" in Heine's historical arsenal, serves to embody the desire for earthly possessions and everlasting fame.[47] Yet while Heine evokes dreams of glorious conquests—erotic and material ones—these conquests always end in death. In "To the Young," the appeal to the younger generation to emulate the Great Alexander's exploits culminates in a kind of bacchantic *Liebestod* as the conqueror celebrates his victory in Babylon (6/I: 99-100). In "Jehuda ben Halevy," the spoils Alexander distributed among his friends are dispersed all over the world, whereas the great conqueror retains but immaterial images and memories. The dreams of the old conquistador Ponce de Leon, finally, end at the river Lethe. In Heine's imaginary, there is no room for lasting conquests, natural surrenders, or marriage of cultures, as eighteenth-century literati had imagined them; the educational or benign developmentalism, the pristine state, the harmonious ending, envisaged by Alexander von Humboldt are absent in Heine: everything is already embedded in history, and history is marked by conflict, oppression, and mortality.

And yet the "fragment" Yehuda ben Halevy may provide us with a clue as to why on his deathbed Heine would come back to the "great

Alexandros," successor to both Columbus and Alexander the Great. In part three of the poem, Alexander of Macedonia loots the property of the defeated Darius and gives away Darius's pearls, which trickle down through Near Eastern and European history. As his only trophy Alexander retains the jewelry casket, into which he places Homer's poems. At night, while Alexander is asleep, the heroes from the past emerge from the casket and populate, as fantasy figures, the conqueror's dreams. In other words, the spoils of great conquests have been dispersed, and nothing remains but memories in the form of heroic poetry. In the fragment, the image of Alexander's dreams is juxtaposed with that of the poet, who once also loved the songs of great deeds and was crowned a victor. Now however, his triumphal chariot is smashed to pieces, while he writhes "here on the ground in torment, / Cripple's torment" (6/I: 145). Clearly, the poet, a conqueror defeated, associates himself with the victorious Alexander: to both, the only thing that will remain of past victories are the songs, the poetry that survives, because it is read. This is all that conquerors can aspire to: to live on through literature. And this is where, I believe, the lives of Heine and Alexander von Humboldt finally touch. In a possibly self-ironic move, the dying Heine, a conqueror in the realm of poetry, recognizes his affinity with the eighty-seven-year old "Great Alexandros," the "physicien du globe,"[48] the intellectual conqueror of the "Kosmos"—over and above all differences. And maybe, their differences were not quite so significant after all, for although one concentrated more on the flora and fauna of the world, and the other on the peoples, poetry, and history, the two were united in their concern for issues that crossed geographic as well as historical boundaries.

So what makes Humboldt and Heine good, or great, Europeans? To be sure, both were culturally rooted in Germany, in France, in Western Europe. Both were appropriated, at different times and for different reasons, as consummate "Europeans," that is, as liberal intellectuals whose work and outlook transcended national boundaries and vindicated Germany before the world.[49] And yet, which part of "Europe" can claim them as theirs, and for what political or ideological purposes? As I have argued, both Humboldt and Heine, but Heine much more than Humboldt, were obsessed with Europe: they were conscious of the pernicious legacies of European history, and critical of contemporary European politics. Their Europe was neither a glorious idea, nor an exemplary political reality. So what are we going to gain from calling them "European," from claiming them for an ever-elusive "European" identity? Maybe we should suspend questions of regional-political identification and ownership, and focus instead on the dynamics of the writers' self-conscious positioning. For they themselves did not insist on rootedness and a fixed regional or cultural perspective, but on change, global conflict, and creative alliances, in order to further their scientific- or poetic-emancipatory projects.[50] After all, it is not their Europeanism but their cosmic "conquests" that finally brought Humboldt and Heine together—the great Alexandros circumscribing his "Kosmos," and the great Heinrich inventing his.

Notes

1. *Briefe von Alexander von Humboldt an Varnhagen von Ense aus den Jahren 1827 bis 1858* (Leipzig, 1860), p. 41. All translations are mine, unless otherwise noted.

2. See, for example, Sander Gilman and Peter Uwe Hohendahl, eds. *Heinrich Heine and the Occident: Multiple Identities, Multiple Receptions* (Lincoln, 1991); or Jost Hermand, *Mehr als ein Liberaler: Über Heinrich Heine* (Frankfurt/Main, 1991).

3. See his "Nietzsche's Colonialist Imagination: Nueva Germania, Good Europeanism, and Great Politics," *The Imperialist Imagination: German Colonialism and Its Legacy*, ed. Sara Friedrichsmeyer, Sara Lennox, Susanne Zantop (Ann Arbor, forthcoming).

4. *Briefe von Alexander von Humboldt an Varnhagen von Ense aus den Jahren 1827 bis 1858* (Leipzig, 1860), p. 313.

5. See Friedrich Hirth's commentary in Heinrich Heine, *Briefe* (Mainz, 1950), vol. 5, p. 7; Michael Werner, ed., *Begegnungen mit Heine: Berichte der Zeitgenossen* (Hamburg, 1973), vol. 1, pp. 250, 547.

6. Heine wanted to travel to Berlin in order to undergo treatment for his eye ailment. See Hirth's commentary in *Briefe*, vol. 6, pp. 28-30.

7. Considering Heine's resentment of the Prussian state, we must take his remark that the names of Humboldt and other "intellectual conquerors" in Prussian services "shine there most brilliantly" with a grain of salt (1: 447). Varnhagen and others relate an anecdote that throws light on Heine's "class anxiety." When Humboldt visited Heine in Paris one day and had to climb several flights of stairs in vain because Heine was absent, Heine, upon his return home, supposedly said to Mathilde: "The man has climbed up much higher than to us." ["Der Mann ist schon höher gestiegen als zu uns," *Begegnungen* vol. 1, p. 575]. In light of his prior skepticism, Heine's affirmation to Lassalle, "I have never doubted Humboldt's sympathy; his letter is sincere, and a warm heart beats in it," (HSA 22: 192) does not ring quite true.

8. Reported in Heinrich Heine, *Briefe*, ed. Friedrich Hirth, vol. 5, p. 32.

9. *Briefe von Alexander von Humboldt an Varnhagen von Ense*, p. 313.

10. As Peter Burke, *The Fabrication of Louis XIV* (New Haven, 1992), states Louis XIV was also apotheosized as "the new Alexander," which adds another layer of complications to Heine's attribution (see pp. 28, 35, 37, 69, 197).

11. Martyn P. Thompson, "Ideas of Europe during the French Revolution and Napoleonic Wars," *Journal of the History of Ideas* 55 (1994), p. 37

12. *Oxford Classical Dictionary* , ed. Simon Hornblower and Anthony Spawworth, 3rd. edition (New York, 1996), p. 547; *Oxford English Dictionary*, prepared by J. A. Simpson and E. S. C. Weiner, 2nd edition (Oxford, 1989), p. 441.

13. Timothy J. Reiss, "Literature and the Idea of Europe," *PMLA* 108.1 (1993), pp. 14-29; here pp. 18, 22.

14. Alan Bance, "The Idea of Europe: from Erasmus to ERASMUS," *Journal of European Studies* 22.1 (1992), pp. 1-19.; here pp. 8-9.

15. José E. Juncosa, "Introduction" to *Europa y Amerindia. El indio americano en textos del Siglo XVIII* (Quito, 1991) p. x.

16. Corneille de Pauw, *Recherches philosophiques sur les américains* (Berlin, 1768/9), pp. iii-v.

17. See Jeffrey L. Sammons' discussion of this issue in "The German Image of America: Is There Any There There?" The Harold Jantz Memorial Lecture. Oberlin College offprint. On the "invention" of America see Mary Louise Pratt,"Humboldt y le reinvención de América," *Nuevo texto crítico* I, 1 (1988), pp 35-53, who adjusted O'Gorman's term to "Re-Invention" to fit her own discussion of eighteenth-century travel writing.

18. Manfred Tietz, "Der lange Weg des Columbus in die 'Historia del Nuevo Mundo' von Juan Bautista Muñoz (1793)," *Columbus zwischen zwei Welten. Historische und literarische Wertungen aus fünf Jahrhunderten*, ed. Titus Heydenreich (Frankfurt/Main, 1992) pp. 357-79; Joachim Schultz, "Columbus für Kinder," *Columbus zwischen zwei Welten*, pp. 325-37. See also Zantop, *Colonial Fantasies*, chapter 10. Curiously, even Juan Bautista

Muñoz, who in 1793 set out to debunk the criticism of the Spaniards by other European authors such as Robertson or Raynal, by presenting an "objective" picture of the Discovery, resorts to this idealizing perspective. In Muñoz's account, as Manfred Tietz reports, Columbus is even attributed a "vision" of the future, a topos that was picked up by every subsequent Columbus drama (pp. 368-9).

19. See Ette,"'Unser Welteroberer'. Alexander von Humboldt, der 2. Entdecker und die 2. Eroberung Amerikas,"*Amerika 1492-1992: Neue Welten-Neue Wirklichkeiten* (Braunschweig, 1992), pp. 130-9.

20. Quoted in Ette, "Entdecker über Entdecker: Alexander von Humboldt, Cristóbal Colón und die Wiederentdeckung Amerikas," *Columbus zwischen zwei Welten*, pp. 410, 413, 414.

21. Alexander von Humboldt, *Personal Narrative of a Journey to the Equinoctial Regions of the New Continent*, trans. by Jason Wilson (London, 1995), p. 12.

22. Ibid.

23. Mary Louise Pratt, *Imperial Eyes: Travel Writing and Transculturation* (New York, 1992), pp. 126-27.

24. See also Eoin Bourke's discussion of Pratt's critique: "'Der zweite Kolumbus?' Überlegungen zu Alexander von Humboldts Eurozentrismus," *Reisen im Diskurs*, ed. Anne Fuchs et al. (Heidelberg, 1995), pp. 135-51. Curiously, although Ette ("Entdecker," fn 8, p. 421) mentions Pratt in his footnotes, he does not engage her argument.

25. *Personal Narrative*, p. 13.

26. *Briefe von Alexander von Humboldt an Varnhagen von*, p. 41.

27. See Jason Wilson, "Introduction" to Alexander von Humboldt, *Personal Narrative*, p. liv. See also Nicolaas A. Rupke, "Introduction" to the 1997 edition of Humboldt's *Cosmos. A Sketch of the Physical Description of the Universe*, vol. 1., trans. by E. C. Otté (Baltimore, 1997), pp. xxx-xxxii.

28. Ralph-Rainer Wuthenow, "Der Reisende als 'Geschichtsschreiber der Natur,'" *Mythen der Neuen Welt. Zur Entdeckungsgeschichte Lateinamerikas*, ed. Karl-Heinz Kohl (Berlin, 1982), p. 243.

29. *Personal Narrative*, p. 13.

30. On Humboldt's concepts of a global market and global trade relations see Ette, "Unser Welteroberer."

31. Ette mentions for example the general map of New Spain that Humboldt had prepared and given to Jefferson and that the United States used to explore its southern border and wage war against Mexico ("Unser Welteroberer," p. 134). Further information in Christian Cortes and Godehard Weyerer, "Verkannt oder überschätzt," *Die Zeit*, Hamburg, Nr. 51 (18 Dec. 1992), p. 20.

32. Quoted in Ette, "Unser Welteroberer," p. 136.

33. On national differences in the reception of Humboldt's oeuvre see also Rupke, xix-xxii.

34. Hermann Klencke, *Alexander von Humboldt. Ein biographisches Denkmal* (Leipzig, 1851), p. 12.

35. Ibid, pp. 47, 92.

36. Editorial in *Deutsche Kolonialzeitung* 19 (1886), pp. 553-54.

37. See Hartmut Steinecke, "'The Lost Cosmopolite': Heine's Images of Foreign cultures and Peoples in the Historical Poems of the Late Period," *Heinrich Heine and the Occident*, pp. 139-162, who characterized Heine's late years as "a turning to history and alien societies, to historicity in its intercultural dimension" (p. 149).

38. See footnote 6. For Humboldt's response to the instrumentalization of his work see Ette, "Unser Welteroberer," pp. 134-35.

39. See Jost Hermand, "Auf andre Art so große Hoffnung: Heine und die USA,"*Amerika in der deutschen Literatur. Neue Welt, Nordamerika, USA*, ed. Sigrid Bauschinger, Horst Denkler and Wilfried Malsch (Stuttgart,

1975), pp. 81-92; Gerhard Weiß, "Heines Amerikabild" *Heine-Jahrbuch* 8 (1969), pp. 21-44.

40. On Heine's "flights" of fancy referring to America see Inge Rippmann, "'Sie saßen an den Wassern Babylons:' Eine Annäherung an Heinrich Heines 'Denkschrift über Ludwig Börne," *Heine-Jahrbuch* (1995), pp. 25-47; here pp. 42-43.

41. See also "Die Götter im Exil" and "Junge Leiden," Lieder IV. All translations of Heine's poetry are taken from Hal Draper's *The Complete Poems of Heinrich Heine* (Boston, 1982). I have taken the liberty to change Draper's "bull" back to "ox," since Heine's insult is directed at both the monarchs and Europa, who succumbed to impotent oxen.

42. For an overview of the critical approaches to "Vitzliputzli" see Roger Cook's summary in *By the Rivers of Babylon: Heinrich Heine's Late Songs and Reflections*, which I saw in manuscript form after completing this paper.

43. Even if Heine did not know Humboldt's "Cosmos," the first three volumes of which had appeared between 1845 and 1851, he must have been familiar with Jean-Louis-Armand de Quatrefages de Bréan's forty-page essay on Humboldt's project which appeared in the *Révue des deux mondes* in 1846.

44. E. g. the plays by Klingemann, Rückert, or Werder. See *Colonial Fantasies*, chap. 10.

45. I disagree here with John Carson Pettey's otherwise convincing interpretation—Pettey, too, stresses the separation, but not the link between the two in Heine's text. John Carson Pettey, "Anticolonialism in Heine's 'Vitzliputzli'," *Colloquia Germanica* 26.1 (1993), pp. 37-47.

46. See Pettey, whose focus is on the religious aspects of "colonialism." In his chapter on "Vitzliputzli," Roger Cook reads the poem as a commentary on the suppression of the senses, of sensuality, in Western discourse. In another context, I have stressed the theme of transculturation, as it is played out by the poem in multiple metamorphoses: "Vitzliputzli's" metamorphosis into a parrot parrots the transformation of the feathered serpent into Quetzalcoatl, just as his move to Europe in the guise of the

"discoverer" replicates and reverses the Spaniards' move to America in the guise of the returning "Quetzalcoatl". See also my "Colonialism, Cannibalism, and Literary Incorporation: Heine in Mexico," *Heine and the Occident: Multiple Identities. Multiple Receptions*, ed. Peter Uwe Hohendahl and Sander L. Gilman (Lincoln and London, 1991), pp. 110-38.

47. See "Die Göttin Diana," 4th tableau (6/I: 434-36), where Alexander the Great, as one of the great "sensualists," joins Goethe and others in the Venus mountain.

48. Bréan's term, quoted in Rupke, p. xxi.

49. See Rupke who describes Humboldt's problematic "European" appropriations after the publication of Kosmos and after World War II (p. xxii). For a lucid, critical discussion of Heine's postwar appropriation as "European" or "cosmopolitan" see Jeffrey Sammons, "Heine as 'Weltbürger'? A Skeptical Inquiry," *Modern Language Notes* 101 (1986), pp. 609-628.

50. Sammons acutely observes the tension between Heine's simultaneous globalism and self-absorption: "His was an imperial mind, colonizing the otherness of the world for what he regarded as his high vocation," ("Weltbürger," p. 627).

The Polish Question and Heine's Exilic Identity[1]

Jennifer Kapczynski, Kristin Kopp, Paul B. Reitter, Daniel Sakaguchi

Introduction

Contestedness is difficult to measure. But certainly Heine's relation to exile must count as one of the most contested aspects of his identity. Critics from Börne through Kraus to Bartels and his nationalist acolytes in the 1920s and 1930s argued that Heine's exile exerted a deleterious influence on his writing. French literary ways and mores infiltrated Heine's prose, rendering it facile and superficial, in other words, un-German. As Kraus put it, "And even in the style of the most modern impressionist poetry the presence of Heine's model is undeniable. That is the French disease that he schlepped home to us."[2]

This reading of Heine's exile has, thankfully, fallen out of favor. For obvious reasons, Kraus's remarks would be considered more incendiary today than they were when he published them. And so, if critics exist who subscribe to Kraus's views they have long maintained a tactful silence.

For equally obvious reasons, exile theory took major steps forward during and after World War II. The compensatory moment in exile, the "second sight" of the exiled thinker, came to be emphasized. Witness Erich Kahler's passionate post-war claims about the link between exile and authentic critical acumen. Or consider Brecht's strikingly, strangely, buoyant comments, made during his own exile:

> Emigration is the best school of dialectics. Refugees are the keenest dialecticians. They are refugees as a result of change and their sole object of study is change. They are able to deduce the greatest events from the smallest hints—that is, if they have intelligence. When their opponents are winning they calculate how much their victory has cost them; and they have the sharpest eye for contradictions, Long live dialectics![3]

In this theoretical context, the effect of Heine's exile took on an overwhelming positive resonance for almost everyone writing on Heine except Adorno. Critics like A. I. Sandor and Marcel Reich-Ranicki stressed and continue to stress the perspicacity of Heine's exilic vision.

The connection between exile and insight had of course been thematized before World War II. Indeed, Heine himself frequently discussed the question of exile in just such terms. And these discussions often figure prominently in contemporary readings of Heine's exile; Heine's own interpretation of exile is appropriated as a kind of poignant immanent hermeneutics by critics as they interpret his exile. This procedure has carried with it certain problematic concomitants. Critics who invoke Heine's theory of exile to reinforce their own theory of exile have tended to press his views aggressively into the service of theirs. Heine's very nuanced, anti-programmatic interpretation of exile gets flattened out as it is pushed into line with a program. Take Susan Bernstein's recent article.[4] For poststructuralists of Bernstein's ilk, exile is, paradoxically, a kind of privileged position. Exile corresponds to the key categories of their critical apparatus: displacement, marginality, the essential lack that makes representation possible, and, of course, all things interstitial. Exile is figured as an epistemologically privileged place in the sense that it is from exile, from a place of absence, that the myth of presence can be effectively debunked.

Now no one is denying that there is some substance to this idea. Our aim here is not to challenge Bernstein's theory of exile directly but, rather, to call into question the way in which she applies it to Heine. In Bernstein's article, as elsewhere, I would add, we hear only of the Heine who does not want to return home because he knows, as a proto-poststructuralist, that his critical incisiveness is a function of his exilic status. We hear nothing of the Heine who was a relentless critic of exile culture, of the Heine who incessantly attempted to distinguish between his own exile and other exiles. We hear nothing, in short, of the Heine who strove to develop a differentiated reading of exile. The contention here is that this Heine is worth listening to at a time when formulaic valorizations of exile (culture) like Bernstein's threaten to eviscerate it into a hollow trope. If Brecht is right, if exile fosters, among other things, dialectical thinking, then it would be a sad irony to pursue Heine's exilic identity undialectically.

Scattered throughout Heine's works is a treatment of Polish emigration and emigre culture according to which Polish exiles are somehow both compelling, potentially emancipatory spectacle and farce. Here, then, the contrasting colorations of exile in Heine's writings become manifest. And so we begin by examining the "Polish Question." Our focus will be that strange and slippery late statement on Polish exile: "Two Knights" ("Zwei Ritter"). Following the trajectory of *Ludwig Börne. A Memorial*, we turn from the question of Polish exile to Heine's reading of his own exile, which also moves back and forth between solemnity and sardonicism. Again and again, just as Heine seems ready to affirm his own exile as over and against Börne's bad exile, a disruptive parodistic note enters his discussion. It is very difficult to determine here, "where irony ends and heaven begins" (2: 166), to speak with Heine. The final section of our presentation takes up the question of Jewish exile. Working primarily with *The Rabbi of Bacherach*, we will try to show how Jewish exile manages to move in two directions at once for Heine. Our argument, then, is that Heine's vision of Jewish exile exhibits the same complexities found in his larger reading of exile and thus reinforces the heterogenous character of this reading. For just as his treatment of Polish exile and exile culture in general is at once disparaging and enthusiastic, in *The Rabbi of Bacherach* Heine criticizes and lionizes diasporic culture in more or less the same breath.

I. Polen. Ein Deutsches Märchen

In her 1991 essay, "Colonialism, Cannibalism, and Literary Incorporation," Susanne Zantop focuses our attention on the intellectual interest of the aging, bedridden Heine. Noting library records that suggest Heine's reading consisted of "histories of discovery and conquest, . . . world travels and. . . colonial endeavors,"[5] Zantop provocatively concludes: "It seems that Heine's own physical decline becomes the point of departure for his renewed preoccupation with the decline of whole peoples and cultures, past and present, in Europe and its colonies."[6] Given this constellation of interests, I am intrigued by the status of the Polish question in Heine's late works. Heine, who is arguably the most differentiated and reflective German author writing on Poland in the nineteenth century, almost completely abandons this subject in his later work.

Indeed, after the 1840 *Börne Memorial*, Heine offers only one final text addressing the Polish question: his poem "Two Knights," published in *Romanzero* in 1851 (6/1: 37-39). The meaning of this poem is highly contested among those scholars who are interested in constructing a narrative of Heine's unique relationship to Poland and the Poles. The resulting discussion is interesting here, as his personal and intellectual relationship to Poland has great relevance to many other contested areas of his life, including his relationship to Judaism, the nature of his relationship with Eugen Breza, and, most important for our current discussion, his relationship to exilic experience.

The poem “Two Knights” was written at a historical moment when Heine was sharing his Parisian exilic with thousands of Poles. In this segment of our paper, I will show how a closer examination of the multiple resonances of this poem problematizes Heine’s views on the situation both of the Pole as well as of exile.

A casual first glance at “Two Knights” is enough to reveal the uphill battle fought by those attempting to locate Heine in any position of unequivocal support for the Poles. The two “knights” depicted in the poem, Polish Parisian exiles, bear the speaking names of *Krapulinski* and *Waschlapski*, and live up to them. They exhibit a counter-intuitive blend of irresponsible aristocratic decadence, slovenly lack of personal hygiene, and devious financial mismanagement, all accompanied by copious alcohol consumption and a homoeroticized portrayal of Polish cultural practice.

Given such a compromised portrayal of these Polish figures, it would be easy to locate this later work within the powerful anti-Slavic backlash that hit Germany in the 1840s. After all, Heine’s poem appeared just four years prior to Gustav Freytag’s *Debit and Credit* (*Soll und Haben*) and seems to share its discourse vis-à-vis the Pole, one that can be captured in the sound-bite “polnische Wirtschaft.”[7]

It would be a mistake, however, to dismiss this poem as part of the reactionary backlash to Poles without taking into account the other complex literary and historical resonances it possesses. To appreciate its context we need an understanding of German-Polish interactions in the period immediately preceding the appearance of Heine’s poem.

When, in November of 1830, the Poles in Warsaw launched an uprising against their Russian occupiers, they became the obsessive focus of German liberal attention. As newspapers delivered accounts of the event’s developments, sympathizers across Germany discussed the news, cheering the progress of the Poles. From the Berlin salon of the Varnhagens to the provincial reading room to the Leipzig café of Richard Wagner’s student days,[8] the “revolution” in Poland captured the imagination of the Germans.

Private support manifested itself publicly in the rapid establishment of *Polenvereine* (organizations for the support of the Poles) across Germany. Their original objective of arranging shipments of supplies to the uprisers was rapidly abandoned when the Russians squelched the insurrection, sending its leaders into exile. During the winter of 1831-32, when some seven to eight thousand Poles trekked through German territory on their way to France, the *Polenvereine* rushed to organize transportation, meals, housing, and supplies for these exiles. Meanwhile, in city after city, the

German populace welcomed the arrival of the Poles, celebrating their journey as if it were a victory march, and not one of defeat.

This enormous enthusiasm was due to the widespread support of German liberals, who projected theirs own revolutionary desire onto the newly-adopted "Polish brothers." Under the strict censorship laws of the post-Karlsbad Restoration period, speech concerning the Polish uprising served as the site of transference for an otherwise silenced desire for effective change in Germany. The emotional impact of the resulting response is evidenced not only in the material effort undertaken on behalf of the Polish insurrectors themselves, but also in the explosive proliferation of poems about Poland *(Polenlieder)*, which gave expression to the strong reaction at home in Germany.

The *Polenlied* was a lyrical genre, recognizable mainly in its fixed set of tropes, most notably that of the "noble Pole" fighting for his nation's freedom against "Russian tyranny."[9] This Pole was an undifferentiated figure that appeared suddenly in the German imagination—and disappeared just as quickly a few years later, at around the time when the German liberals came to realize that granting Poland autonomy would mean giving them back some significant portion of the land which Prussia had seized in the annexations from 1772 to 1795.

Despite this radical change of sentiment, the Germans could not rid themselves of the memory of their pro-Polish euphoria, as it had been captured in an estimated one thousand *Polenlieder* written by some three hundred poets, including von Platen, Lenau, Gutzkow, Herwegh, Freiligrath, Grabbe, Schubart, Uhland, Laube, and Anastasius Grün; even writers whom one would not have expected to be enthusiastic for the Polish cause, such as Grillparzer, Droste-Hülshof, and Hebbel, made contributions to this genre.[10] These poems served as social currency, marking membership within a larger political sentiment. Many *Polenlieder* were set to music, sung at significant political events, and thus established themselves as folksongs.[11] A memory of the events of the early 1830s therefore lingered in the air for quite some time.

That Heine did not write a *Polenlied* in the 1830's is, on the one hand, quite understandable. A genre so dominated by Platen and the Swabian romantics was bound to cause Heine to distance himself as much as possible from it.[12]

On the other hand, however, Heine's relative silence during this period is surprising, due to his unique past relationship with Poland. During a period when German texts on Poland were growing in popularity, yet exceedingly formulaic, Heine was singular in his open-minded, critically inquisitive approach. In this regard his essay *On Poland* is of central importance. Written in response to a trip Heine took to Poland to visit his friend, Eugen Breza, in 1822, this essay engages and critically contests a well-established set of notions and stereotypes regarding the Poles. It was the most important work to do so prior to the 1830s, and is monumental in this respect. Heine's ability to create a new language with which to discuss the Pole is in part due to the underlying function of his appraisals. Heine's statements about Poland, after all, were meant to serve as veiled criticisms of the then-current situation in Prussia. The very title of the essay, as been Jost Hermand has pointed out,[13] is itself already a provocation, since Poland recently ceased to exist as a political entity due to the division and annexation of the country by Prussia, Austria and Russia.

Given Heine's specific early interest, one would expect to find, if not the unbridled support evinced by his contemporaries, then at least a critical appraisal of the events related to the November uprising; but neither is present in his writings. Early in 1831, Heine buries comments about the events in Poland in two articles discussing the situation in France, but even here he does not directly state his views on either the situation of the Polish exiles or the German response to them. This silence is even more pronounced in Heine's text, *From the Memoirs of Herr von Schnabelewopski*. This fragmentary work has been characterized convincingly as a heterobiography, in which Heine merges versions of himself and the above-mentioned Eugen Breza in the figure of Schnabelewopski, a Polish Jew.[14] Schnabelewopski travels from Poland through Germany to Holland in a time frame roughly matching that of Heine's own movements, but interestingly Heine stops short of his current situation. If Heine is using the figure of Schnabelewopski to investigate aspects of his own identity, or to try to imagine that of Eugen Breza, then it is interesting that he does not imagine this conglomerate figure existing as an exile in Paris, despite the fact that both he and Breza were in Paris in 1834, when he reworked and published this text.

It will, in fact, take Heine almost a decade to write his first statement synthesizing his experience of these events of the early 1830s, and it will take two decades for Heine to publish his version of the *Polenlied*. It is in this context that we must approach the poem "Two Knights."

That Heine was frustrated by the conduct of many of the Polish exiles with whom he came into contact in Paris is well-documented. This frustration has led some scholars to focus solely on the offensive rhetoric and to dismiss this poem as an ill-executed *anti-Polenlied*. But for this function, the poem arguably arrives twenty years too late. Surely, if rendering a criticism of the activities of the Polish exiles were his sole motive, a different generic form would have been a better vehicle for his message. Reading this text simply as a negative *Polenlied* only raises the question of why Heine would make use of this particular genre at all.

My argument is that the historic *form* of the *Polenlied* is itself the site of a memory of the role this genre once played in German consciousness, and that this memory must be an integral part of any reading of this text.

Like the essay *On Poland*, the title of the poem "Two Knights" itself maintains an ironic tension with the main body of the work.[15] The title conjures a romantic regression into the medieval world of knights and chivalrous adventure, an image obviously at great odds with the figures of Krapulinski and Waschlapski. Perhaps this title functions not only as a conjuring but as a summons, and Heine is addressing those who had previously used such medieval imagery to exalt the Poles, evoking not only a memory of the events, but also the specifically sentimental, Romantic *Polenschwärmerei* that arose in response those events, and that was expressed through the vehicle of the *Polenlied*.

Understanding this multiple meaning of the formal genre also places the language of the poem in a new tension. Heine does not infuse this reappropriated form with a random assemblage of slanderous language, but instead draws heavily on the traditional German "Polonist" discourse. The rhetoric of this discourse identified an uncultured, yet decadent and wasteful Polish aristocracy, which was destroying that country's natural resources and oppressing its backward, squalid peasantry. This "understanding" of the Other served as a justification for Prussia's colonization of Poland at the end of the eighteenth century: if Poland could not take care of herself, then Prussia was doing her people a favor, while at the same time protecting herself from what threatened to become an unbuffered border with Russia. The temporary suspension and inversion of this discourse resulted in the image of the "noble Pole" in the 1830s; the more traditional rhetoric, as noted above, was then firmly reinstated in the debates in the late 1840s concerning the boundaries of a projected German state.

By this time, German liberals had realized that the goal of their formerly exalted "noble Poles," namely the nationalist project of establishing an independent Poland, would involve a major German loss of colonized territory in the East. Many who had seen the Polish uprisers as their spiritual brothers now found it advantageous to remobilize the former version of the weak, degenerate Pole who needed strong neighborly safe-keeping (Lenau stands out in particular in this regard). It is from this reinstated anti-Slavic discourse that Heine takes the stereotype of alcoholic excess, financial mismanagement, and decadent aristocracy found in his poem.

In adopting the earlier form of the *Polenlied*, emptying it of its content of enthusiasm for Poland (*Polenbegeisterung*), and reinfusing it with a new content based on the current discourse vis-à-vis Poland, Heine is making a deft statement about the initial meaninglessness and blind interchangeablity of the genre. He is criticizing those who now so easily turn their backs on their earlier convictions, while at the same time showing how shallow those convictions were.

But underneath this criticism of the former *Polenschwärmer* lies a critique of the basic exilic behavior of the Poles, indeed, perhaps of the exilic situation in general. For underneath the slanderous language, we are still left with a narrative of two exiles who waste their time in Paris and wait for the arrival of the next generation to take up the struggle. For Heine, it is not enough that these Polish exiles fought against the tyranny of the Russians if all they do now is bide their time in Paris. Perhaps underlying Heine's disgust at the Poland fanatics (*Polenschwärmer*) and the Poles themselves is a questioning of his own exilic identity, a questioning of the degree to which he himself is waiting for the next generation to carry his torch.

Where does such a reading leave us? Is Heine this time using Poles as a foil for his own personal message? If so, perhaps the reason Heine's imagination shies away from the Poles in his later life is that they have come to represent for him weaknesses that, indeed, fall too close to home.

II. Poetic Exile?

In what follows, I wish to point out Heine's ambivalence to exile, his wariness of its seductive and romantic aesthetic, and his double-edged means of expressing how he felt about it.

Judging from what he did write in the early 1830s, Heine was enthusiastic about Poland's uprising and despondent when Warsaw fell. His despairing solidarity, voiced in *French Painters* of 1831 (3: 69), lies at quite a remove from his disparaging remarks about Polish exiles in the third book of the *Ludwig Börne Memorial*, a work that, we would do well to remember, was completed at the end of 1839. Once supportive of the revolutionaries, Heine takes a skeptical tone when commenting on the overly enthusiastic fanaticism (*Schwärmerei*) that prevailed in Germany as the beaten survivors made their way through to Paris. German daughters are seduced by woeful tales told by Polish knights beneath the moonlight, and mothers are scandalized by visions of the Tsar eating Polish children. Or in Heine's words,

> The German mothers fearfully clasped their hands over their heads when they heard that Tsar Nicholas, the cannibal, would eat three small Polish children each morning, completely raw, with oil and vinegar. But most deeply smitten were our young maidens, as they lay in the moonlight against the heroic breasts of the Polish martyrs and wailed and wept with them over the fall of Warsaw and the victory of the Russian barbarians. (4: 78)

In comparison to the enthusiastic *Polenlieder* of the early thirties, Heine's much later reception is mostly dry, only sappy—that is to say, dressed up with oil and vinegar under the moonlight—when he wishes to make a critical point. The sorrowful spectacle—Heine uses the word *Anblick*—of exile radicalized many a sympathizer, he observes, as Germany came closest to revolution in the wake of the Polish processions of mourning (*Trauerzüge*). And yet the Poles, Heine insists, were ill-equipped for revolution, as least as unready as the Germans themselves were, and would have only inspired further tragedy if Germans had followed their lead. "A revolution is a misfortune," writes Heine, "but an even greater misfortune is a failed revolution; and it was with the latter sort that the emigration of these Nordic friends threatened us. They would have brought that same confusion and unreliability into our affairs through which they themselves went to ruin" (4: 78-79). The danger of premature revolution in Germany as portrayed by Heine calls attention to a perhaps more overarching danger: if exile is aestheticized, and viewed as compelling in and of itself, the effect can be blinding. Heine does not shy away from aestheticizing experiences; that is not the point. But all modes of aesthetic reception are not alike, and clearly ones that pay adequate attention to complexity and contradiction are more favorable to Heine. In his estimation of the German scene vis-à-vis the Polish exile, Heine seems to say that not all suffering leads to wisdom, but often only leads to more suffering.

Heine underscores his point a few pages later. A walk in the Tuilleries sets the stage for one of Börne's sermons, in this case, a rhapsodic flurry of speech that begins with a dream about unwary turtles marked for death, sweeps through the dreadful subject of exile, and ends with the proclamation that Paris' holy stones and freedom trees have more to teach about human martyrdom than all the history professors in Berlin and Göttingen. Yet at the point where the speech should have reached its climax, a rotten branch falls from a so-called "freedom tree," striking the rapt and slow-moving Börne on the hand with a ponderous and prosaic thud. "Börne, who did not rescue himself as quickly as I, was wounded on the hand by a twig of falling branch and muttered peevishly, 'A bad sign'"(4: 88). Heine's message is this: Börne may know the sorrows of exile, but this knowledge has not necessarily sharpened his critical acumen; he is certainly not the agile figure that Heine depicts himself to be.

The question arises: How does Heine manage to present his own exile in a way that is neither uncritical nor demagogic? To be honest, he does not entirely manage this. In book five of the Börne *Memorial*, Heine sets himself apart from other exiles because he is a poet. It is his extraordinary sensibility that allows him no refuge, he claims; hence he is doubly exiled, even from his fellow exiles. In contrast to the poet in exile, political prisoners in Germany are happy, because they hear German spoken, the poor in exile are fortunate, because they need only struggle with hunger, the insane are blissful with their delusions, and the dead, like Börne, are the luckiest of all. "Perhaps you have a conception of bodily exile, however only a German poet can imagine spiritual exile, who would see himself forced to speak French every day, to write, and even to sigh at night at his lover's breast in French. Even my thoughts are exiled, exiled in a foreign language" (4: 124)

We do not have to look far to find reason to read Heine's lamentations somewhat ironically. According to Heine, it was Börne who complained that he would be unhappy even in heaven, where the angels would not speak German: "they speak no German, and smoke no cigars" (4: 86). And it was in this same speech that Börne claimed to envy the failed republicans: "Ach! how I envy the French Republicans! For they suffer in the fatherland" (4: 87). I have already described how this speech ended, so unceremoniously, with a literal slap on the wrist. In his own complaints about exile, Heine seems to parody Börne to a certain extent. When Heine compares his spiritual exile to exiles in which hunger and poverty are of chief concern—"O golden misery with white kid gloves, how infinitely more torturous you are!" (4: 124)—this is hardly a line to be read seriously. Or is it? There is a refined edge to be found even in this last quote. Despite the hyperbole, the finesse, there is at the same time the message that exile is indeed hell. Whereas his not-so-flattering imitations of Börne do indeed pose a critique and a differentiated reading of exile, it seems that Heine uses what I have just called a parody to express also more straightforward feelings without irony. In this way, his complaints about exile serve as a vehicle for his criticism while carrying a note of confession or self-implication at the same time.

Heine's Börne is a cigar-smoking, egalitarian demagogue, not a poet, and it is poetry that underwrites Heine's claim to a differentiated and tragic exile, even or perhaps especially when he uses parody to express it. This is not to say that his claim is necessarily valid, but it certainly is well written.[16] Börne declares that even the stones and trees offer testimony to mankind's martyrdom, and yet he cannot distinguish a rotten branch from a symbol of freedom. Heine, too, is inclined to read the stories that stones tell, as the next section of our paper will show, but he also wants to be seen as the better and more dialectical reader.

If we go back to the third book of the *Memorial*, to Heine's disparaging comments on Polish exiles and their uncritical reception in Germany, we may see a positive note as well. "I am speaking of 1831 and 1832," he begins. "Since then eight years have flowed by, and just as the heroes of the German tongue, the Poles have had some bitter but useful experiences, and many of them have been able to use the muse of exile to study civilization. Misfortune has schooled them, and they have been able to learn something worthwhile." In passing, he adds this remark: "As once Israel after the fall of Jerusalem, so perhaps after the fall of Warsaw will Poland raise itself to the highest of destinies" (4: 81)

III. Situating Exile: *The Rabbi of Bacherach*

As in the discussions of Polish exile, Heine's depiction of Jewish exile in his unfinished work *The Rabbi of Bacherach* is characterized as much by pettiness as by greatness. And although, as in the Börne *Memorial*, Heine suggests the possibility of a positive, fruitful exile, it is not offered as the certain or even likely outcome. Earlier segments of this paper argue against a simplistic view of Heine's relationship to Polish exile. I will argue that much ambiguity is also found in his relationship to Jewish exile. I will also make an argument for viewing exile as a situated experience, through the issue of the landscape's importance in the construction of exile. *The Rabbi of Bacherach* offers a view of history as complex and multi-layered, and perhaps the most significant site of these historical layers is found in the landscape.

In her recent article in *New German Critique*, Susan Bernstein suggests that for Heine the *Heimat* is a sort of utopian "no place"—in both senses of the word. She writes: "His metaphorical homeland portends to no actualization and remains strictly an image named as such. The German poet is merely a name, a set of signifiers with a hollow resonance, pointing to no interior substance."[17] This reading, while somewhat seductive, misses something when it conflates Heine's notion of a poetic realm with the homeland. Such an approach elides any distinction between "material and metaphorical space."[18] Here I should note that this sort of elision is an unfortunately widespread phenomenon, by no means limited to Bernstein's article. The emphasis on the metaphoric significance of exile over a discussion of its material aspects has important consequences, for euphoric declarations about the liminal position afforded by exile often overlook its frequently devastating causes and results. Such readings overlook—if they do not outright override—the significance of the spatial as well as political aspects of exile.

Rather than conflate the material and metaphorical, I would insist on maintaining the distinctions and interconnections of these spaces. Heine's idea of exile as expressed in *The Rabbi of Bacherach* is rooted in real places, and this rootedness has important implications. Borrowing a term from feminist theory—"situated practice"—I will contend that Heine's view of exile should be understood as dialectical and situated: exile constitutes a moment that is both dynamic and bound up with specificities of time and place.[19]

The aborted novel begins with a view of the town of Bacherach, a view that gives an account of both its present dilapidation and its former glory, of the political and religious history of the town. Thus the castle ruins that line the river are revealed as monuments to the instigators of mass killings of Jews in the Middle Ages. In a similar passage later in the text, Heine describes the state of the medieval Jewish ghetto in Frankfurt, which is not yet the ramshackle heap of buildings it will become in his day.

These passages resonate with one out of the *Börne Memorial*. Heine accompanies Börne on a trip through the Jewish ghetto. Börne bemoans the glorification of the Middle Ages and remarks: "... where the dead are silent, the living stones speak all the louder." Heine then notes that: "Indeed the houses of that street gazed upon me, as though they wanted to tell me sorrowful tales. Tales that one knows, but does not want to know, or that one would rather forget than recall to memory" (4: 22).

This historically informed perspective has two implications. First, it offers a view of the landscape as imbued with history. It is not simply an empty location in which events unfold, but rather marked by events. The landscape bears the traces of the human structures within it, which one must simply know how to read; in fact, the landscape seems veritably to speak. Second, the omnipresent view permits an acknowledgment of change through time, a point to which I will later return.

During Sara and Abraham's flight up the Rhine, Sara lapses into a kind of reverie—at times comforting, at times nightmarish—which also incorporates several different moments in time. Memories from her childhood, images from the Hagadah, of the Bacherach community, and of the landscape of the Rhine are woven together in her dreams. While the narrative certainly draws a connection between their sudden exile and a broader history of Jewish oppression, it also connects Jewish and German cultural traditions: the Rhine, ever-popular symbol of Germany, and not the Red Sea, whispers the melody of the Hagadah. As tradition shapes her memory and understanding, so too does Sara's presence in Germany.

These images of the landscape in the frame text and in Sara's dreams suggest that German and Jewish history and cultural traditions cannot be separated from one another, but rather are interwoven, integrated on the level of memory, on the level of literature, and on the level of landscape. This integration, however, must not be viewed as a static relationship, which brings me back to my discussion of the omnipresent narrator's insight into the changes that have occurred through time.

There are several significant changes the narrator brings to light, notably the gradual deterioration of the town of Bacherach and the increasing dilapidation of the Jewish ghetto in Frankfurt. Following the description of the none-too-innocent ruins peppering the Rhine, the narrator observes: "But the more the Jews of Bacherach were visited by hatred from without, the closer, the more intimate grew their domestic life, the firmer their piety and fear of God" (1: 463).[20] The cohesion of the Jewish community, established in relationship to outside pressures and not simply born from within, resonates in another passage in the text, whose subject is the Frankfurt ghetto:

> For in those days the houses in the Jewish quarter were still trim and new, and much lower than they are now; it was only later, when their numbers multiplied and they were prevented from extending the Jews' quarter, that the Jews of Frankfurt commenced to build one story upon another, and pressed together like sardines—and in this way were crippled both in body and soul. (1: 486)

In both these passages the narrator makes clear that the community is both physically and spiritually shaped by forces from without. These outside forces may exercise both a positive and negative influence—the community is spiritually enriched in one moment, spiritually impoverished in the next. The Jewish community is not simply constructed by outside forces, however; note, for example, the edict passed down through the family of Bacherach rabbis, to remain in Bacherach unless confronted with mortal danger. The pressures from within the community shift and seem always to be in relation to the pressures from without.

The positive and negative aspects of exile are again highlighted through the issue of childlessness in the text. Significantly, Sara is unable to conceive; unlike their Biblical namesakes, Sara and Abraham do not seem likely to found a Jewish line, although the Jewish community is hardly without progeny: "The cantor took the book as if it were really a child, a child for whose sake much has been suffered, and which is, for that reason, all the more precious. He rocked it in his arms, dandled it, pressed it to his heart (1: 488-89). The child-like status of the book is emphasized again when the book is unwrapped from its covering of a "Mäntelchen," meaning "cover" but also "jacket," and "Windeln," meaning "wrapping" but also "swaddling cloth" or "diaper" (1: 489).

Again Heine provides a conflicting image of exile; for while it may not result in a physical regeneration, it does seem to encourage spiritual and intellectual growth (though never in an unqualified fashion). Heine alludes to this aspect of exile again in Book III ("Hebrew Melodies") of *Romanzero*, where the Hagadah is likened to a garden, another image of fecundity (6/I: 132).

Heine's idea of exile is fundamentally dialectical: born of conflict, produced from within and without, and simultaneously positive and negative. Exile emerges from both a dialogue between the present and the past, and as the result of pressures from inside and outside of the parameters of the Jewish community. This conflict does not find resolution, is not fixed. The significance of this lack of resolution should not be underestimated: it reveals the borders and limits of exile and isolation as flexible, as always in the process of being produced. Rather than an exile that bases itself exclusively on an historical tradition of diaspora, it is created through situated practice—that is, practice linked to specific locations and historical moments. Thus although exile in this text is not fixed, it is not a "homeless" exile of purely metaphoric content.

Heine's text indicates a real concern with a particular presence. While in Heine's writing Germany is not simply synonymous with "Heimat," it is clear that his historical and geographical situatedness were significant in the construction of *Heimat* and in figuring the parameters of exile. Although its meaning is unstable, there is a real place to which Heine refers in *The Rabbi of Bacherach*: the specific landscape that "speaks" the history of German-Jewish relations.

Conclusion

Heine's relation to exile—the effect of exile on his writing and his reading of exile, in short, his exilic identity—has long been debated. What has gotten lost in the noise of programmatic polemics against and valorizations of Heine's exile is the paratactic tension or dialectical resonances that make Heine's reading of exile so richly nuanced. These nuances need to be brought to light. The three significant moments in Heine's writings on exile we have analyzed—his representations of Polish exile culture, of his own exile, and of Jewish exile—are pervaded by irony, ambiguities, and ambivalences. The bombastic poem "Two Knights" can be read in antipodally opposed ways: as a chauvinistic indictment of Polish emigres in Paris and as a caricature of such indictments, as, in other words, an indictment of an indictment. Both readings are available, for the poem maintains a subtly ironic distance to the crude invective it launches. Paradoxically enough, then, Heine positions himself here as both a critic and a defender of exile culture. These countervailing tendencies in Heine's writings on Polish emigration persist after the failed revolution. Indeed, Heine's treatment of Polish exile in *Ludwig Börne: A Memorial* exhibits the same radical movement we find in "Two Knights." Heine's reading of his own exile is just as complex. While Heine sets up a crude dichotomy pitting Börne's rabble-rousing exile against his own exalted poetic exile, when we look closely at the Börne *Memorial*, we see that Heine subjects both his critique of Börne's exile and his self-flattering vision of a poetic exile to a destabilizing irony. Finally Heine's representation of Jewish exile in *The Rabbi of Bacherach* is dialectical in the sense that it moves back and forth between lamenting the state of Jewish culture in exile and emphasizing its positive possibilities. At issue here is also the historical specificity of exile culture. In response to recent poststructuralist readings of Heine's exile, according to which the homeland is exposed as illusory and the universality of exile is acknowledged, we contend that for Heine exile is embedded in a historically specific, sensuously particular landscape. To lose sight of Heine's sensitivity to the materiality of exile is to attenuate his exilic vision. For precisely the process situating exile within a specific historical landscape or context makes substantive critical reflection on exile possible. As we have tried to show, in Heine's case this kind of critical reflection yielded a pointed dialectical reading of exile culture, one that should not, indeed cannot, be reduced to a simple theoretical formula.

Notes

1. Paul B. Reitter wrote the introduction and conclusion to this paper; Kristin Kopp wrote "Polen. Ein Deutsches Märchen"; Daniel Sakaguchi "Poetic Exile"; and Jennifer Kapczynski "Situating Exile: *Der Rabbi von Bacherach.*"

2. Karl Kraus, "Heine und die Folgen," *Gesammelte Schriften*, ed. Christian Wagenknecht (Frankfurt/Main, 1989), vol. 4, p. 186: "Und selbst im Stil der modernsten Impressionslyrik verleugnet sich das Heinesche Modell nicht. Ohne Heine kein Feuilleton. Das ist die Franzosenkrankeit, die er uns eingeschleppt hat."

3. Quoted in Martin Jay, *Permanent Exiles: Essays on the Intellectual Migration to America* (Columbia, 1986) p. 28.

4. Cf. "Susan Bernstein, "Journalism and German Identity: Communiqués from Heine, Wagner, and Adorno," *New German Critique* Nr. 66 (Fall 1995) pp. 65-93.

5. Susanne Zantop, "Colonialism, Cannibalism, and Literary Incorporation: Heine in Mexico," *Heinrich Heine and the Occident: Multiple Identities, Multiple Receptions*, ed. Sander Gilman and Peter Uwe Hohendahl (Nebraska, 1991) p. 110.

6. Zantop, p. 110.

7. A pejorative term which translates as "Polish (lack of) economic management" or "Polish (lack of) housekeeping."

8. *Dokumente zur Geschichte der deutsch-polnischen Freundschaft 1830-1832*, ed. Helmut Bleiber and Jan Kosim (Berlin, 1982) p. 455ff.

9. For a critical discussion of the tropes of the *Polenlieder*, see: Marek Jaroszewski, "Der Novemberaufstand von 1839-31 in der deutschen Polenlyrik," *Germanica Wratislawiensia* 45 (1981), pp. 3-29.

10. See Gerard Koziolek ed, *Polenlieder: Eine Anthologie* (Stuttgart, 1982).

11. See, for example, Günter Berndt and Reinhard Strecker ed., *Polen—ein Schauermärchen oder Gehirnwäsche für Generationen: Geschichtsschreibung und Schulbücher: Beiträge zum Polenbild der Deutschen* (Reinbeck bei Hamburg, 1971), pp. 19-21 for a discussion of the role *Polenlieder* played in May of 1832 at the Hambach Festival staged by republican nationalists such as Philipp Jakob Siebenpfeiffer and Johann Georg August Wirth.

12. I thank Jeffrey Sammons for pointing out that Platen's own *Polenlieder* were not published until 1839, and thus the poems themselves would not have played a role for Heine in the early 1830's. Platen, however, was perhaps the most dominant figure in the *Polenlieder* movement, and it is thus highly probable that Heine was aware of his activities. See: Ernst Josef Krzywon, *Heinrich Heine und Polen* (Vienna, 1972) p. 345.

13. Jost Hermand, *Der frühe Heine: Ein Kommentar zu den "Reisebildern"* (Munich, 1976), p. 44.

14. Krzywon, pp. 272-290.

15. Cf. Helga Whiton, *Der Wandel des Polenbildes in der deutschen Literatur des 19. Jahrhunderts* (Bern, 1981), p. 155.

16. When Heinrich Laube reproached Heine for his dangerous confusion of the political and personal in this book, Heine replied, "But is it not well-phrased?" ("Aber ist's nicht schön ausgedrückt?"). In Michael Werner, ed., *Begegnungen mit Heine: Beritchte der Zeitgenossen* (Hamburg, 1973), vol. 1, p. 417.

17. Bernstein, p. 92.

18. I have borrowed this term from Cindi Katz and Neil Smith, cited in Matthew Sparke, "Displacing the Field in Fieldwork: Masculinity, Metaphor, and Space," in *BodySpace: Destabilizing Geographies of Gender and Sexuality*, ed. Nancy Duncan (New York, 1996), p. 217.

19. "Situated practice" is a term that originates from feminist standpoint theory; however, I am specifically interested in Donna Haraway's notion

of "situated knowledge," as described in her book *Simians, Cyborgs, and Women* (New York, 1991), especially in chapter 9.

20. Translations are from Heinrich Heine, *The Poetry and Prose of Heinrich Heine*, trans. Frederick Ewen (New York, 1948).

Tribune of the People or Aristocrat of the Spirit? Heine's Ambivalence Toward the Masses

Jost Hermand

I

Two views of Heine's relationship to the masses have dominated in literary criticism from the middle of the previous century up to and to some extent past the end of the Cold War. These views differ so extremely that they are often described with the recently fashionable term "binary." Though they tell us little about Heine himself, they are extremely revealing in terms of the strategies of justification used to support different ideological standpoints. The representatives of the one position, extending from *Nachmärz* reactionaries to fin-de-siècle aesthetes, and finally to the cold warriors among the New Critics, were usually out to represent Heine as an inveterate individualist, a hedonistic dandy, or a neurotic aristocrat of the spirit; in short, as an egotist who was only concerned with his own well-being and who despised the masses as crude, boorish, and simple-minded.[1] The proponents of the other position, including voices as diverse as those of the Social Democrat Franz Mehring[2] and GDR scholar Hans Kaufmann,[3] saw in Heine above all the pugnacious enlightener, the tribune of the people, the champion of progress, the friend of Marx who fought not just for the rights of the privileged bourgeois upper classes but who also supported the liberation of oppressed peoples and groups such as the Poles, Jews, Irish, Black slaves, and all the poor of the world, and who toward the end of his life even sympathized with communism.[4] Proponents of both positions aimed to support their points of view with quotes extracted from Heine's oeuvre which most closely matched their own positions, thereby lending to their strategies of justification the necessary scholarly "objectivity."

There is no doubt that such mutually contradictory statements coexist in Heine's works. This is obvious upon even a superficial perusal, and the contradictions persist even when we subject the works to a deeper ideological examination. Yet neither the advocates of the individualist thesis nor the advocates of the populist thesis were especially bothered by this. Imagining themselves in exclusive possession of the "truth," they always saw only that which was easily reconciled with their own political views—and suppressed from the outset anything "disturbing." Thus it is not surprising that as early as the nineteenth century, a new perspective emerged that challenged any such one-sided approach within Heine scholarship and the broader Heine reception. By attempting to emphasize the basic contradiction of Heine's entire existence and underlining his ambivalence toward the so-called masses, this new perspective held that he was a bourgeois left-liberal but fully in accord neither with the "left" nor with the "liberals"; rather, he oscillated constantly and indecisively between these two poles. Yet even within this new perspective two clearly distinct positions can be delineated. Representatives of the one maliciously used Heine's contradictoriness toward the masses only in order to point to his alleged political opportunism, irresponsibility, or superficiality. The others gave it a positive twist to accent his democratic openness and pluralistic way of thinking. Whereas the former defamed Heine as a chameleon-like *filou*, the latter presented him, precisely because of his conspicuous subjectivity, as the perfect example of a good liberal who shied away from all ideological appropriation like Beelzebub from holy water.[5]

Certainly no words need be wasted today against proponents of the opportunism thesis, who up to and through the Third Reich had no qualms about invoking terms such as Jewified, Frenchified, or subversive.[6] Obviously their numbers have dwindled sharply in the face of world-wide revulsion at the atrocities of Auschwitz. By contrast, we have seen a considerable growth in the number of those who regard Heine's alleged fickleness as perfectly acceptable, indeed even exemplary within the context of their own suspicion of ideology and contempt for so-called master discourses. For them, Heine is neither a tribune of the people nor an aristocrat of the spirit, but one of those proverbial liberals who manages to straddle the fence rather comfortably, and from the outset dismisses all political engagement as pointless. Thus Fritz J. Raddatz—in his perennial polemic against any "leftist" appropriation—sees Heine as a thoroughly "unpolitical person" who had nothing to do with "either revolutionaries or democrats or demagogues" and who "avoided any sort of political scribbling" in order to maximize his "freedom of movement" and to remain a "loner."[7] Similar if somewhat more sophisticated statements of this kind can be found in the writings of other advocates of the liberal Heine legend, such as Dolf Sternberger or Marcel Reich-Ranicki. Heine is indeed a "liberal" for all of these critics, but in the end politically uninvolved and disinterested—a prime role model for justifying their own political waffling.[8] In this way, Heine has evolved over the last four decades from a representative of Cold War anti-totalitarianism into a postmodernist.

Those critics who misuse him as a figurehead for their own ideological detachment feel no need to find anything politically relevant in his writings, for they want his world view to exhibit the same uncertain wishy-washy character as their own feuillitonistic chit-chats.

The motives underlying such argumentative strategies are all too obvious. And having established this, we have no need to launch a full basis-superstructure analysis in order to reveal the ideology behind them. Nonetheless, one problem in such an analysis has commonly been overlooked. As the starting point for their claims, not only the advocates of the individualist thesis or the populist thesis but also many of their critics have typically reduced Heine to a radically one-sided author. Seduced by the stylistic unity of his works, they have almost always spoken of a Heine with either an unambiguously individualist or a clearly populist stance; they have developed only those recurrent elements in his works which agree with their model. Though there are such constants in Heine's oeuvre, there are also equally important shifts in ideological emphasis—hardly surprising in an author as eminently interested in the politics of his day as Heine. Many critics, especially those hostile to him, have recognized these shifts, but they have usually used them to demonstrate Heine's alleged "opportunism" and unreliability.

The uncovering of this contradiction brings us to a point where a new approach is needed in order to advance fruitfully our reflections and debates. This new approach consists in realizing that when Heine changes politically, he hardly ever does so opportunistically, but almost always situationally. In other words, he consistently proceeds, within the limits of his perspective, from the shifting social situation at any given time. Rather than poutingly withdrawing to the sidelines after individual failures, he remains steadfastly committed to the possibility of political progress, of more inclusive social justice, and of more comprehensive individual liberation. Moreover, in doing so he adopts the newest philosophical and political theories that could advance such social aims. Seen in this way, it is not so much the differing ideological contents that are the decisive factor or standard in judging Heine, but rather the single engaged "stance" underlying them. There are, therefore, no dogmas, no orthodoxies, and no rigidly fixed utopias in his works, but only a constant changeablitiy, always rooted, however, in the same emancipatory intention.

In the following essay, I will try not to drift off into pointless byways of intellectual history or structuralism by alternately celebrating or condemning Heine as either solely tribune of the people or solely aristocrat of the spirit. Rather, I will first offer a short outline of his socio-political views, keeping in mind the question of his possible readiness to take part in a revolution for the benefit of the socially disadvantaged and the ideological consequences derived from this readiness. Given the sheer breadth of the topic "Heine's ambivalence toward the masses," this will not be possible without a few over-simplifications, despite all efforts to remain as concrete as possible. Such a historical outline must nevertheless be attempted so that the arguments that follow may have a real foundation. By and large, one can distinguish roughly five phases in Heine's life and work: 1) the early period in Germany, i.e., the years before the Paris July revolution of 1830; 2) the first years in Paris between 1831 and 1835; 3) the period from the ban on Young Germany in 1835 until the onset of the *Vormärz* unrest after 1840; 4) the period directly before the Paris February/German March revolution of 1848; and 5) the period after the failed revolution, that is, the period until Heine's death in 1856.

II

As early as the 1820s, Heine developed a highly critical perspective on contemporary social conditions around him. As a Rhinelander with direct and positive experience of the Napoleonic *Code civile* who was later obliged to become Prussian, as a son of a Jewish textile merchant in Düsseldorf, as a business apprentice in Frankfurt, as nephew of a rich Hamburg banker who financed his studies, and as a student of Hegel in Berlin, he had received substantially deeper insight into the political, social, and economic life of the times than most other young writers of his era. Admittedly, Heine's first priority was "literature," but a literature that he never detached from its social basis or let slip into the non-committal vagueness of mere daydreams. Even his earliest writings—such as the "Letters from Berlin," the essay "On Poland," the "Harz Journey," the "Northsea III," the "Book Le Grand," the "Journey from Munich to Genoa," as well as the subsequent "Travel Sketches"—fairly burst with politically subversive passages in which Heine attempted to rebel against the oligarchic politics of the Metternich Restoration, that is, against the continued dominance of nobility and church. Whereas in the beginning, during his studies in Bonn, nationalistic tones occasionally surface,[9] after his semesters in Berlin a definite turn toward liberalism and cosmopolitanism, toward "Washingtonian freedom" becomes evident (2:

81). Instead of setting his sights solely on the liberation of Germany, as the "dilettantes of the revolution" among the Germanophile fraternity members had done, Heine already supported in these years the liberation of the Poles, Jews, Irish, Italians, and the Black slaves of America with equal fervor (2: 47). Indeed, through his consideration of these cases, Heine arrived at a model of dialectically unfolding history. He was not inspired by any uncontrolled emotional exuberance, but firmly grounded in the highly circumspect insight that every historical process of development, even as it enters a state of change and despite any tendency toward revolution, always contains within itself counter-revolutionary elements, and that true historical progress arises only through a synthesis of these two forces. Heine attempted to illustrate this through the example of Napoleon in "North Sea III" (2: 235).

A noticeable radicalization of these emancipatory hopes began in Paris in 1830 with the outbreak of the July revolution, which Heine consistently portrayed as one of the most important, if not the most important formative event of his life. Elated by the news from Paris, which reached him on Helgoland in August of 1830, he was delighted by the fisherman who assured him full of pride: "The poor people have won!" (4: 54), and was at the same time deeply gratified that this time in Paris there was no recurrence of the "mad terror" that had marred the Jacobin rule of 1793/94. Indeed, so much did he identify with this revolution that in the end he wrote jubilantly: "I am all joy and song, all sword and flame!" (4: 53). Heine suppressed for the time being his subliminal fear of the masses, whom he had initially observed with a certain mistrust. As a bourgeois intellectual and simultaneously as a Jewish outsider, he was wary of the masses' underdeveloped intellectual state that could so easily result in political unpredictability, particularly after this had been demonstrated by the German Hep-Hep pogroms of 1819.

This change of mood becomes especially evident in the two last pieces Heine wrote while still in Germany, between the outbreak of the July revolution of 1830 and his move to Paris in May of 1831. For example, in the conclusion to the fourth volume of the *Travel Sketches*, written in November 1830, he regretted that no revolution had yet occurred in Germany, and that the henchmen of the Restoration were already preparing to lock the "poor German people" within "prison walls" even thicker than before (2: 603). He wrote in yet sharper tones in his introduction to the pamphlet *Kahldorf Concerning the Nobility*, published in March 1831. Here he reproached German princes for keeping the masses in a condition of "mental immaturity" through their rigid censorship (2: 658), which might, he warned, have very bitter consequences one day. "Darkness," he wrote, often "does more harm than passion." The less certain "views and opinions" are discussed beforehand, the more "violently and horribly" they could later "influence the blind populace," or they might even be "used as battle cries by the parties." For this reason, Heine argued, nothing could be more beneficial than the introduction of freedom of the press. As proof of this, Heine provocatively pointed to the Paris revolution, which, he held, was carried out with "legendary moderation and touching humanity" (2: 660).

Once he arrived in Paris, Heine realized sadly just how little his characterization of the 1830 Revolution corresponded with reality. After all, the upper middle class, not the "poor people" had been victorious there. This was progressive insofar as it represented a defeat of the prior rule of nobility and church, but at the same time it reinforced all Heine's prejudices against monied magnates, who had rankled him already in Hamburg with their ostentation and philistinism. Moreover, the "poor" of Paris proved to be in no way practitioners of "legendary moderation and touching humanity," as he had previously believed, but were rather uncouth. They were urbanites who did not shy away from even the most rude speech and behavior, all of which was fairly shocking to a sensitive writer like the young Heine.

In order to salvage some revolutionary emancipatory hopes for a general liberalization of conditions, however, Heine took refuge in subsequent years in the anti-authoritarian utopia of Saint-Simonism, replacing socio-economic goals with sensual and erotic ones. Accordingly, rebellious sensuality, a desire for pleasure, and aesthetic raptures are common topics in his writings between 1832 and 1835. Against the backdrop of the postrevolutionary dead-end situation, Heine no longer viewed rebellion exclusively as a vehicle to a better future. Rather he now came to believe that the actual revolution consisted in how one lived one's immediate life (3: 23). In the long essay *On the History of Religion and Philosophy in Germany* written in 1835, Heine explained that in this point, the contemporary Saint-Simonians were fundamentally different from the Jacobins and the Babouvistes among the previous "men of the revolution," who with a Rousseauian zeal for renunciation had rhapsodized about the poverty of the poor. This is followed by the famous passage in which Heine emphatically turns against all spartan, puritan, and neo-Babouviste interpreters of the revolution and counters them with his concept of the aesthetically, culinarily, and erotically enhanced liberation of all people:

> We do not want to be sansculottes, nor simple citizens, nor venal presidents; we want to found a democracy of gods, equal in majesty, sanctity, and in bliss. You demand simple dress, austere morals, and unspiced pleasures, but we demand nectar and ambrosia, crimson robes, costly perfumes, luxury and splendor, the dancing of laughing nymphs, music and comedies. (3: 570)

The deeper meaning of these oft-quoted, but usually decontextualized sentences can be understood only by taking into account Heine's underlying disappointment with French political reality in the mid-1830s. The *juste milieu* of the Citizen King Louis-Philippe, while endurable, did not afford the newly Parisian Heine the cosmopolitan "fulfillment" of his earlier dreams. Thus, his revolutionary hopes for emancipation increasingly gave way to subjectivism, aestheticism, and even elitism, as evidenced in the poem cycle "Various Women." This explains how Heine ended up strongly opposed to the "friends of the revolution" grouped around Ludwig Börne in Paris at this time. After initial overtures of friendship, they became increasingly persuaded during the course of the 1830s that Heine was a traitor, and in statements both public and private did not hesitate to indict him for putting on aristocratic airs.[10] Heine endured this silently at first. But after Börne's death in 1837 and the simultaneous rise of republican revolutionary forces whose outlook reminded Heine more of the Jacobin terrorists of 1793/94 than of the "holy men of revolution" of 1830, he finally sat down and retaliated with his *Ludwig Börne* memoir of 1840. Here he spoke out against those Jacobin fanatics and egalitarian Babouvistes for whom revolution meant a government led by prudish guardians of public morality who would enforce their regime with a guillotine, surrounded by bloodthirsty masses. As an alternative, Heine once again offered those "Hellenists" who, in good Saint-Simonian tradition, hoped for something far more utopian from a future revolution.

Fearful that the revolution of 1789 would recur, Heine repeatedly spoke out in his *Börne* memoir against the Paris "people's congresses" (4: 74) at which, he claimed, tribunes attempted to stir up a "red fury" among the people (4: 71) by painting the coming revolution in wildly exaggerated terms as a triumph of good over evil. Heine, for his part, liked to cite Mirabeau's saying at this time: "One does not make a revolution with lavender perfume" (4: 75). "As long as we read about revolutions in books," he wrote in the *Börne* memoir, "everything looks very neat. It's like a landscape, which, artfully engraved on white parchment, appears quite pure and charming. Seen *in natura*, however, though it may well gain in grandiosity, its details give a very dirty and shabby impression indeed" (4: 75). A few pages later he wrote even more succinctly: "A revolution is a disaster" (4: 78), because "in the times of revolution we are left with no choice other than to kill or be killed" (4: 91).

Heine expressed with equal clarity his abhorrence of the French neo-Jacobins around Louis Blanc, who, he wrote in the *Lutetia* articles of this period, wanted to introduce the same "kitchen-equality" as Ludwig Börne (5: 328). In comparison to such a fanatic, Louis-Philippe seemed increasingly acceptable to Heine, who even went so far as to call him a "great king" (5: 330). Again and again in these years he stressed that a constitutional monarchy, understood as a synthesis of absolutism and democracy, was greatly preferable to the rule of the masses, who, as an "equally shorn, equally braying herd of people," would surely subordinate themselves to the first persuasive demagogue (5: 407). One should desist, he wrote, from using the "red cap" to awaken "demonic destructive powers" among the lower classes, for this might launch a revolution so tumultuous it would make all the scenes of 1789 "seem like cheerful midsummer night's dreams" (5: 319). Instead, one should preach peace. After all, he declared, there were about "400,000 crude fists in Paris, which await only the word to make the idea of absolute equality which smolders in their crude heads a reality" (5: 375). Heine's greatest fear concerned the potential chaos of a new revolution, particularly the "shady types" who would certainly "emerge from the ruins of the current regime like rats" (5: 414) and profess with the "most hackneyed, shallowest of platitudes" a "communism" devoid of all higher values (5: 412).

Heine nursed an equally great fear of a new outbreak of anti-Semitism in France, possibly inspired by the 1840 outbreak of anti-Semitic violence in Damascus, on which he wrote lengthy reports for the *Augsburger Allgemeine*. This is why he finally decided to dust off the secret manuscript of *The Rabbi from Bacherach* and publish it that year. In this narrative fragment, he sided with those people with whom he shared a heritage, if not a creed. Anti-Semitism, as another kind of "fanaticism," seemed to him a "contagious evil" (5: 208), which in times of crude egalitarian leveling could take on highly dangerous forms for people of his heritage. In short, his fear of the masses was intensified by a Jewish fear of pogroms.

Thus the "French conditions" of the years around 1840 plunged Heine's empathy with the hardships of the populace and his revolutionary zeal for emancipation into a deep crisis, because they caused him to fear a simultaneous relapse into the Jacobin terror and the darkest anti-Semitism of the Middle Ages. The "German conditions" at this time also led him to fear the worst, in this case a recurrence of the fraternities' cult of teutonism. After all, Heine knew all too well that there was still an abundance of "former Germanophiles" among the *Vormärz* activists, as we call them today, whose "single idea of progress" was a nationalistic and chauvinistic vision of a "Unified Germany" (4: 90). This aggravated Heine's recurring fear that the "German thunder," should it ever actually break loose, would take on even worse forms than the French, as he had expressed as early as his *History of Religion and Philosophy in Germany* (3: 640), and that this "thunder" could provoke a murderous rebellion that would make "the French revolution seem only a harmless idyll" (3: 640).

Heine's view of the German situation remained quite pessimistic through the publication of his *Timely Poems* and *Germany: A Winter's Tale*. He continued to believe that the crude, unenlightened power of the people could change during a revolution into a blind fury against anything different, higher, or finer, due to prejudices spawned by nationalism, communism, and anti-Semitism. This gloomy view brightened to a certain extent in 1843 and 1844, however, when Heine's association with Karl Marx in Paris led him to cast off a few of his prejudices against social revolution. Evidence of this new optimism, of the feeling that he had climbed aboard a "new boat" with new comrades and was being carried along by a renewed revolutionary elan, can be found in such familiar verses as

> Drum the people out of their sleep,
> Drum reveille with youthful aplomb,
> And drumming march ahead of all,
> That is the ultimate wisdom (4: 412)

or in the equally famous quatrains from Caput I of *Germany: A Winter's Tale*:

> A new song, and a better song,
> O friends, I'll sing for you.
> Here on earth we mean to make

Our paradise come true.

We mean to be happy here on earth—
Our days of want are done.
No more shall the lazy belly waste
What toiling hands have won (4: 578).

Heine addressed these lines not just to intellectuals, but also, as he had in 1830, to the oppressed and hungry.

This hopeful phase, to the extent one may call it such, was relatively short-lived. Heine's world view darkened again just a short time later. In 1844, he professed that he was frightened, on the one hand, by the "revolutionary fury" and "communist frenzy" of the French republicans and, on the other hand, by the unspeakably narrow-minded bigotry of German nationalists, "who carry only race and pure-blood and such thoughts worthy of a horse peddler around in their heads," as he wrote in his testimonial to Ludwig Marcus (5: 185). Moreover, his physical afflictions, which worsened substantially after 1844, caused him to see the state of the world from the morose perspective of a seriously, and eventually mortally ill person. For these reasons, he did not greet the outbreak of the Paris February revolution of 1848 with the enthusiasm expected of him by many liberals and left liberals. At that time, he was convalescing at the Foultriers Sanatorium and experienced a confrontation with the rebels first-hand. After paying a visit to his empty apartment on February 23, he was dragged out of his carriage by rebels who appropriated it for barricade construction.[11] Despite such indignities, he did not seek to flee from the turmoil of the times to any sort of quieter venue where he could concentrate on convalescing. Rather, he followed the course of the revolution with pain-wracked attentiveness, writing a number of correspondence reports on the Parisian events for the *Augsburger Allgemeine* (5: 207-215) whose inner ambivalence is hardly to be surpassed.[12] In wild succession we read here about "demonically criminal tones," "frenchified devil's song" (5: 208), the "fury of the folk" (5: 209), and the "blood red flag" (5: 212), but also about the "heroic deeds" of the French people who even at the height of revolutionary unrest "never misappropriated foreign property" (5: 209). In letters from the same year, like the one to Julius Campe on July 9, Heine went so far as to use terms such as "universal anarchy," "world in a muddle," and the "madness of God made manifest" to characterize the events in Paris (HSA 22: 287).

Nearly everything that Heine wrote or stated about the German revolution of 1848/49 is similarly ambivalent. Despite his sympathy with a few of the attempts at revolt, he sensed from the beginning that this was a maneuver of the nationalistic big-mouths and hot-aired rabble rousers whom he had ridiculed as early as 1844 in his *Timely Poems*. What Heine felt Germany lacked at this point was a "personality of genius," someone the likes of Lassalle, Garibaldi, or Bonaparte.[13] Even Georg Herwegh, who mustered an armed German democratic legion made up of "militarily untrained artisans" that suffered a crushing defeat at the hands of Würtemberg troops in the first weeks of the revolution, did not impress Heine but rather struck him as a faint-hearted Philistine.[14] He was even less impressed by the majority of the deputies who sat in the St. Paul's Church. He explained in a conversation with Fanny Lewald that the story of this parliament provided the "most marvelous material" for a comedy one could ever hope to find: "Everything as if made for a work of art: unity of time, place, and stupidity! What a menagerie sat there together in St. Paul's! A jester should have been there to describe it. What was all gathered together there, all these fossil relics! All the old trash!"[15] By "fossil relics" Heine meant primarily Germanophiles such as Friedrich Ludwig Jahn and Ernst Moritz Arndt, who as the "main representatives of conservative chauvinism"[16] in St. Paul's had a much greater following than the truly upright democrats. Heine penned prophetic words about men of this ilk in an August 29 letter to the Paris bookseller Jean-Jacques Dubochet, whose liberal views he found appealing. He wrote:

> Our enemies have the upper hand in Germany. The so-called 'national party', the rootin' teutons, are all puffed up with a ridiculous and ill-founded euphoria, their bragging is unbelievable. They dream of nothing less than playing the leading role in world history and of reincorporating all the lost tribes of Germany from the East and the West. And if they [the French] don't hurry and give them back Alsace, they will not hesitate to demand the Lorraine as well. God knows where they will stop with their Teutonic demands. (HSA 22: 289)

The poem "Michel—After March" of 1849/50 probably best summarizes Heine's attitude toward the role played by the masses over the course of the German March revolution. Here he does not hide his initial hope for a German "fairy-tale miracle," that is, for a transformation of the German Michel into a bold revolutionary. But then the graying fraternity brothers and the "old warriors of Roman law" had prevailed in the St. Paul's Assembly, ineffectually blustering away any revolutionary momentum, and the German Michel had once again subordinated himself to the "four-and-twenty monarchs" (6/I: 270). Heine wrote at the same time how courageously the Hungarians had revolted against Austrian dominance. When this revolution, too, was bloodily beaten back, Heine penned his bitterly tormented poem "In October 1849," which tells of the final victory of the counter-revolution and the resultant return of the German *misere*. After once again praising the Hungarians for their heroic courage, the poem closes with the following lines, referring to Germany:

> Yet we are bowed beneath the yoke
> Of heartless wolves, and common dogs, and swine.
>
> They howl, and bark, and grunt—my nose
> Can scarcely bear the victor's reek.
> Poet, be still; your anguish grows—
> You are so sick . . . it were wiser not to speak." (6/I: 118).

Yet how could Heine, the most important German political poet of the nineteenth century, have kept his silence after such incidents? He could not and would not. In the last years of his life, Heine did not shy away from once again raising all the basic political issues that had occupied him in the previous decades. These include a concern for social progress, a commitment to a more just distribution of worldly goods, an interest in the possibility of future revolutions, and speculation on the role of art in an emancipated society. And as before, he again acted in situational adaptation to changed circumstances, without ever betraying his left liberal stance. Indeed, whereas other *Nachmärz* activists became more accepting of compromise during this time, Heine became in certain respects more radical than before.

The unjustly maligned *Confessions*, frequently interpreted by liberals as Heine's relapse into a theistic belief system, speak for this turn toward radicalism, as does the better-known "Slave Ship" (6/I: 194-197) and other poems of the *Romancero*. In fact, precisely the ill-reputed *Confessions* prove on closer examination to be the most important social-ethical writing of any of the late works of Heine.[17] Here, because his own extreme physical infirmity had made him sensitive to the hardships of the oppressed and dispossessed, he passed highly critical judgment on his privileged status as a poet isolated from the common people. Rather than thinking only about expanding privileges for already favored bourgeois liberals, he shifted noticeably to focus on those same suffering classes who in his *Börne* memoir were still too "unclean" for him to come into closer contact with them (4: 75). He wrote that, after waltzing about for many years "on the dance floors of philosophy" and, as novelty-hungry theoretician, "living in sin with all sorts of philosophical systems," he now realized that his intellectual isolation had blinded him to the main problem of contemporary society—namely, the gap between the famished and the feasting, in short, "the great stomach question" (6/I: 480). On the subject of "Hellenism," earlier heralded as the polar opposite of "Nazarenism," Heine was suddenly silent.

As usual, he did not simply indulge in theoretical speculation, but also used two anecdotally concise stories to illustrate memorably this change of perspective on social and ethical issues. The first is the story of his encounter with Wilhelm Weitling, the leading representative of German artisanal communism, in Campe's Hamburg bookstore. At the time, in August 1844, Weitling's ingratiating presumptuousness embarrassed Heine—this fellow did not hesitate to expose the place on his leg where prison chains had left deep scars. But ten years later, with the changed perspective in Heine's *Confessions*, Weitling's steadfast belief in social progress allows him to appear in a much more positive light. Even more striking is the passage in which Heine describes Uncle Tom, the black slave with Bible in hand who had become world famous in 1852 along with the eponymous novel by Harriet Beecher Stowe. Heine wrote:

> What a humiliation! With all my learning I've gotten no farther than that poor ignorant Negro who barely knew how to spell. Poor Tom, of course, appears to see even greater profundities in the Holy Book than I do, especially in the latter part, which I still don't find completely clear. Perhaps Tom understands it better because there are more beatings in it—I mean those whiplashes that, when I read the Gospels and the Acts of the Apostles, sometimes caused me a very unaesthetic disgust. A poor Negro slave reads with his back as well as his eyes, and therefore grasps the meaning much better than we do. (6/I: 480).

One can hardly believe that these are the words of a poet as philosophically learned as Heine. Toward the end of his life, he suddenly realized that the highest human goals are perhaps not art and personal comfort, but rather the precepts of social responsibility—and that it would be boundlessly arrogant to wrinkle one's nose at a socially critical novel such as *Uncle Tom's Cabin* for imperfections of language or form.

To the earlier Heine, bent on enlightenment, religion had been the "opium of the people," that "song of renunciation / By which the people, that giant clown, / Is lulled from its lamentation," as he wrote at the beginning of *Germany: A Winter's Tale* (4: 577). The later Heine, however, is interested in religion primarily for its social message, expressed in both Testaments of the Bible. Unfortunately, he wrote, this message was taken much more seriously by the spiritually poor than by those intellectuals who, in their egoism and craving for novelty, avoided all questions of belief. The great religious men, he continued, had always worked for greater social justice. Thus Heine did not balk at labeling Moses and Jesus "socialists" in his *Confessions*, in order to give voice to a different kind of communism. For Heine, this communism did not rely on the "comfortless negations" of a sobering atheism, but was instead religiously inspired, taking a genuine interest in the crises of the common people rather than merely advancing new theories of social criticism (6/I: 487).

The famous quote in the foreword to the French edition of *Lutetia*, published one year later in 1855, should also be understood in this sense. Here, Heine summarized these thoughts once more in the form of a small manifesto, in which he expressed even more explicitly his changed outlook. For example, he stated that although he was still put off by the atheistic slogans of the communists, they nonetheless held a growing "fascination" for him because of their postulate of social justice (5: 232). In what Heine termed an act of "desperate magnanimity," he struggled to overcome his inner resistance to communism for two reasons. The first was its doctrine of "world-citizenship for all people, which is in complete agreement with the basic dogma of Christianity" and differs fundamentally from the world view of those "false patriots whose love for Fatherland consists only in a stupid hatred of foreign countries and neighboring peoples" (5: 233). Second, it embodies a strong sense of social justice, which it sets ahead of all desires for intellectual or aesthetic segregation. If under a future communist regime a grocer would use the pages of his *Book of Songs* to make paper bags, Heine wrote, he would have no objection provided those bags were filled with "coffee or snuff" and given to "poor old grannies" who "in our present world of injustice perhaps have to do without such comforts" (5: 233).[18] Heine died on February 17, 1856, shortly after writing these lines.

III

The development plotted here can in no way be described as linear. It does not exhibit the logical coherence claimed for it by those who attempt to fit Heine into a clearly delineated liberal poet type, one who was always true to himself and whose work therefore forms an unquestionable unity of style and content. Yet neither was this development as contradictory as has been claimed by those Heine opponents who dismissed his way of thinking for subversiveness. The actual truth is, of course, much more complicated. A number of the questions raised by this essay must therefore—despite all attempts to situate Heine historically—remain unanswered. One thing, however, should now be clear: Heine's relationship to the masses went through a number of major changes, which for the most part were linked with the radically changing political situations during his lifetime. Heine's view of the masses, however, as ambivalent as it was, was never totally negative, and it became increasingly perceptive, especially during the last phase of his life. There were certainly moments when he was gripped by a panicked fear of the masses, brought about by his intellectual isolation and a deep-seated fear of pogroms. Yet in his clearer, more enlightened moments, this fear always gave way to a feeling of profound kinship with the common people whose troubles and oppression he came to understand.

We should, however, not paint too positive a portrait. After all, even in Heine's later sympathy for the "poor Negro" and for the "poor old grannies" there is an undeniable remnant of ambivalence, or at least an assumption of difference. As a true Enlightener, however, who longed throughout his lifetime for a democracy of cultural and social equals, Heine regarded this difference not as absolute, but rather as correctable. What he criticized was therefore not the common people themselves, but rather the circumstances under which they had to live—and this saved him from lapsing into either an aristocratic contempt for the rabble or the pseudo-populist panegyrics of many a phrasemonger. Thus Heine's seeming ambivalence towards the broad masses never takes the form either of snobbish remoteness or of phoney familiarity, but instead is always linked to the socioeconomic situation of the lower classes. A passage from the

Confessions bespeaks this perspective. It is so concrete and insightful that it merits quotation in full length.

> These court lackeys of the plebs constantly extol its virtues and excellent qualities, crying out fervently, "How beautiful the common people are! How good! How intelligent!" No, you lie, the poor common people are *not* beautiful. They are, on the contrary, quite ugly. But this ugliness comes from dirt and will disappear with it, as soon as we build public baths where Their Majesty the people can bathe for free. . . . The people, whose goodness has been so highly praised, are not good at all, they are often as evil as other potentates. But their malice is due to hunger, and we must see to it that the sovereign people get enough to eat. As soon as (and this is the crucial point) they have fed and filled their bellies, they will smile at you with gracious condescension, like other sovereigns. Their Majesty the people are likewise not very intelligent. They are perhaps stupider than the others, almost as bestially stupid as their favorites. The masses bestow their love and confidence only on those who speak or howl their passionate jargon, while they hate every good man who addresses them in the language of reason, to enlighten and ennoble them. So it is in Paris, so it was in Jerusalem. When the people judge between the most just of the just and the most loathsome highwayman, you may be sure they will cry, "We want Barabbas! Long live Barabbas!" The reason for this perversity is ignorance. We must try to extirpate this national disease with public schools, where along with instruction, bread, butter, and other provisions will be given out free of charge. And when everyone among the people has been able to acquire all different sorts of knowledge, before long you will see intelligent masses. In the end, perhaps, they will be just as educated, as ingenious, as witty as we are, that is, as you, my dear reader, and I (6/I: 408-9).

Behind all the concentrated wit of this passage is a demand still waiting for its fulfillment. Economic and social relations have of course improved on many levels in the meantime. Yet the equality hoped for by Heine is far from realization, especially in the area of education. For this reason, the social message of the *Confessions*, namely, the call to create a democracy that rests on an actual "rule of the people," remains as relevant as ever. Catch phrases like "back-to-work programs," "widespread prosperity," or "growing the economy" should not deceive us about this fact. On the contrary, the frequency and emphasis with which such phrases are invoked point to the distance still remaining between us and the goal of true democratic equality.

Translated by Melissa Sundell

Translator's note: English translations of Heine's poetry were taken from: Heinrich Heine, *Poetry and Prose*, ed. Jost Hermand and Robert C. Holub (New York: Continuum, 1982). Excerpts from *On the History of Philosophy and Religion in Germany*, the introduction to *Kahldorf Concerning the Nobility*, and the French preface to *Lutetia* were taken from: Heinrich Heine, *The Romantic School and other Essays*, ed. Jost Hermand and Robert C. Holub (New York: Continuum, 1985). Excerpts from Heine's *Confessions* were taken from: Heinrich Heine, *Confessions*, trans. Peter Heinegg (New York: Joseph Simon, 1981). All other prose was translated by Melissa Sundell.

Notes

1. Cf. especially the statements on Heine's "aristocracy of the spirit" in Friedrich Sengle, "Trommler und Dichter. Zum 175. Geburtstag Heinrich Heines 1972," *Heine-Jahrbuch* 35 (1996), p. 228.

2. Cf. my essay "Franz Mehrings Heine-Bild," *Monatshefte* 88 (1997), pp. 310-320.

3. Hans Kaufmann, *Heinrich Heine. Geistige Entwicklung und künstlerisches Werk* (Berlin and Weimar, 1967).

4. Cf. Jost Hermand, *Streitobjekt Heine. Ein Forschungsbericht 1945-1975* (Frankfurt a.M., 1975), pp. 21-25.

5. Cf. Robert C. Holub, "Zwischen allen Stühlen. Zum Bankrott der liberalen Heine-Legende," *Heinrich Heine*, 4th ed. (*Text + Kritik* 18/19, 1982), pp. 117-128.

6. Cf. Paul Peters, *Heinrich Heine "Dichterjude". Die Geschichte einer Schmähung* (Meisenheim, 1990).

7. Fritz J. Raddatz, *Heine. Ein deutsches Märchen* (Hamburg, 1977), p. 97.

8. Cf. Marcel Reich-Ranicki, *Über Ruhestörer. Juden in der deutschen Literatur* (Munich, 1973), p.64.

9. Cf. Jost Hermand, "Eine Jugend in Deutschland. Heinrich Heine und die Burschenschaften," *Jahrbuch des Instituts für deutsche Geschichte*, Supplement 4 (Tel Aviv, 1982), pp. 111-136.

10. Cf. Klaus Briegleb's commentary to his edition of *Ludwig Börne: A Memorial* in *Sämtliche Schriften*, vol. 4, pp. 741-750.

11. Cf. Fritz Mende, *Heinrich Heine. Chronik seines Lebens und Werkes* (Berlin, 1970), p. 246.

12. Cf. Michael Werner, "Heine und die französische Revolution von 1848," *Der späte Heine. 1848-1856. Literatur — Politik — Religion*, ed. Wilhelm Gössmann und Joseph A. Kruse, (Hamburg, 1982), pp. 113-132.

13. Cf. Walter Grab, "Heine und die deutsche Revolution von 1848," *Der späte Heine* (Hamburg, 1982), pp. 147-174.

14. Ibid., p. 163.

15. Cf. *Begegnungen mit Heine. Berichte der Zeitgenossen*, Michael Werner, ed., vol. II (Hamburg, 1973) p. 196.

16. Cf. Walter Grab, "Heine und die deutsche Revolution von 1848," p. 166.

17. Cf. my essay "Die soziale Botschaft der 'Geständnisse,'" *Ich, Narr des Glücks*: *Heinrich Heine 1797-1856*, ed. Joseph A. Kruse, (Munich, 1997), pp. 313-317.

18. Cf. Leo Kreutzer, *Heine und der Kommunismus* (Göttingen, 1970), among others.

Heine's Critical Intervention: The Intellectual as Poet

Peter Uwe Hohendahl

There is little doubt among scholars that Heinrich Heine conceived of himself as a writer who publicly intervenes through his texts, who might even have an impact on his own time. But how did this intervention express itself? Has Heine left his mark primarily as a poet or as an intellectual? While nineteenth-century criticism for the most part understood Heine's contribution to German and European culture as that of a poet, more recently, and specifically during the last three decades, the pendulum has swung in the other direction. During this period Heine was celebrated as one of the first and most significant intellectuals in Germany. It was none other than Jürgen Habermas who foregrounded this aspect in his provocative essay "Heinrich Heine and the Role of the Intellectual in Germany."[1] For Habermas, who intervened in the current debate about the fate of the public intellectual when he first presented this paper in 1985, Heine served as an early example for a responsibility that remained underdeveloped in modern German culture. What set Heine off from contemporary and later writers or public figures was, according to Habermas, his accurate understanding of the task of the intellectual, namely to participate in and steer public debates, but not in the name of a political party or as the spokesman of a particular social group. This approach to Heine's works, which could build on the critical scholarship of the 1970s, places the emphasis upon Heine's prose. The question whether Heine was an important poet or what his poetry contributed to his achievements as an intellectual does not come up in Habermas's essay. Yet Heine clearly also thought of himself as a poet. One of the frequently quoted statements we find in his late *Confessions*:

> A witty Frenchman—some years ago the term would have been pleonastic—once called me a *romantique défroqué*. I have a soft spot for every sort of wit, and, malicious though it was, the characterization gave me the greatest delight. It's on target. Despite all the murderous campaigns I waged against Romanticism, personally I always remained a Romantic, and more than I ever imagined. I had dealt the taste for romantic poetry the most lethal blows, but then I felt an infinite longing for the

> "blue flower" in the dreamland of Romanticism steal over me once more. And so I took up the enchanted lute and sang, abandoning myself in that song to all the rapturous excesses, all the moony intoxication, all the blooming nightingale madness of the once beloved melody. I know it was "Romanticism's last free woodland song," and I am its last poet. With me the old lyrical German school comes to an end, while at the same time I inaugurate a new one—the modern German lyric. (6/I: 447)[2]

Heine sees himself as a fierce critic of Romanticism, who nevertheless remained indebted to the very language and style he attacked. At the end of his career he emphatically reinforces the importance of the poetic side of his oeuvre. Heine describes himself as a poet rather than a mere writer of prose. Moreover—and I will have to come back to this aspect—he claims to be the transitional figure between romantic and modern poetry. I am inclined to take this claim very seriously, precisely in the context of my topic. But Heine does not provide his readers with a definition of the new poetry. Therefore I will have to examine this question after I have more rigorously explored the relationship between the roles of poet and intellectual in Heine's persona.[3]

Heine's self-assessment that I just quoted may be witty and appealing, but the question remains: how accurate is it? Can we truthfully describe the author of *Conditions in France* and *Lutetia* as a secret romantic for whom poetry remained the essential part of his work? With equal force and conviction, it seems, Heinrich Heine has argued that he was first and foremost a warrior for the cause of human emancipation who had little regard for those writers who would care exclusively about the formal perfection of their works of art, a critique that would even include Goethe. The late poem "Enfant perdu," published as part of the *Romanzero* in 1852, gives us a very different understanding of Heine's role in the public sphere:

> I fought to hold positions that were lost
> In Freedom's war for thirty faithful years.
> Without a hope to win, despite the cost
> I battled on, expecting only tears.

The life of the author is represented as that of a fighter in the war of history, an ongoing war between progressive and reactionary forces. The writer has to choose between these forces and consequently he also has to be ready to kill the enemy or to receive the fatal wound. The last stanza reads:

> My wounds are gaping wide—A post's unmanned!—
> One sentry falls, another takes his part—
> And yet I fall unvanquished, sword in hand—
> The only thing that's broken is my heart. (6/I: 120-21.; D 649-50)[4]

In this poem Heine seems to be much closer to Habermas's definition of the critical intervention of the intellectual than to the secret romantic searching for the "blue flower." And yet we have to note that this statement is not presented in the form of a reasoned argument but rather as a poem. Its force is allegorical.

It was precisely the rhetorical nature of Heine's poetic language, its reliance on poetic convention that Theodor W. Adorno, who, by the way, equally praised the critical spirit of Heinrich Heine's prose, found problematic.[5] Measuring it against earlier romantic poetry, Adorno concluded that Heine's poetic language fell short since it could not break away from poetic conventions. In other words, one could play out the intellectual Heine against the poet, his critical and journalistic prose against his lyrical poems.

The contradictions and tensions that I have shown in Heine's attitude towards his own work and his public role bring me to the central question that I want to raise in this paper. How do we understand Heine's identity as a writer? How do we make sense of the many sides that the author presents to us in his work? In particular I want to focus on the relationship between the strong claim to be essentially a belated romantic poet and the equally strong assertion that he was primarily a warrior in the struggle for the emancipation of humanity. Obviously, the question of Heine's identity is complex and cannot be reduced to an either/or.[6] There are additional aspects that one would have to take into account, among them certainly Heine's Jewish or German identity, as well as Heine's social and political identity. But these aspects will enter my discussion only as part of a more specific argument about Heine's role as a writer.

For Heine, it seems, the question of his identity as a writer remained an unresolved problem throughout his career. At various times he tried to come to grips with it by publicly articulating his own position, frequently in a polemical fashion, i.e., by attacking other contemporary writers or by using historical examples (Lessing and Voltaire among them) as a way of defining his own role in the public sphere. The public nature of these statements is significant: for Heine the place of the writer (*Schriftsteller*) is the forum rather than the interiority of the private sphere, as much as private matters can become the material for his work. This emphasis is the result of Heine's heightened sensitivity for the historical transformations that occurred during his lifetime. More specifically, I would argue that Heine's continuing struggle to define his role as a writer is closely related to a keen awareness that the role of the writer lacked stability because of the fundamental changes that were occurring in the political and social sphere. A self-definition that seemed adequate in 1830 was already problematic in 1835, and a solution that appeared to be successful in 1840 would come across as outdated in 1850. Thus Heine always felt the pressure of history to "update himself," to reflect continuously on his shifting positionality. To put it differently, Heine saw his career as a writer as marked by significant turning points, turning points that were by and large not private but public in nature. For him the revolutions of 1830 and 1848, as we will see, were clearly the most important and most instructive ones. He felt encouraged or even forced by these political events to redefine the boundaries and the emphasis of his work as well as his self-presentation in the public sphere (in the case of Heine these two aspects were closely related if not identical). And Heine was also aware that this moment of heightened self-fashioning (frequently criticized by his opponents as personal vanity) reflected not only his personal needs—as a way of stabilizing his conflicted and possibly fragile personality—but at the same time revealed shifts in the historical constellation of the public sphere.

Hence for Heine the role of the writer was historical through and through; it could not be conceived outside of history. This understanding implies, I want to argue, that the relationship between the role of the intellectual and that of the poet is equally unstable. It would be highly problematic to assume that statements in Heine's early and his late work are necessarily compatible. In fact, the question of continuity has to be raised in principle. We have at least to acknowledge the possibility that the unity of Heine as an author is a fiction. At the same time I want to note that Heine himself, as skeptical as he remained about the possibility of self-knowledge, felt and explicitly argued that his entire career as a writer could and should be understood as a totality, although a conflicted one.

For the purpose of my discussion I will have to limit myself to a number of examples from different periods of Heine's oeuvre. I will focus on three crucial turning points in Heine's self-fashioning.[7] The first is the revolution of 1830 and his decision to move to Paris, thereby becoming a cosmopolitan author who consciously transcends the boundaries of a national literary system; the second is articulated in the essay on Börne of 1840, which emphasizes Heine's attempt to mark the difference between the mere political intellectual and the "true" poet, and finally the turning point of 1848, when personal and historical events, as I will show, reinforce each other as crucial determinants for a very different solution of the problem. Not only did Heine reposition himself within the political debates of the 1850s, but he also revised his concept of the poet.

Although in recent years Heine scholarship has done important work on the late Heine,[8] I believe that this phase is still the least understood, especially compared with the early period which stood at the center of Heine criticism in the 1970s, when the politics of Heine became the central issue. I will argue that the shifts that occurred in Heine's writings after 1848 mark a decisive break with his former conception of the poet and the poetic. The tendency to foreground mythology in his late poetry has to be noted as an index for this change; for this tendency, as we find it expressed in "Vitzliputzli" or "Bimini," suggests that the poetic intervention is specific and qualitatively different from that of the intellectual—not only in the sense that the poem as a work of art is autonomous and cannot be reduced therefore to the level of historical reality (an argument that Heine already presented in his Börne essay), but more importantly in the sense that it opens up a realm of meaning which is not accessible to the intervention of the public intellectual. At first glance, therefore, after 1848 the critical and poetic function seem to move apart. Does this mean that the late Heine retreats from his claim to intervene in the public debates of his time? Has the conception of the intellectual lost its centrality for the late Heine? These are the questions that call for closer examination.

During the 1820s Heinrich Heine was primarily identified as the author of the *Book of Songs* and the *Travel Pictures*, i.e., as a lyrical poet and a writer of fiction. The decision to move to Paris after the Revolution of 1830 was at the same time a resolution to change his image. Instead of fiction and poetry Heine foregrounded critical prose in the following years, writing interventions designed to connect the backward German conditions with the advanced political and cultural consciousness of the French metropolis. As it turned out, however, the task of informing his German readers about the French situation had to go hand in hand with informing his French readers about the poetic and philosophical revolution that had occurred in Germany during the late eighteenth and early nineteenth century, since the Hegelian notion of progress to which Heine was very much indebted at that point makes it mandatory to reflect on the totality of the historical process, i.e., both on the political events in France (as well as their social consequences) and intellectual life in Germany, where continued political repression blocked the very changes that took place West of the Rhine. Heine's self-imposed role as the premier mediator between France and Germany would call for a specific revision of the author's position. Like Ludwig Börne, whom he met in Paris again, Heine took upon himself the task of national representation. While Heine presented himself as the intellectual historian of Germany to the French, to the Germans he took on the role of the critic and commentator of contemporary life in France. In both instances prose became the most appropriate medium for this task. This is precisely the constellation to which Habermas refers when he describes Heine as an intellectual in the burgeoning literary public sphere.

Heine soon realized that this new project would also have an impact on his concept of the poet. Particularly in his essays on German history, for instance in *The Romantic School* and *On the History of Religion and Philosophy in Germany*, he seeks to pinpoint the radical transformations that the concept of the poet underwent around 1770 and then again around 1830. Especially the analysis of Goethe's significance within the history of German literature and the critical examination of the German romantics allows Heine to define the concept of the *Dichter*, thereby also positioning himself vis-à-vis the older German literary tradition.

Heine's assessment of Goethe focusses less on his biography and his works than on his reception by the German reading public and his role as the central literary figure of his age. In the third book of *The Romantic School* Heine tries to explain the dynamics of the literary evolution around 1800, when the Schlegel brothers began to support Goethe in their critical writings in order, as Heine clearly understands, to develop the new literary theory of the Romantic School. For the romantics Goethe became the representative literary figure in Germany. While Heine remains largely unsympathetic to the projects of the romantics and especially to that of the Schlegel brothers, he agrees with them as far as Goethe's position is concerned. But this agreement is not without reservations. The very celebration of the aesthetic qualities of Goethe's works and the assertion that the artwork has its autonomous realm of existence (its separate reality) fills him with doubt. As he puts it:

> Insofar as the admirers of Goethe adopt this point of view, they perceive art as an independent second world, which they place so high that all human activities, as well as human religion and morality, since they continued to change and stay in flux, remain at a lower level than art. However, I cannot unconditionally swear allegiance to this position; the followers of Goethe were tempted by this point of view to proclaim art to be the highest value and thereby turn away from the demands of the first real world, which after all deserves precedence. (3: 393)

As Heine explains a few paragraphs later, the works of Goethe are like beautiful statues, but they are not alive: "Goethe's poetic writings do not produce the deed, unlike those of Schiller. The deed is the child of the word, and Goethe's beautiful words are without children." (3: 395) Please note the distinction that Heine makes between Goethe and Schiller. Schiller's works, for instance his plays, are given the power to produce the "deed," i.e., to change reality. In other words, art and literature are not by definition "childless," but there is in Heine's mind a specific mode of art and a specific kind of artist that are exclusively concerned with aesthetic perfection and therefore not interested in the task of human emancipation. While Heine expresses high regards for Goethe's artistic accomplishments, he equally emphasizes the deficiencies of Goethe's position and that of his followers. It is a position of historical and moral indifference.

In the early 1830s Heine emphasizes the ideological implications of this position: he argues that the celebration of the aesthetic as an ultimate value can function in support of the political status quo.[9] To put it differently, Goethe and Metternich are largely compatible. It is against this position that Heine defines the new project of the contemporary writer, who is not content to perfect his artistic skills but means to intervene in the historical reality (the first world) of his time, who sees him- or herself as part of the crowd and not as part of a small circle of aesthetic connoisseurs. He calls explicitly for a new "totality" of the writer. Hence in his brief assessment of the Young German writers Heine states: "This quality, this totality, we also find among the writers of today's Young Germany, who also do not want to distinguish between life and writing, who never separate politics from science, art from religion. They are at the same time artists, tribunes, and apostles" (3: 468).

This famous quote deserves closer attention. For the most part Heine scholarship has stressed the moment of political activism implied in this definition of the writer. This reading is certainly correct. From the perspective of my questions, however, there are other elements that have to be noted as well. By invoking the concept of the artist, the tribune and the apostle, Heine stresses a synthesis that will bring together spheres that had been increasingly separated in the modern age, namely art, politics and religion. In Heine's view, this synthesis is crucial for the project of the young generation; they want to transform the world through the word. In this constellation the boundaries of the concept of the poet have to be broadened in such a way that the poet can equally address the aesthetic, the religious and the political sphere.

However, this synthesis seems to favor the critical rather than the poetic element. As a result, the concept of the intellectual, which is not mentioned in Heine's assessment of Goethe or his critical evaluation of the romantics, comes into the foreground. This occurs in two ways, first, in the emphasis Heine places on certain writers whom he considers as essential for the German tradition (Lessing would be the most important example; unlike Goethe, Lessing is seen as a critical and moral force in the German tradition, as someone who is concerned with the history of human progress); second, through the treatment of German philosophy from Kant to Hegel as a revolutionary project that will ultimately bring about a major political revolution in Germany as well. Heine's presentation of the history of German philosophy in *On the History of Religion and Philosophy in Germany* uses the perspective of the philosophy of action (*Tatphilosophie*), which underlines the transition from the philosophical to the political discourse. In this context the figure of the poet and that of the philosopher begin to merge into that of the politically active intellectual. As a type this figure is closer, I would argue, to the French *philosophe* of the eighteenth century than to the systematic German philosopher of the early nineteenth century. What the German philosopher lacks, as Heine notes more than once, is a form of writing that can reach the people, the simple style that Heine claims for himself when he describes himself as the modest and faithful scribe who will put Hegel's complex and obscure thoughts into simple and understandable sentences.

In the configuration of the early 1830s the concept of the intellectual does not replace that of the poet in Heine's discourse, but it dominates the structure of his thought. If one wanted to press the point one, could argue that the more limited concept of the poet as the artist who produces literary artworks is absorbed into the broader concept of the intellectual who effects changes in the historical world through the use of language. This concept is very powerful because Heine as a radical though irreverent student of Hegel assumes that the word is a primary force in the historical process.

Around 1840, i.e., only five years after the publication of *The Romantic School*, Heine's position had changed considerably. The former opposition against the celebration of art as the highest cultural value and the concomitant critique of the poet's indifference to the life of the people had lost much of its relevance.[10] Instead, Heine, now confronted with the radical politics of republicanism in France and Germany, developed a different dichotomy. On the one side, we find the politically motivated critic and ideologue who struggles for immediate political change, on the other, we see the true poet whose works contain a broader and deeper meaning. In this scheme the poet remains removed from the mundane frictions of political struggle.

In his *Ludwig Börne: A Memorial* of 1840 Heine uses the appraisal of the former confederate and estranged friend Börne to work out the conceptual opposition between poet and political writer/journalist. While he admits to a certain amount of appreciation of Börne's accomplishments as a literary critic and essayist, the logic of the dichotomy that defines the book focuses on Börne's political and moral motivations at the expense of his purely literary achievements. To put it differently, Börne serves as the model for the narrowly defined political writer who is obsessed with specific political goals and strategies.

Heine's critique of Börne has to be read against the background of Börne's criticism of Heine, which had reached the German reading public through his *Parisian Letters* and his late newspaper articles.[11] In these writings Börne had accused Heine of a lack of moral and political commitment for the liberal cause, a critique that Heine was certainly not willing to accept. But before Heine takes Börne's polemic apart, he allows his adversary to have his own voice. Here is Börne's voice in Heine's text:

> Given Heine's sybaritic nature, the mere drop of a leaf of a rose can disturb his sleep. How should he rest comfortably on Freedom, who is so very knotty? He should stay away from her. He who gets tired by every unevenness, he who is confused by every opposition, should not walk, should not think; he should go to bed and shut his eyes. . . He who has weak nerves and shies away from danger should be only in the service of art, of

> absolute art, which cancels all savage thoughts before they become deeds, and polishes all deeds until they are too delicate to become misdeeds. (4: 135)

According to Börne, the aesthetic approach to life, where the question of truth becomes a question of style, is closely connected with another character flaw: the pure poet is unreliable in politics. Hence Heine's political attitude is seen as anything but stable. In short, Heine finds himself placed in a position that very much resembles his portrait of Goethe in *The Romantic School*. The synthesis he had claimed for himself is now reduced to the moment of one-sided aestheticism. The definition of art and the artist attributed to Heine in the *Memorial* (whether it was Börne's real opinion matters ultimately very little) is focussed on the moment of beauty and deliberately excludes the moment of truth and consequently the aspect of praxis in the lifeworld.

I want to argue that the pressure from the radical political left in Paris forced Heine to revise both his concept of the poet and his self-representation in the public sphere. Strategically the Börne essay became the locus for this revision. By setting himself off against the figure of Börne, who is presented as obsessed with petty political conflicts, Heine arrived at a new stage in his self-fashioning.

In his answer to Börne's abstract radicalism Heine develops two arguments: on the one hand, he criticizes in strong terms the narrow project of the committed political writer; on the other hand, he begins to explore a new realm of truth for the artwork. The first strategy leads to a concept of the intellectual that is quite different from that of the early 1830s. Now the intellectual is conceived in terms of a rational, goal-oriented discourse. In this context the moment of critique, which was so prominent in the concept of the activist writer, takes on a less positive meaning: it is primarily associated with the limits of rationalism. The second argument leads to a reassessment of certain aspects of the romantic project that Heine had viciously attacked in 1835. Heine begins to take seriously the possibility of a continued importance of pre-modern culture. The search for a moment of truth in the work of art that is not identical with its beauty or formal perfection leads Heine to a re-evaluation of myth and mythology.[12] Consequently, the opposition between art and life, which had determined Heine's self-understanding around 1835, turns out to be unreliable. It shifts in such a way that now art (as Poesie) and life seem to merge and face the political sphere as a common enemy. Heine predicts a situation in which modern society has completely drained life of its poetic moments: "All traditional serenity, all sweetness, all the fragrance of flowers will be sucked out of life: and there will be nothing left except the Rumfordian soup of utility. In the community of our new puritans there will be no place for beauty and genius..." (4: 140). In this configuration the aesthetic position deserves our attention because it rescues the meaning of life from the narrow pragmatism of the political intellectual. Unlike the intellectual, the poet is life-affirming. Accordingly, Heine's new self-image foregrounds the creative rather than the critical aspect of the writer. And this creative moment, as he suggests at the end of *Ludwig Börne*, can find its expression through the use of mythology. Yet in 1840 this suggestion still remains only an aperçu; the problem of myth and mythology is not extensively treated.

Before I can discuss the period after 1848 I have to examine, at least briefly, Heine's position during the pre-revolutionary years.[13] As far as the conception of the writer is concerned, they are characterized by two conflicting tendencies, which, however, are ultimately caused by the same socio-political phenomenon. On the one hand, Heine observed the growing social and political unrest in France, which resulted in an increasing destabilization of the constitutional monarchy. On the other hand, he noticed the rapidly expanding commercialization of the cultural public sphere in Paris, the fact that works of art were as much for sale as other consumer goods. As a result, as Heine pointed out in his reviews of the Salons and the opera, the artist had become an entrepreneur who consciously or unconsciously produced for the market and had to adapt to its changing forces. The undeniable commodification of the artwork, however, also devalued the romantic notion of the poet as a completely independent creative force. The poet had become part of the very society that Heine considered a threat to the aesthetic realm. For Heine the opposition to modern bourgeois society could take two forms: it could either take the form of a defense of aesthetic autonomy and an idealized notion of the artist, or it could follow the path of a critique of the social conditions that caused the unrest. This critique, then, would have to deal with the class conflict of the 1840s in France. In response to the quite visible class struggle in France and the continued political repression in Germany Heine repoliticized his concept of the writer, he reintroduced the notion of critique and polemic as part of the poetic process.[14] *Germany, A Winter's Tale* would be a good example for this reaction. Similarly, in response to the commodification of art and literature, he developed a strong critical defense of aesthetic freedom. Therefore we once again find the idea of the poet as an intellectual. The real difficulty consisted in the coordination of these two moves, since the defense of artistic freedom and the critique of social repression under the constitutional monarchy did not necessarily go hand in hand. Heine was aware that his support of the inevitable social revolution and his assertion of aesthetic autonomy were in conflict and would potentially undermine his concept of the intellectual poet. Heine's self-ironical statement in the preface to *Lutetia* of 1855 makes this tension very clear: "In fact, only with dread and horror can I think of the time when those sinister iconoclasts [the communists] will gain power: with their brutal fists they will smash all the marble statues of my beloved art world; they will destroy all those fantastic games [*Schnurrpfeifereien*] that were so dear to the poet; they will cut down my laurel trees to plant potatoes instead" (5: 232). Looking back at the essays he had originally written for the *Allgemeine Zeitung* during the early 1840s and then collected in the volume *Lutetia*, he not only claims for himself the role of the visionary critic who saw the revolution coming long before it actually occurred, but also deliberately foregrounds the tension within the model of the intellectual poet. Heine makes fun of and sacrifices the traditional trope of the poet in order to assert the self-critical aspect of writing. But where does this move lead him? What is the role of the writer after the failure of the revolution?

The understanding of Heine as an intellectual presupposes, as Habermas rightly pointed out, the existence of a public sphere. While in the German case this public sphere was still primarily defined in literary terms,[15] in France there was a fully developed political public sphere. As I have shown, Heine's attempt to clarify his role as a writer was from the beginning tied up with the function of the writer in the public sphere. In other words, for Heine his life as a writer was a public matter, i.e., the private and the public were inseparable. This means that for him the question of his identity as a writer was always both a personal and a public issue. It is typical therefore that Heine responded in the same manner to the most severe personal crisis of his life, namely the physical breakdown in 1848, the outbreak of an illness that would slowly but surely kill him. The *Confessions* are the site where the public discussion of this illness and its emotional and intellectual consequences is carried out. It is a discourse in which the private elements have become much more prominent than before; at the same time, however, Heine continues to view himself and his role as a writer within the larger context of post-revolutionary history.

The failure of the 1848 revolution and the physical breakdown together provide the framework for the renewed discussion of Heine's identity as a writer.[16] Heine invokes his personal crisis primarily to explain an important turn in his philosophical position. I am referring, of course, to his much-discussed religious conversion, namely the abandonment of radical Hegelianism (atheism) and the return to a more traditional concept of god as a figure with whom the individual can develop a personal relationship. The details of this religious crisis are not part of my discussion; it suffices to point out that Heine's embrace of a personal god who can be addressed and who is ultimately responsible for the world because it is his creation has significant consequences for the concept of the writer. For Heine the logic of Hegel's philosophy and especially the logic of its radical derivations, for instance in the work of Feuerbach and Marx, would result in atheism and what he calls the deification of man, a condition that has become, as he now believes, more of a burden than a relief from the religious oppression that he had once stressed.

If the artist and the philosopher are the most creative representatives of the human species, as Heine had assumed, then the problem of "deification" would be a particularly severe one for both of them. Hence in *Confessions* Heine admonishes his old friend Karl Marx to repent and to revise the fundamental assumptions of his doctrine. It seems to me that during the early 1850s Heine was more concerned with rescuing the figure of the poet than the figure of the philosopher, which means that the concept of the intellectual moved again into the background. Heine tried to accomplish this task in two different ways. First, in his late poetry he turned to the past in order to find models for the figure of the ideal poet; second, he vigorously resumed his discussion of mythology as a form of truth that only the poet can present. In the latter approach he was generally much in tune with ideas that Richard Wagner developed more or less at the same time and that a generation later the young Nietzsche would propose as the solution to the impasse of modern knowledge in *The Birth of Tragedy from the Spirit of Music*.

The poem "Jehuda ben Halevy" is possibly the most prominent example for the tendency to use a historical figure—here, the medieval Rabbi and poet Jehuda from Spain—as a medium for a discussion of the poetic existence. The poem rehearses the search of the lyrical persona for the historical figure:

> I could recognize his pallid
> Forehead, proudly worn with thinking,

And his eyes, so gentle-stubborn—
Pained, inquiring eyes that pierce me—

But I recognized him mostly
By his enigmatic way of
Smiling with those rhyming lips
Which are found in poets only. (6/I: 130; D 655)

What marks the formation of the medieval Jewish poet is his grounding in the Torah and the Talmud, that is, in the central texts of the Jewish tradition. Poetic inspiration, in other words, is based on and is nourished by the religious foundations of Jewish life. More specifically, however, Heine emphasizes Jehuda's training in both parts of the Talmud, in the Halacha and the Haggada. While the first one represents for Heine the intellectual aspect of the tradition (its form of dialectic), the second represents the poetic aspect that allows Jehuda to develop as a poet.

Thus Jehuda ben Halevy
Grew to be not just a scholar
But a master of poetics
And a great and mighty poet. (6/I: 134; D 658)

Between the two sides of his training the poetic facet seems to be more important for the figure of the poet since it articulates the suffering of the Jewish people in exile. It is a role that God has bestowed on the poet, who therefore is only answerable to God. As we see, the assertion of artistic autonomy, so important for the Börne essay, returns in the *Romanzero*. But there is a difference. One does not have to take the religious references of the poem literally, as an actual dogmatic affirmation of the Talmud on the part of Heine, in order to appreciate the serious nature of these allusions.

I want to argue that Heine explores, to be sure, through the language of the poem, resources of meaning that are no longer available in the modern world. This raises the question whether these resources can be transferred to the modern world without losing their power. The identification of the modern author with the medieval poet cannot erase the difference between their cultural conditions. Any attempt to return to the medieval world is therefore open to the very critique that Heine developed in *Die Romantische Schule*; the return becomes regressive and potentially ideological. Heine's poem demonstrates its awareness of this problematic when the lyrical persona of the author moves the discussion to the present in part IV ,where the wife of the modern poet is presented as dissatisfied with him.

> My good wife's dissatisfaction
> With the chapter just concluded
> Bears especially upon the
> Precious casket of Darius. (6/I: 149; D 670)

Mundane financial problems interrupt the celebration of the medieval poet's life and work. The sudden and unmediated shift from the past to the present destroys the illusion of an organic restoration of the past. The tension between the two ages, the split between a medieval and a modern consciousness, is integrated into the poem itself.

The figure of the medieval poet whose life and work are grounded in his religious tradition serves as a model for the modern author, although, as I have tried to show, not without an ironic twist.[17] At the same time, the religious allusions of the poem hint at a larger problem for which Judaism would be only an example, and not even a particularly good one for that matter, since Judaic monotheism is fundamentally hostile to the concept of myth. The mere fact that Heine was also considering a poetic renaissance through the restoration of myth and older forms of Greek mythology would suggest that he did not want to reinscribe himself dogmatically into the Judaic tradition. The purpose of the project lies elsewhere.[18] The return to mythology allows a rupture with the logic of modernity. Since for Heine with the failure of the 1848 revolution the idea of historical progress has lost its utopian propensity, i.e., the notion that the future will contain not only the guarantee of a better material life for the people but also the promise of happiness through aesthetic and sensual pleasure, the search for meaning has to turn elsewhere. The question arises whether a new ground could be found, whether a different model of history could preserve moments of meaning that are being erased by the graying of the world, namely the expansion of modern institutional rationality. If myth could be revitalized, the poet as the bearer and translator of mythology would become a central cultural figure.

It seems to me that Heine took this question quite seriously. In his late work myth is not merely an allegorical construct that allowed him to visualize abstract intellectual positions, as he had done during the 1830s. In *Die Götter im Exil* (1853) the secret return of the Greek gods in the disguise of monks, who seemingly uphold Christian spirituality but once every year regain their old powers and celebrate the Dionysian mysteries far away from modern civilization, is surrounded by an atmosphere of the uncanny that cannot be neatly redeemed through an allegorical use of the strange and to some extent scary figures. The young fisher who first secretly observes them and then tries to inform the Christian authorities about their secret festivities is clearly frightened by their power, especially when he finds out that the abbot to whom he wants to report the scandalous behavior of the monks is none other than the god Dionysus himself. Older forms of religion have not disappeared; instead, they survive in new and different guises. History, therefore, is no longer defined as a Hegelian process moving from the primitive to the modern; rather, it is conceived and narrated as a process in which the old and the new remain intertwined, although the older elements are not always visible.

One might expect Heine to use his narrative for an emphatic celebration of the mythic ground as a site of sheer rejuvenation. Actually, Heine's narrative strategy is considerably more complex. First of all, the return of the Greek myth in the form of a bacchanal is presented through a language that is quite ambivalent in its praise of the sensual moment in as much as sensuality is at the same time presented as an extreme moment, as a form of excess that would break down normal social life. Not unlike the Romantics (Hölderlin), Heine refers to Dionysus as the savior and thereby establishes a connection with Jesus Christ, but the Greek god is called the "savior of sensual pleasure" (6/I: 406) in clear distinction from the Christian savior.[19] By juxtaposing Greek and Christian mythology, Heine's narrative maintains a precarious and unstable balance. In this structure the beliefs of the young fisher who wants to restore a Christian order are problematized but not erased. Secondly, Heine adds another level of consciousness through a dialogue between the narrator and the modern reader, who is understood as explicitly distinct from the medieval fisher. The modern reader appears as a sophisticated connoisseur of mythology who cannot possibly be frightened by the return of the old Greek gods. "But helas, dear reader, unlike you, the poor fisher of whom we tell was not well versed in mythology; he had not undertaken archeological studies; thus he was scared and terrified by the sight of the beautiful triumphant god together with his two strange acolytes when they jumped out of their monks garb" (6/I: 406).

This rupture in the text marks the difference between a religious consciousness that claims to be superior to ancient myth and a modern consciousness for which the old mythology is merely a field of scholarly study. For this modern attitude the return of the old gods becomes a problem insofar as it is caught up in the very process of modernity from which it would like to escape. It is important to note that Heine's narrative does not try to evade this question simply by positing an actual renaissance of the old myth. Similarly, the modern poet, who addresses his contemporary readers and shares the consciousness of his age, cannot be expected to recreate a mythic age through poetic language alone. Thus the moment of reflection cannot be given up without the danger of regression. The poet, it seems, must remain an intellectual precisely when he or she is confronting the power of myth. One of the reasons is the likelihood that the modern age underrates the ambiguous power of myth. Moreover, I want to underline that the encounter with myth differs qualitatively from other historical experiences. In the poem "Vitzliputzli," part of the first book of the *Romanzero*, Heine attempts to articulate this difference. Ostensibly the poem deals with the conquest of the New World by the Spaniards and more specifically with the fate of Montezuma and Cortez in Mexico.[20] The sacrifice of the Spaniards who were captured in the battle by the Indians foregrounds the violent and uncanny side of myth that is traditionally de-emphasized in the European tradition. It is the belief of the Aztec priest that through human sacrifice the angry god Vitzliputzli can be manipulated. Yet it is precisely this belief that the poem ultimately questions when the voice of the god is heard: He anticipates the end of his life as a god. With the conquest of the Spaniards and their imposition of Christianity on the natives the age of the old Indian myth has come to an end.

> Smashed to bits will be my temple,
> I myself will fall and founder
> In the ruins—dust and ashes—
> None again will see me ever.
>
> Yet I shall not die. We gods are
> Apt to grow as old as parrots,
> And, like them, we can be moulting
> Grow a whole new change of feathers. (6/I; 74: D 613)

In the Christian context the old Indian gods will turn into negative forces, into devils, just as the old Greek gods turned into demons when Christianity displaced ancient polytheism. The old myth returns as a power of revenge on those who carried out the conquest.

> My beloved Mexico—
> I can save her now no longer,
> But I'll wreak a dire revenge for
> My beloved Mexico. (6/I: 75; D 614)

Here the old Aztec mythology is anything but harmless; it still contains the violence that once determined its logic. Consequently, the modern age, supposedly far removed from the brutality of human sacrifice, remains in its debt. The belief that human emancipation can be achieved through historical deeds is ultimately subverted because they themselves are saturated with mythic violence. This insight, however, also throws a different light on the sophistication of the modern reader Heine invoked in *The Gods in Exile*. Their sense of security vis-à-vis the myth may be false because their knowledge is exclusively based on modern archeology (science).

At the beginning of this paper I claimed that after 1848 a significant, possibly even fundamental break occurs in terms of Heine's concept of the poet. To describe this transformation exclusively as a move towards myth and mythology, however, would blatantly simplify Heine's development. The undeniable attraction of myth for the late Heine positively transcends the idea of a rejuvenation of modern, overly rationalized culture. For two reasons the notion of an emphatic return to the origin of myth is insufficient in the case of the late Heine. First, the power of myth is rather ambiguous. Its sensual vitality, which Heine celebrates in *The Gods in Exile*, stands in sharp contrast to the violence in "Vitzliputzli," where human sacrifice is an essential part of the pattern. The survival of mythic structures in the modern world, which both texts suggest, therefore turns out to be as much a threat to modern claims for reliable standards of civilization as an enrichment for an overly rationalized society. To put it differently, the poet who rediscovers the mythic ground by studying mythological narratives is dealing with potentially explosive material, material that also contains destructive forces. It seems that Heinrich Heine was keenly aware of this potential, an insight that did not, however, diminish his interest in the subject matter. Yet this interest is definitely channeled through a modern aesthetic consciousness. Neither *The Gods in Exile* nor "Vitzliputzli" operates in the mode of simple identification. The narrator, as well as the lyrical voice of the poet, keeps his distance from the mythological material, that is to say, in these texts the modern world is equally present either through narrative strategies or stylistic means. One such stylistic device is the comparison of the Indian god with a "parrot," hardly an appropriate image for a deity (6/I: 74).

This observation would suggest that the concept of the poet in Heine's late work cannot be reduced to the notion of a naive creative force that retells or makes use of mythological narratives. Instead, the use of specifically modern strategies such as irony and parody would suggest that the idea of the poet stays in rather close contact with the concept of the intellectual. In other words, the poet is conceived as a highly self-conscious writer, but not necessarily as an activist who is working for specific political goals. Apparently the function of the intellectual aspect has changed, but it remains my task to clarify in what sense.

The majority opinion of more recent Heine criticism assumes that after 1848 Heine not only abandoned his former philosophical and religious point of view but also the ideological commitments of the 1840s, among them the ideas of progress and emancipation.[21] Such a reading could result in the supposition that the late Heine moved towards an arbitrarily constructed concept of the self. Along these lines Norbert Altenhofer has suggested that the mature and late Heine was almost exclusively concerned with his role as an artist who is not bound by conventional rules of morality or ideological commitments. Hence Altenhofer argues that the various roles Heine developed for himself in his writings are the different masks of the artist who consciously evades any form of determination. Altenhofer concludes: "The play of the artist with interchanging identities is the fiction—admittedly a fiction—of a freedom that in reality cannot be found anywhere."[22] While this approach enables the critic to explain the complexity and the contradictions of Heine's late writings, it also reduces them, it seems to me, to one common denominator, namely the aesthetic. The emphasis that Altenhofer, especially in his interpretation of "Jehuda ben Halevy," places on the "literarische Kalkül"[23] could also encourage a problematic reading that comprehends the poem exclusively as a form of literary play. While I agree with Altenhofer's warning against a literal understanding of Heine's supposed return to the Jewish faith, I would argue that the aesthetic dimension, which seems to be the ultimate legitimation for Altenhofer, has to be seen as *one* aspect within an intricate configuration of meaning. In the final analysis, Altenhofer's reading, I believe, underestimates the stakes involved in the concept of the poet by reducing him to the role of the playful and unreliable "Artist." Only by perceiving the "Artistentum" as part of a larger configuration in which concepts such as history, philosophy, religion and myth also actively participate can we explore and specify the function of Heine's artistic strategies.

One way of addressing this complicated issue would be to focus on the idea of the intellectual that Heine's late writings either articulate or imply. The European intellectual of the eighteenth and nineteenth century was by definition part of the public sphere and assumed a number of potential public roles, among them that of critic, adviser and educator.[24] Did Heine forsake these public roles after 1848 in order to refashion his conception of authorship in terms of a primarily private use of poetic language? If we understood the various identities articulated in Heine's work as masks of a self-conscious artist, it would be plausible to argue that Heine conceived of his late literary production as a private expression whose public dimension was established merely *post factum* by the apparatus of the literary market. Only through its reception did the work become a public event. One could claim, then, that Heine's transformation after 1848, the way he rejected the philosophical outlook of Hegel's radical disciples, amounted to a process of privatization that diminishes the public persona of the author and places the emphasis on an idea of "Poesie," privileging thereby the intrinsic literary aspect of the writing process.

Against this position Luciano Zagari has rightly asserted that the literary accomplishment of the late Heine was grounded in a modernist rather than a belated romantic sensibility, a sensibility that was self-consciously concerned with the construction of a post-conventional poetic language. "The poem is a net composed of words, which does not show loose stitches; still, it is unable to retain anything concrete in its mesh, anything coming from the realm of reality."[25] Yet the poetic language of the late Heine did not restore the sphere of romantic intimacy. The possible increase in subjectivity after 1848 did not reduce the public involvement of the author Heine. By foregrounding the difference between Heine's late poetry and the romantic tradition Zagari correctly underlines a significant shift in the (implied) conception of the poet: "The new intellectual, even if he had no insight into the novel and different problems involved in living together in society, could not help notice how problematic the poet, values, communication, and the reader had now become."[26] Please note Zagari's use of the term "intellectual" when he undoubtedly refers to Heine's poetry. The late Heine deliberately remained a public author who meant to test and to provoke his readers. But for Zagari this public stance—and here I would disagree with him—has pretty much shed all former beliefs and commitments and is left therefore with the cynicism of interior and exterior emptiness. It seems to me that Zagari conflates the critical role of the poet, who deconstructs the stylistic and thematic repertoire of Romanticism, with cynicism. In any case, the role of the poet embraced by the late Heine is not affirmative. It would be misleading therefore to claim an organic use of mythology on the part of Heine. His project remained self-consciously dissonant. In this respect it was clearly distinguished from that of Richard Wagner, for whom the new work of art, the all-embracing drama of the future, would open up a qualitatively different public sphere.

Wagner insisted on the harmonious correspondence between a general and socially undifferentiated public, on the one hand, and a new type of drama based on myth, on the other.[27] "The material of *this* drama, however, was myth," Wagner notes with respect to the Greek tragedy,"and exclusively on the basis of this essence we can comprehend the highest form of the Greek artwork and its seductive form."[28] For Wagner myth is the ultimate collective resource of meaning for the people; it therefore always transcends the project of the individual artist, whose work will resonate with the general public only when it partakes in the common beliefs as they are articulated in myth. Obviously Wagner's ideas center around a notion of community (*Gemeinschaft*) as socially and ethnically undifferentiated, standing in sharp contrast to the fragmented class society of his time. Hence in Wagner's program, the modern artist, by returning to the origin of myth, also transcends the limitations of contemporary art. In other words, Wagner conceives the feasibility of a real exit from the prison-house of modernity. Heine, on the other hand, was ultimately not prepared to provide a map for a mythical rejuvenation. His late work invokes mythical figures and narratives in order to mark temporal cultural alterity, but it foregrounds the dissonance. His own positionality is located within modernity, viewing pre-modern, and specifically ancient culture, as an ambiguous other. In this respect the late Heine reaffirmed his commitment to the figure of the intellectual poet, although his interpretation of poetic intellectuality changed considerably between 1830 and 1855. The role of the political intellectual, who is defined in terms of an ideological commitment, was still fairly new in the 1830s. As it turned out, however, the initial promise of a synthesis of poet and intellectual (poet, tribune and prophet) was bound to a particular historical configuration and could not be sustained during the 1840s. In this decade Heine recognized that the poetic principle (aesthetic autonomy) would not automatically resonate with the program of progressive politics, that poetic and political logic were by no means identical. This more cautious and skeptical stance would then move Heine towards a recognition of the substantial role of myth within the structure of modernity. Yet this search for a new collective resource of meaning did not result in a rejection of modernity and an unconditional embrace of the sphere of myth; rather, Heine reinserted the force of intellectual reflection into the equation. The creative force of the poet cannot succeed without the moment of subversion that is tied to reflection. One might call Heine's self-determination, therefore, the refusal of a final synthesis or the tenacity of keeping contradictions unresolved.

Notes

1. Jürgen Habermas, "Heinrich Heine and the Role of the Intellectual in Germany," in Habermas, *The New Conservatism. Cultural Criticism and the Historians' Debate* (Cambridge, Mass., 1989), pp. 71-99.

2. Heinrich Heine, *Confessions* and Leo Tolstoy, *A Confession*, transl. and ed. Peter Heinegg (New York, 1981), p. 21; unless otherwise indicated all translations are mine.

3. For a more detailed discussion of Heine's position as an intellectual in the early nineteenth century see Peter Uwe Hohendahl, "Heinrich Heine: Macht und Ohnmacht des Intellecktuellen," in *Responsibility and Commitment. Ethische Postulate der Kulturvermittlung*, Festschrift für Jost Hermand, ed. Klaus Berghahn, Robert Holub and Klaus Scherpe (Frankfurt/Main, 1996), pp. 91-107.

4. The translations of Heine's poems are consistently taken from *The Complete Poems of Heinrich Heine. A Modern English Translation* by Hal Draper (Boston, 1982); page references are given in the text (for instance, D 15).

5. Theodor W. Adorno, "Heine the Wound," in Adorno, *Notes to Literature*, vol. 1 (New York, 1991), pp. 80-85. For an extensive discussion of Adorno's critique of Heine see Hohendahl, *Prismatic Thought Theodor W. Adorno* (Nebraska, 1995), pp. 107-117.

6. See, for instance, Jost Hermand, "One Identity is not Enough. Heine's Legacy to Germans, Jews, and Liberals, in *Heinrich Heine and the Occident*, ed. Peter Uwe Hohendahl and Sander Gilman (Nebraska, 1991), pp.19-41.

7. The most extensive discussion of Heine's self-understanding as a poet and writer can be found in Sabine Bierwirth, *Heines Dichterbilder. Stationen seines ästhetischen Selbstverständnisses* (Stuttgart, 1995), Bierwirth suggests seven distinct phases in Heine's development from 1820 to 1856.

8. Among the recent monographs see Ernst Pavel, *Heinrich Heine's Last Years in Paris* (New York, 1995); Henner Montanus, *Der kranke Heine*

(Stuttgart, 1995); Sabine Schneider, *Die Ironie der späten Lyrik Heines* (Würzburg, 1995).

9. For an extensive discussion of Heine cultural politics see Albrecht Betz, *Ästhetik und Politik. Heinrich Heines Prosa* (München, 1971); see also Jeffrey Sammons, *Heinrich Heine. A Modern Biography* (Princeton, 1979), pp. 159-246.

10. See Sammons, *Heinrich Heine*, pp. 249-275; also Hohendahl, "Art Evaluation and Reportage: The Aesthetic Theory of the Later Heine," in Hohendahl, *The Institution of Criticism* (Ithaca, 1982), pp. 83-125.

11. For a discussion of Börne's position see Wolfgang Labuhn, *Literatur und Öffentlichkeit im Vormärz. Das Beispiel Ludwig Börne* (Königstein, 1980).

12. For a thorough recent treatment of Heine's use of mythology see Markus Küppers, *Heinrich Heines Arbeit am Mythos* (München, 1994).

13. For the following see Sammons, *Heinrich Heine*, pp. 249-293; see also Hohendahl, "Art Evaluation and Reportage" (note 8).

14. Heine's journalistic articles for the *Allgemeine Zeitung* (1840-1843) would be a case in point; see Michael Werner, "Der politische Schriftsteller und die (Selbst)-Zensur. Zur Dialektik von Zensur und Selbstzensur in Heines Berichten aus Paris," *Heine-Jahrbuch* 26 (1987), pp. 29-53; for a discussion of the change in the conception of the writer see Bierwirth, *Dichterbilder*, pp. 296-358.

15. For an extensive discussion of the political and literary public sphere see Hohendahl, *Building a National Literature: The Case of Germany 1830-1870* (Ithaca, 1989).

16. See Bierwirth, *Heines Dichterbilder*, pp. 359-430.

17. An extensive discussion of irony in Heine's late poetry is offered by Sabine Schneider, *Die Ironie der späten Lyrik Heines*, especially pp. 97-165.

18. For a critical discussion of this topic see Habermas, *The Philosophical Discourse of Modernity* (Cambridge/Mass, 1987), pp. 51-74.

19. See Manfred Frank, *Der kommende Gott. Vorlesungen über die neue Mythologie* (Frankfurt/Main, 1982, pp. 245-284.

20. For a critical discussion of the colonial aspect see Susanne Zantop, "Colonialism, Cannibalism, and Literary Incorporation: Heine in Mexico," in *Heinrich Heine and the Occident*, pp. 110-138.

21. For a good summary see Sammons, *Heinrich Heine* (Stuttgart, 1991), pp. 119-149.

22. Norbert Altenhofer, *Die verlorene Augensprache. Über Heinrich Heine* (Frankfurt/Main, 1993), especially pp.207-233, here p. 226.

23. Altenhofer, *Augensprache*, p. 229.

24. See Zygmunt Bauman, *Legislators and Interpreters. On Modernity, Postmodernity and Intellectuals* (Ithaca, 1987); see also Dena Goodman, *Criticism in Action. Enlightenment Experiments in Political Writing* (Ithaca, 1989).

25. Luciano Zagari, "'Das ausgesprochene Wort ist ohne Scham' Der späte Heine und die Auflösung der dichterischen Sprache," in *Zu Heinrich Heine*, ed. Luciano Zagari and Paolo Chiarini (Stuttgart, 1981), pp. 124-140, here p. 126.

26. Zagari, "'Das ausgesprochene Wort ist ohne Scham,'" p. 137.

27. See Frank, *Der kommende Gott*, pp. 226-231

28. Richard Wagner, "Oper und Drama, " quoted from Frank, *Der kommende Gott*, p. 229.

German Life and Civilization

German Life and Civilization provides contributions to a critical understanding of Central European cultural history from medieval times to the present. Culture is here defined in the broadest sense, comprising expressions of high culture in such areas as literature, music, pictorial arts, and intellectual trends as well as political and socio-historical developments and the texture of everyday life. Both the cultural mainstream and oppositional or minority viewpoints lie within the purview of the series. While it is based on specialized investigations of particular topics, the series aims to foster progressive scholarship that aspires to a synthetic view of culture by crossing traditional disciplinary boundaries.

Interested colleagues are encouraged to send a brief summary of their work to the general editor of the series:

Jost Hermand
Department of German
University of Wisconsin
Madison, Wisconsin 53706